Uncovering the Sources
of Love and Hate

Excerpts from letters and comments

on Dr. Rule's *A Theory of Human Behavior*,
first published in The American Journal of Psychiatry.

It was a pleasure to meet you at J.'s. Your fascinating mss.
reached me at Sarah Lawrence College just as the year was
closing, excuse the delayed reply. Since receiving it I have
become a chimpanzee fan. All my thanks and best wishes.
—*Joseph Campbell*

Thank you for your letter and the reprints of your paper
that I requested. I am certainly not surprised at the world
wide requests for copies. I regret that I could not attend the
AAAS meetings in Montreal and meet with you but I'm
sure our paths will cross in the future.
—*Professor Harry Harlow, University of Wisconsin*
Pioneer Investigator of Primate Behavior

It was a very great pleasure to read and I was keenly
interested in your manuscript. As you no doubt will quess I
am of the school that believes deeply in the relativity of
human-animal behavior. I feel sure that you should have it
published.
—*Fairfield Osborn,*
President, New York Zoological Society

Loved your psychiatric paper. Knowing my feeling for
animals you can understand how very interesting it was to
me. Look forward to seeing you.
—*Consuelo Vanderbilt*

I have read with great interest your manuscript, "A Biologically Based Theroy of Human Behavior and its Implications
for Psychiatry." I like your concept very much and would
like to discuss it with you as soon as we can get together.
—*Frank Fremont-Smith, M.D.,*
Director, New York Academy of Sciences

PROMINENT THINKERS
comment on Dr. Rule's theory:

I finished reading your manuscript today. Once having started it, I could not put it down. Until I read your paper I had not encountered an original thought about women and psychiatry in decades. Yours is not only original, it is a signal contribution.

— Florence Powdermaker, M.D.
Psychiatrist, Author

Your theory is an excellent synthesis of modern behavioral thinking. Our era is ripe for your concept of "mothering."

—Betty Locker Pope, Anthropologist

It is scarcely necessary for me to mention how stimulating your theory was as you presented it to our "standing room only" audience. I do believe you are on the verge of great discoveries.

—Louis Wolberg, M.D., Director,
Postgraduate Center for Mental Health, NYC

Your concept that the "mothering team" was fundamental to social evolution should revolutionize psychiatric thinking.

—Louis Reuling, M.D., Psychiatrist

Your theory should become a "Bible" for every therapist.
—William Lemmon, Ph.D.
Professor of Psychology
University of Oklahoma

UNCOVERING the SOURCES of LOVE and HATE

A Theory of Human Behavior

COLTER RULE, M.D.

Foreword By Joseph Post, M.D.

Former President, The New York Academy Of Medicine

SUNSTONE PRESS

SANTA FE
NEW MEXICO

First edition

Printed in the United States of America

10 9 8 7 6 5 4 3 2 1

Library of Congress Cataloging in Publication Data

Rule, Colter, 1911-
  Uncovering the sources of love and hate: a theory of human behavior/
Colter Rule; Foreword by Joseph Post.—1st ed.
          p. cm.
    ISBN 0-86534-102-8, —ISBN 0-86534-229-6 (pbk)
      1. Mothering. 2. Mother and child—case studies. 3.Psychology,
Comparative. I. Title.
HQ759.R833 1955
306.874'3—dc20
                                                                95-1450
                                                                CIP

Published by Sunstone Press
             Post Office Box 2321
             Santa Fe, New Mexico 87504-2321 / USA
             (505) 988-4418 / FAX: (505) 988-1025
             orders only (800) 243-5644

DEDICATION

First of all, to the many, many patients who have shared their pain, their memories and their thoughts and who supplied the bricks and mortar of this theory.

To the memory of my mother and father. To my sisters and their families who endeared and endured and to all the humans who helped me grow up.

To the primates of my own troupe—my wife, Betty; my children, Marquerite, Jeanette and Colter along with their families.

To colleagues who encouraged me or argued with me—and to colleagues who rejected my views and dismissed me as well; they were all important contributors.

Lastly, beyond humans to the world of the non-human primates which led me to the sacred kinship and bonding to all that breathe.

—Colter Rule, M.D.
New York City, March 1995

CONTENTS

FOREWORD / 7

Chapter One / 9
Debbie and Her Mother

Chapter Two / 21
Robert and His Grandfather

Chapter Three / 27
Trouble: The Case of Angie L.

Chapter Four / 34
Siblings, Playmates, Classmates:
The Search for Friends

Chapter Five / 41
Sex: Nature's Mandate

Chapter Six / 52
Transference: Funny Business in Therapy

Chapter Seven / 58
Territoriality in Animals: Humans, Too?

Chapter Eight / 71
Dominance: Who Pushes Who Around?

Chapter Nine / 77
Spacing: Hold Me Tight But Don't Fence Me In

Chapter Ten / 82
Whose Invention is Fathering?

Chapter Eleven / 90
The Family: Another Riddle

Chapter Twelve / 96
Human Beginnings

Chapter Thirteen / 110
Some Feminine Input

Chapter Fourteen / 119
The Case of Greg C.

Chapter Fifteen / 128
Psychiatric Problems Are Family Problems

Chapter Sixteen / 133
Greg and Silvia: Happy Ending

Chapter Seventeen / 145
The Power of the Group

Chapter Eighteen / 161
New Ways in Therapy

Chapter Nineteen / 173
Turbulent Times: East meets West

Chapter Twenty / 185
Summing Up

Chapter Twenty-One / 210
A Hopeful Tomorrow

Appendices / 227
Articles by Colter Rule, M.D.

Article reprinted from *The Graduate Journal* / 228
Article reprinted from
Perspectives in Biology and Medicine / 266
Article reprinted from the *American Journal of Psychiatry* / 291

FOREWORD

Doctor Rule has experienced life through many roads, some of them paths through imagination and fantasy, some of them through the rigors of medical and biological disciplines. He was trained at The Johns Hopkins School of Medicine and the Rockefeller Institute for Medical Research (now Rockefeller University), was certified as a specialist in Internal Medicine and, then—giving up a busy practice of medicine—undertook years of psychiatric training.

He has been enabled—as a psychiatrist—to roam freely in considering diverse areas of the human situation, including all important non-verbal forms of expression and communication. His patients' widely variant accounts of mothering care and the tragic consequences of the lack of it—encountered repeatedly in his practice—led him to long, intensive and fascinating studies of primitive primate behavior.

To focalize the many roots Doctor Rule's researches and explorings have taken, he has written, among other books and papers, this book, which serves to bring together the many and rich avenues Doctor Rule has explored with patience, delight, amusement and steadily increasing knowledge. Sharing his cases he provides us with many examples of knotted human behavior which he untangles before our eyes.

He offers us a profusion of ideas about our relationships with our parents, siblings, friends, spouses and enemies and their roots in the primate world. He is one of the few scientists who continue to explore our primitive past and profound relatedness to other forms of animal life. His humor and sense of wonder, as well as his breadth of knowledge inform and delight us. Women will be particularly pleased and invigorated by Dr. Rule's delineation and assertion of their true place in all of society as well as basic mothering. His views, indeed, sound a keynote resolute and resonant for any discussions of the role of Women, a keynote whose echoes may well be tomorrow's Wisdom.

—JOSEPH POST, M.D.
FORMER PRESIDENT,
THE NEW YORK ACADEMY OF MEDICINE

Chapter One
DEBBIE & HER MOTHER

As she had since the first visit, Debbie W. took her usual chair and said nothing. I got ready for another hour of silence.

Debbie W., 22, was an intelligent and attractive young woman. Her parents, however, were at wit's end, according to the referring physician Dr. D. According to him they genuinely loved her and had given her everything that money could buy—private schools, summer camps, annual trips to Europe, all topped off by a debutante party at the Plaza Hotel. Although bright and full of energy, she had been expelled from college for breaking rules and was managing to make a mess of everything. She had wrecked several automobiles, run up debts and broken several engagements to be married—the result of her uncontrolled spells of temper which, on occasion, approached pure rage. Recently her drinking had increased and she had been seen with a crowd that her parents described as "dangerous." The most recent scandal had been precipitated by her seducing the fiance' of a former college roommate on the eve of the wedding.

She had been seen by a number of psychiatrists who dismissed the notion that Debbie was just spoiled and headstrong. All agreed that she suffered from a mental illness but, as happens so often, the psychiatrists disagreed about the diagnosis. Some said it was schizophrenia, others said it was a manic-depressive disorder and still others said it was schizoaffective in nature. Debbie refused treatment and would have nothing to do with any of them. She had agreed to see me only because she had always listened to Dr. D. who had been her pediatrician throughout the years of childhood. Dr. D. suggested a few visits just to get acquainted with me and assured her that she could stop whenever she wanted.

I felt certain that I would be dismissed as were the other psychiatrists when, during our first visit, it became clear that answering questions made Debbie acutely uncomfortable. At one point she looked around furtively, glancing at the door as if she were about to bolt from the consultation room. She behaved, it occurred to me, as though the power to question was the power to destroy. I suggested, casually, that it might be a good thing if she just went through the motions of seeing me. I would ask no questions. She would not have to talk about herself if she didn't feel like it. This might make things easier, and besides, I hinted, it might get her parents off her back for a while. She seemed to accept the suggestion and so began our silent therapy.

She took a chair in the corner of the consultation room farthest from my desk, turning the chair slightly so that our eyes wouldn't meet. Every so often, I would try to lessen the tension by making some neutral or playful remark but I stuck to my promise that there would be no questions. Session after session she would go directly to the corner, sit down and grip the arms of the chair. At first, I thought this indicated her readiness, at any moment, to jump up and escape but later it seemed to me that she was, tentatively, establishing possession of the chair, as though it might be the safest place available.

With the passing weeks she stuck to her corner, her face turned away most of the time. Occasionally, she would steal a quick glance at me, or in my general direction, but I could not read its meaning. Months went by. In view of the lack of progress, I suggested to Dr. D. that we might have to end the sessions and explain to the parents that therapy was ineffective. Dr. D. had been a close friend of the parents for years and he was quick to disagree. He pointed out that I was the first psychiatrist Debbie had seen for more than a single visit, and, he added, the parents were greatly relieved that Debbie was, finally, seeing a therapist.

"You must be doing something helpful," he said.

I wondered. Maybe he's right, I thought. Maybe just being there helps. This was many years ago, not long after my going into practice; remaining silent and doing nothing was not easy. The passing hours, day after day, became periods of frustration. I groped for some meaning in Debbie's posture, facial expression or actions and hoped for a clue that would lead to some understanding or clarity.

Aware for some time of Debbie's sensitivity, I was concerned that she would interpret any restlessness on my part as hostility but maintaining an amiable presence was becoming difficult. Furthermore years of training as resident physician in a psychiatric hospital plus the years at a psychoanalytic institute hadn't helped me find answers or even guidelines for a case like Debbie's. Perhaps she was, as the other psychiatrists had said, simply another chronic schizophrenic unable to appreciate or process reality as the result of some mysterious brain defect or some profound undiscoverable trauma. If so treatment would, very likely, be futile.

While sitting hour after silent hour, my thought processes dutifully ran through their multiple functions, observing, scanning, searching for a pattern, checking out the various theories of human behavior. In those years, Freud's theories of the instincts dominated psychiatric thinking. Adler, with his views of the inferiority complex, and Jung, who described the collective unconscious, had submitted alternative views of human mental development but their theories, at least in medical circles, were mentioned only in passing.

Here and there, a few newer thinkers, such as Karen Horney, Harry Stack Sullivan and Erich Fromm, were challenging Freud's views that human behavior was the result of instinctual drives which led to conflict. According to them, humans were, first and foremost, social creatures. What people did, or thought, or felt was determined less by their genes than by their relationships with others. Emotional disorders stemmed from troubled relationships; the difficulties were interpersonal not instinctual.

That Debbie suffered from disturbance in relationships, as these thinkers emphasized, went without saying. But what relationship could it be? There wasn't a clue; it certainly did not seem to relate to father and mother.

Debbie's father and mother loved her deeply. This was not based alone on what Dr. D. had told me; I had talked with Debbie's parents in Dr. D.'s office even before I had met Debbie and had been impressed by their sincerity, directness, and the simple declaration of love for their only child. They had willingly described their daughter's negative behavior and open rebellion toward them and had warned me that if Debbie knew I had talked to them she would never agree to see me. Desperate for information after months of frustration, I had deviated from a fundamental tenet of practice; I had visited with the parents without Debbie's permission and without her knowing.

Among psychiatrists there is a saying to the effect that if you can't reach a diagnosis after talking with a patient, the diagnosis usually turns out to be schizophrenia. With Debbie it was different. Although the weeks went by without any signs of progress, I was beginning to understand why I could not simply relegate Debbie to a category of chronic schizophrenia or, indeed, provide any formulation carrying a dark or dismal prognosis. There was something mysteriously intriguing about Debbie; there was something challenging about her problem. I began to see in those furtive glances just a trace of a plea for help, interrupted, on rare occasions, with what looked like a twinkle of playfulness—or mischief. I couldn't be sure.

Continued questioning of the parents revealed that Debbie's troubles went back to early childhood with tantrums, feeding difficulties, and adjustment problems in the early school years, culminating in truancy and Debbie's repeatedly running away from home by the time she was in third grade. I asked Dr. D. if he recalled Debbie's runaway behavior.

He tilted his head this way and that, then, a light of recognition dawning, he blurted out, "Oh, that wasn't running away, it turned out that she just wanted to visit her grandmother." This was the first I had known that Debbie even had a grandmother.

In those years, psychiatry had shown no particular interest in the events of the early months of life. Formal research into newborn behavior had not been done; infancy was generally accepted as just "one big buzzing confusion". The infant was in its own world, busy getting its eyes to focus, its other sense organs and its muscles to work and would become interested in the world outside only after it developed some awareness that its needs were met by some external source.

Debbie had been coming to see me for several months when, browsing at lunch-time in the hospital library, I came across the first scientific reports describing the effects of depriving infants of a mother's care. The research, however, was not with humans but with monkeys. A University of Wisconsin professor, Dr. Harry Harlow, described what happened when infant monkeys were taken away from their mothers. Most of us would have guessed that nothing much would happen. After all, we routinely take a kitten or a puppy from the litter without thinking much about it and without apparent damage.

With monkeys, however, separation from the mother had profound effects on every aspect of growth and development. The abandoned baby was a picture of anguish, crouching in a corner, whimpering and hugging itself, incessantly rocking back and forth, periodically sucking or biting its fingers and toes. As the deprivation continued, even though nutrition sufficient for growth was provided, signs of extreme fear and distress continued.

If two deprived monkeys were put into a cage together, they would grab one another and cling desperately. The clinging would continue for hours with little or no efforts to explore or play. If five or six mother-deprived monkeys were placed together in a play area, they would form a chain of clinging monkeys. The lead monkey, having no one to cling to, would struggle to free itself causing the whole chain to jerk along the floor in a fashion that observers labeled "choo-choo" behavior.

Further exploring the mechanisms of deprivation, Dr. Harlow offered a deprived infant a choice of two artificial "mothers" constructed of wire. One of the wire models offered a nipple which supplied milk, the other offered no milk but was covered with terry cloth. The preferred substitute for the lost mother was the fuzzy one, the one covered with terry cloth. This lifeless object, with buttons for eyes, resembled a monkey mother less than a scarecrow resembles a human, but the infant monkey would grab hold and hang on for dear life. The need for attachment, the yearning for contact, or touch, or support was powerful. The infant would cling to the terry cloth mock-up for fifteen hours daily, leaving only to nurse periodically on whatever source was available. A basic law of primate behavior— still valid after millions of years for humans—seemed to be: When in trouble *grab hold of the nearest primate and hold on tight*.

The pitiful substitute for a real mother was a lot better than no mother at all. A baby monkey who had experienced no other mother than the terry cloth-covered dummy would, given the chance, timidly join a group of playful, non-deprived youngsters and, learning from its age-mates, manage somehow to grow up and become a socialized, functioning monkey, taking its place among adults and becoming capable of courtship and sexual behavior.

The infant monkey not provided with a terry cloth-covered substitute never grew up, never made it into the world of playmates or adults. Its behavior became more and more psychotic, like pitiable humans I had seen on the back wards of mental hospitals. It remained a terrified and isolated creature gnawing out pieces of its own flesh.

Instinct, for hundreds of years thought to be all any animal needed to guide its growth, was apparently insufficient. A baby monkey, clearly, needed an extended period of nurturing, of protection, of learning, and this required mothering. If the mother was taken away, even temporarily, the damage to the infant was profound and growth into the juvenile and adult stages of living was seriously disturbed.

To what extent could these observations be applied to humans? Probably not at all, was my immediate thought. A human baby wouldn't be nearly as vulnerable. In the wild, a baby monkey that loses its mother perishes, the intense mother-infant bonding insures survival, hence, the terror. The human baby, on the other hand, doesn't perish if it loses its mother; a father, granny, auntie, older sister or other guardian takes over. Human babies routinely have access to an assortment of foster mothers, less nurturing and affectionate, perhaps, but a lot better than terry cloth scarecrows. By comparison, the human mother would seem optional.

Speculations came readily; facts, however, were lacking. Reports of wild children, raised without human parents, and scattered comments about orphans provided only fanciful theories. Reading in the psychiatric journals yielded little. Reliable scientific studies of the psychology and behavior of newborn infants were few and far between.

As therapy with Debbie went on in a futile parade of days and weeks, I began to get an image, not of the attractive woman that my eyes saw, but of a baby monkey hiding its face in terror. It made no sense. This wasn't an orphaned or abandoned human; Debbie had a mother and, as far as I had been able to determine, a loving and nurturing one. At a loss, I continued to ask questions of the parents and Dr. D. about Debbie's early years.

One day, a chance remark of Dr. D.'s puzzled me. He said that it was a pity that the grandmother had died as she would be able to answer all those questions about the beginning years. I had heard nothing of a grandmother and questioned him further. He recalled that the grandmother had taken care of Debbie because of the mother's illness. Finally, with the help of the parents and much questioning, fragmented memories were recovered and the complete story assembled as the bits and pieces fell into place.

Shortly after returning from her honeymoon, Debbie's mother had been excited and happy to discover that she was pregnant, but the happiness was short lived when it was found that she had contracted tuberculosis. This was in the days before streptomycin, the miracle drug discovered shortly after penicillin, and doctors knew that to continue the pregnancy would gravely endanger the mother. Mrs. W., nevertheless, insisted on going ahead with the pregnancy, although she was aware of the risk and knew that a long cure would be necessary. She spent the entire pregnancy in bed.

Immediately after Debbie was born, Mrs. W. was taken to a tuberculosis sanatorium where she spent the next two years pining for her baby. Separated by a glass partition, she was allowed to see Debbie for only a few minutes once a month. On one occasion, her nose and mouth covered by a mask, she was allowed briefly to hold her baby. The grandmother, Debbie's father's mother, assumed the mothering chores and raised the baby—with some assistance from the father, who worked long hours and was frequently away on business. Meanwhile, the mother, in bed at the sanatorium, dreamed again and again of her baby and the day she could return to her.

More than two years had gone by when she was, finally, allowed to return home. She was instructed to continue wearing the mask when she tended to Debbie. After a few weeks, Mrs. W.'s mother-in-law, not wanting to be in the way, left the house and moved to a distant city. By this time, Debbie was no longer a cuddly infant, she was an active toddler, walking and talking—with a mind of her own. Her mother in her excitement and happiness accepted anything and everything that occurred without complaint.

Dr. D. eventually recalled that there had been a never-ending series of feeding difficulties, temper tantrums, physical ailments and, with the advent of school, learning and disciplinary problems. Mrs. W. kept trying to hold on to her belief that there was no such thing as a difficult child and continued to do her best.

Debbie's delinquency took a more serious turn when, at a very young age, she began running away from home. Dr. D. had remembered correctly what Debbie had been up to. At the age of eight, she had managed to steal money and find her way by train and bus to her grandmother's home in a city many miles away, a remarkable undertaking for one so young. This was repeated on several occasions and stopped only with the grandmother's death.

A possible explanation of the mystery crossed my mind. The infant Debbie had "bonded" to her grandmother with all the primitive intensity of an infant monkey, and the inadvertent and arbitrary interrupting of that bond had caused all manner of difficulties. The possible truth of this formulation was one thing; applying it to help Debbie was quite another. I could not risk telling Debbie what I had found out and how I had done so. It would, I felt certain, jeopardize the fragile trust that had begun to develop between us.

Weeks passed before we came across a subject that we could share and in which Debbie would join, namely, the games and fun we had as children. I would tell some little anecdote of my childhood, a pleasurable event or an episode of childhood mischief. Debbie would respond, at first with some hesitancy, but, on occasion, we would break into a laugh. We agreed that recalling things in childhood was a little like pretending and could be a lot of fun. When, on recalling a memory from childhood, she mentioned her grandmother I would mention my grandmother, too. Debbie's memories began to tumble out.

On several occasions, caught up in sharing a memory with me, she would leave her chair and move around the office seemingly less concerned about controlling the distance between us. Her memories began to include a long series of frustrations, hurts and defiant behaviors. She would frequently flare up in anger after she became certain that I would not disapprove or try to control. I suggested that whenever she wanted to she could pretend I was a friend or an older brother which she once said she had always wanted. Or, if that didn't work, she could imagine me as a favorite uncle. Were there no other people in her imagination, I wondered, who could be as loving and playful as her grandmother?

"At least, you could pretend that I'm not a psychiatrist," I ventured.

Debbie burst out laughing. "You aren't," she said, and laughed some more.

"Only incidentally." We both laughed.

Searching for understanding we managed to form an alliance, a kind of club with two members. It could have been called Childhood Hurts But You Can Have Fun, Anyway.

Debbie became much more free; the space between us was no longer fixed and rigid, and some days she would sit in the chair by my desk, but months passed before we could share and discuss the full story without tension or emotional outbreaks. Months more passed before I could get Debbie and her mother to sit down together and discuss what had happened.

So many years had gone by; so much pain and misunderstanding had occurred.

Gradually, the facts were brought into the open. As each painful episode was discussed, one after the other, I suggested that the three of us just sit quietly, acknowledge it and try not to run away. The tragedy of the mother's illness, I explained, had destroyed any chance for the development of the mother-baby bonds of deep love and trust that develop soon after delivery. Both of them had suffered greatly, I went on, the mother by the failure of her dream to experience her baby's love, the daughter by losing the grandmother she had learned to love as a substitute for the lost mother.

The only option I could see that was open to them would be to set aside their bitterness, to share their suffering as honestly as they could, and to see if they could retrieve just a little from long lost hope by building some kind of friendship. There were many tears—and, occasionally sobs from both or an angry outburst from Debbie—but over the next few months things began to happen. Expressions of vengefulness and resentment on Debbie's part lessened.

Debbie's wild and erratic behavior stopped. Problem drinking ceased. Our visits became less and less frequent. She fell in love and married. She had babies of her own. In time, a genuine friendship between mother and daughter did develop and, on a number of occasions, they took trips together to visit the grandmother's grave. Over the years, I would see Debbie on the street, with friends or with her husband or the children, or walking her dog. There was always a smile and sometimes what seemed to me like an expression of gratitude—or love.

The experience with Debbie gave me a renewed sense of hope and optimism for patients with severe emotional disturbances. It made me wonder more than ever about the origins of human behavior but could knowledge of animal behavior, a field at once vast, uncertain, confusing, help solve human problems? The question wouldn't go away.

Published research, like Harlow's with Rhesus monkeys or Kohler's and Yerkes' with chimpanzees—dealt with captive animals. Reliable observations of monkeys or apes in their natural surroundings were few—most were from travelers or hunters who lacked formal training in animal study. Pioneer field observers, like George Schaller who studied gorillas and Jane Goodall whose studies of chimpanzees made her name known the world over, had not yet appeared on the scene. In years to come their studies would provide crucial information and stimulate an interest in animals and the environment which would spread to millions of people.

Among psychiatrists, none took animal studies seriously. Official psychiatry held and still holds, generally, to the view that the proper study of mankind is Man. Harry Stack Sullivan, a leading psychiatrist whose theories carried much weight, summarized the prevailing view which dismissed animal studies with firmness and finality. He wrote, ". . . the only worthwhile study for psychiatry is of things ubiquitously human." Where a study of animal behavior would lead I did not know, but, wherever it was going, my colleagues weren't likely to be interested.

Chapter Two
ROBERT & HIS GRANDFATHER

These were the years just after World War II, a period of change-over to peacetime, a period of adjustment and confusion. Science had been focussed on the war effort, knowledge of animal behavior was limited, little research had been done on child development and virtually none on newborns. Among my psychiatrist friends, for instance, no one seemed to know much about what went on or what could go wrong between infants and their mothers. Asking questions at hospital staff meetings yielded little. Nobody seemed to know how babies behaved when they were deprived of mothering.

Time spent searching the literature at the hospital library was not informative. Newborns were startled by a loud noise and reacted with alarmed stiffening to the threat of being dropped but that was about it. There were measures of childhood learning, developmental scales for school aged children and some papers on juvenile delinquency, but no studies of newborns. Research on behavior, said one observer, seemed limited to studies of white rats and college sophomores. Reliable studies of newborns—studies that have begun to reveal the amazing abilities of babies have all been done since today's parents were young, the last three or four decades.

After some months of unrewarding search on my part, the librarian at the New York Academy of Medicine library managed to come up with a few interesting studies. John Bowlby in England had published the first detailed observations of orphaned or abandoned babies in asylums and had noted their failure to thrive. They grew more slowly than normal, they were apathetic, they explored their environment less, and they walked and talked late. In one area, however, they were precocious. They showed increased care-soliciting behavior: that is, until apathy set in, they exhibited skill in appealing for attention.

A researcher in this country, Sybil Escallona, working at the Menninger Clinic, had published observations of mothers nursing their babies, noting that mothers varied widely in their sensitivity to their baby's signals. One case in particular impressed itself on my memory. This mother, described as preoccupied and distracted, seemed confused by almost anything the infant did. On hearing a slight cry of distress she would push the baby's head further against the breast, shutting off its air supply; only when it struggled and turned blue would she notice. Within a short time, the very act of nursing would send the baby into spasms of terror. The mother then wondered why the baby had become a feeding problem. What other ways could a mother's distress effect her baby? How did such difficulties come about and how much could they effect the baby's growth and development? No one knew.

In another study, Dr. Rene Spitz, a pediatrician, had made careful observations of the newborn's reaction to the human face and had made a documentary film of newborn behavior. Dr. Spitz took an ordinary balloon, painted two dark spots on it for eyes and gently waved it above a baby in its crib. The baby would make its typical effort to focus, slowing its random movements as it endeavored to keep its head still. On recognizing a face, even this crude disembodied imitation, the baby would break into a smile. When the balloon was slowly rotated so that one of the spots disappeared, the smile on the baby's face would disappear also.

For the newborn, apparently, a face is something with two eye-spots that invokes a joyous 'yes' expressed as a smile. There must be, I thought, other words beside 'yes' in the newborn's vocabulary. With its cries of distress, of pain, of anger it certainly had many ways of saying, 'no.' What was it really like for the infant in these early months? I was convinced of the importance of this but until more research was done the only source of information would have to be my own patients.

The case of Debbie had taught me a great deal but it wasn't long before I realized that, for all the struggle it entailed, her case had been easy. Debbie's parents and Dr. D. had supplied the much needed facts; without their help the case would never have been solved but such a fortunate situation was an exception.

Dependent on information I could get from patients themselves, I soon discovered that, for most all of them, their first weeks, months and years were a total blank. Questioning patients about their mothers turned out not to be simple either. Usually, they expressed how they felt about her at the present time. Some described her as an angel, others, vindictively, as the opposite. For most, she was something in between, but their views were often based on the flimsiest of facts and, sometimes, were just transparent rationalizations. Only on occasion would helpful information be forthcoming.

Such was the case with Robert S. He was a successful advertising man in his mid-forties, referred to me by his medical doctor who was concerned about Robert's high blood pressure and his failure to respond to the standard treatment. Robert had a reputation as a kind of genius in his field. He had set up a unique method of research, helping clients select precise media placements which led to remarkable increases in the sales of their products.

In our first talk, it became clear that his career was his life. He had virtually no outside interests except evenings spent in discussing his work and drinking with business associates. He had not married. He had no close friends, only a following of admirers who sought his help and enjoyed listening to his theories. Some referred to him as "the Professor."

I had changed my way of questioning when trying to get information from patients about their mothers. Asking patients to tell me about their mother elicited more emotion than information. A better question, even though it seemed strange at first, was to ask them to tell me about the persons who had provided them with "mothering behavior." Often, they would go blank or laugh but with a little further discussion, when I explained that I meant care that had warmth and meaning, they would see the point. This way of questioning often elicited important information about the years of early childhood.

In Robert's case, the question led to some key facts about his early life. When Robert's mother was pregnant, her own mother, on whom she had always been dependent, died. After giving birth to Robert his mother went into a severe depression which lasted for many months. Her father, Robert's grandfather, assumed the care of the infant with, apparently, no help from either Robert's father or the mother. He fed, diapered, bathed and dressed the baby for more than two years. Then he died. Robert recalled a family story about himself. Age two and a half, he had fought like a tiger, screaming and biting, when his parents attempted to remove the grandfather's clothes from the closet of the room he and his grandfather had occupied together.

Robert's recollection of the early years was that he had been in a total daze. Although seemingly intelligent, he had a severe learning difficulty until the second or third grade, when a teacher told him that the story he had written was excellent and that he was a good boy. He had never been told, he said, that he was a good boy.

The teacher's words, good boy, triggered what seemed almost like an explosion in his head. The words, good boy, seemed to produce a vague but powerful image of his grandfather, urging him to be a good boy, and it put him, momentarily, into a blissful trance. Further questioning revealed that the thought had crossed his mind, "If I am a good boy, I will get my grandfather back."

The teacher's remark brought about a complete revolution in his life and his behavior. From then on he was guided by one vast and primitive injunction; Be Good. A year or so later, the family moved from the town where they had always lived to New York City. Robert had gone into a panic but couldn't recall why this had occurred. At first, he reasoned that he must have missed visiting the clothes closet every day where the smell of his grandfather's clothes made him feel that his grandfather was near in spite of the five years that had elapsed since his grandfather's death. Then, he remembered the real reason for his panic. There were too many people in New York City. His fear was that he could not possibly continue to study intently the face of every passing human to see if it was his grandfather.

"Being good" meant not only to excel in every activity, whether in studies, in athletics, or in social behavior, but to be absolutely honest and absolutely obedient. Robert went on to build an excellent, virtually flawless, record in school, in the armed services and in the business world. Of pleasure or joy there was none. Nor was there time or place to express the pain, the suffering, the loneliness of existence. His being good had become heroic in its dimensions; after his father's death, he supported his depressed and demanding mother with generosity and without complaint. He was totally indifferent to financial reward or honors of any kind, colleagues had ready access to him for counsel or advice, he was an easy touch and loaned or gave money freely.

Our discussions about the origins of his behavior triggered insights that slowly broadened into understanding. He became more relaxed. In the next few years he began to make friends and enjoy them, he fell in love, and married a devoted and understanding woman. Although he said that he was happier than he had ever been, a thoughtful, almost mystical attitude remained a prominent part of his life. He told me that he always felt most comfortable on those occasions alone out in vast open spaces, particularly at night staring into the sky, when he knew that somewhere out among the stars was his grandfather and that he was certain to find him.

Working with Robert made me wonder more than ever about those early months of life, the mystery of mothering and its vicissitudes, because his case seemed to illustrate with clarity and focus what I was finding with an increasing number of patients. The belief was slowly taking shape in my mind—the image of the baby monkeys was still vivid that, if one could uncover what happened to the mother-child relationship during the first months and years, many, perhaps most, psychiatric problems might be resolved.

When young we often jump to conclusions. Now that I have grey hair, walk with a cane, and spend a fair amount of time in a rocking chair, I can smile as I look back. Fifty years ago we were all so confident and earnest—unaware of the extent of our ignorance.

My views of human behavior would go through all kinds of twists and turns as the years flowed by.

Chapter Three
TROUBLE: THE CASE OF ANGIE L.

Angie L. was a young doctor at the hospital where I was a staff member. She was brunette, bright and very serious. She was appreciated by patients, who took her seriousness as dedication, and she was chased after by many young men, doctors and others—not surprising in view of her looks and her graceful figure. She had been raised in the south on the campus of an exclusive preparatory school where her parents were teachers. Both parents were young and this was their first teaching experience. When Angie was born her mother gave up active teaching for several years so she could spend more time with the baby but kept up peripheral chores such as tutoring or grading papers.

Early in her visits with me, Angie's seething hostility toward her mother came out in the open. She made no secret of it. She hated her mother with a consuming passion explaining that her mother had never loved her, had never wanted her in the first place, had feigned concern and love only to keep up appearances. Appearances, according to Angie, were crucial to both parents. Appearances and proprieties were their "religion."

Her attitude toward her father was not so much hatred as it was disdain or scorn. Although she was an obedient child and excelled as a student, she had no happy memories of childhood and declared that it was an unremitting experience of suffering without hope, joy or happiness. She had no friends and was not permitted to play with the wealthy and exclusive students. "Remember, we are just teachers, it wouldn't look right," her parents had said.

Her father died unexpectedly of a massive heart attack during Angie's first year at college. He had carried a sizeable life insurance policy, which was divided equally between Angie and her mother which enabled Angie to continue her education. At first, we were unable to discover why she had chosen the profession of medicine. As a young girl, she had spent much time wandering alone in the fields and woods near the campus. She liked the birds and the other animals and had gravitated toward biology in college. Medical school seemed a natural continuation of this interest.

After graduation and her first postgraduate year as a medical resident, she seemed to have come to a dead end. The reason for her consulting me was her discovery that she had no real interest in helping patients. Further, she was not interested in pursuing a specialty, doing research or even shifting to a completely new career. When I suggested that she might be suffering from a temporary depression, she replied that she had always felt this way, that she had kept going through college and medical school not because she enjoyed it, but because what to do the next day seemed clear, there always seemed to be an assignment. Now there weren't assignments and she realized that she had really never cared in the first place.

Months passed. No explanations of the hatred for her mother came to light. I was reluctant to pursue the matter further for fear that Angie would become angry and stop therapy, which, I was convinced, she needed badly.

She went off on a month's holiday with a young doctor on the staff. He had pursued her relentlessly, with wining, dining, flowers and gifts. She didn't love him but didn't dislike him either. On her return, she related the experience to me, saying that she had hoped that it would bring her some pleasure. Everything had been fine, she said, a nice holiday in the sun and sand. They had been compatible sexually. But nothing had changed, she saw the young doctor for a few more months and the relationship, in the absence of encouragement from Angie, finally withered away. She would spend her weekends driving around the country roads of New York and Connecticut, breaking the monotony by occasionally getting a traffic ticket for speeding. I could not fathom what was going on; I could only continue seeing her and hope for a break.

"My mother's coming to New York," said Angie, "would you like to talk to her?"

"If you feel comfortable about my seeing her it might be helpful," I answered.

A few days later Angie brought her mother to the office. Angie was a big girl, striking without being imposing. I had expected to see someone as big or even bigger, possibly with an intimidating manner. What I saw was a delicate little creature with a very sweet face. I looked at her more intently, almost as though I expected to see a lavender dress and a lace bonnet. Could this be the fierce and hateful mother Angie had been telling me about?

The mother was en route to Boston to visit relatives, but I was able to have several visits with her. Some weeks later, on her return, we had several more visits. She was fully aware of Angie's rejection of her; it had been the pervasive anguish of her life.

"How sharper than a serpent's tooth," I said, nodding my head in understanding.

". . . it is to have a thankless child," she completed the quote, then added, "I doubt that a doctor, or anyone really, can feel a mother's anguish." There was a faint smile.

She said that Angie had always been a puzzle to her, had always avoided and resisted every effort on her part to love, care for, or help in any way. I began to pursue every avenue of inquiry I could think of. Was there a family history of mental problems? None. Were there any childhood illnesses? Only the standard ones, measles, mumps, chicken pox, and Angie had always been unusually healthy and free of illness. It was as though her hatred fueled her health and energy. Had the delivery been uneventful? Well, Angie had been a big baby, over nine pounds, and labor had been somewhat prolonged but, otherwise, nothing very serious. How about nursing? Did you have plenty of milk, I asked? There was a long pause during which the mother, squinting and with furrowed brow, searched to recollect.

All she could remember was that she had made many visits to the doctor in those early months. She seemed to have forgotten just what the difficulty had been except that she knew it was not for any ailment of Angie's. At first, she guessed that it might have been because of a slow recovery from the prolonged delivery but, finally, memories burst through.

Angie's mother had had a series of breast abscesses which began within days of her returning home after the delivery. Nursing became almost impossible. At first, she had been able to nurse from the less painful breast but within a matter of weeks the abscesses of both breasts were equally bad. Although nursing was anguish she refused to give up trying to breast feed Angie. She had plenty of milk but it would cease to flow freely as the pain got worse and she would have to interrupt nursing every few minutes. She recalled tears and pain with every nursing, shifting Angie from one breast to the other. She also recalled Angie's development of biting behavior which, on occasion, caused such pain that she let out a scream.

After months of the doctor's insistence she reluctantly gave up and began substituting bottle feedings. From then on it was an endless ordeal. Angie would fight being bottle fed and no formula seemed to agree with her. She would have colic, seemed resistant to being put on any kind of schedule, would scream to be fed at any hour of the day or night. This struggle eased off only when Angie began to eat solid foods but a series of tensions, one after the other, paraded through the growth years.

No signs of love or affection were ever expressed, not even on birthdays or holidays when gifts and pleasures were provided. It was as though not only the mother but the whole human race was for Angie a source of pain rather than pleasure. Angie, apparently, owed her mother, her father and the world civility and impersonal cooperation but nothing more.

The only option left was to try what I had done, a few years before, with Debbie and her mother, bring the two of them together. Angie was reluctant but I insisted. Nothing came of it. The mother, taking an open, almost begging posture, pleaded with Angie to explain what had been so bad. Angie would either brush the questions aside or, with a hint of desperation, come up with a series of trivial accusations. They hadn't allowed her to have a dog. The school forbade it. She had been called home from summer camp. There was an outbreak of measles. My recounting of the mother's breast abscesses and the nursing experience made no impression on Angie; she had no memory of any such difficulty nor was she the least bit interested.

I urged the mother to extend her stay in New York but she did not feel comfortable at Angie's apartment and longed to get back to her home in the south. They never saw one another again. The mother died of cancer a few years later.

Meanwhile, Angie, even in the absence of insight and understanding, did show some improvement in mood and motivation. Was I, the psychiatrist, functioning like the terry cloth mother substitute, having some healing affect just by being there? I crossed my fingers and hoped.

She began to socialize a little more and met a young Russian opera singer, very much on his way up, and being groomed for top roles. He fell head over heels for Angie, assumed complete charge and wasn't taking no—or nyet—for an answer. They married. Angie stopped seeing me but, after a year or so, returned. The joylessness, the purposeless feeling was the same as always.

It had all been very colorful, international travel, meeting celebrities but what did it all mean? Nothing. Was she depressed? No, just empty. I continued to reassure her, with gentle hints of her lovabilty, of her basic goodness, urging her to be kinder to herself, to explore her potentials for growth. Month followed month. I encouraged her to try exercise programs, massage, hobbies, religion. I finally convinced her over considerable resistance to try the newly discovered anti-depressant medications although she resisted. A year's trial on several different medications and dosage schedules brought no improvement. At my insistence on a second opinion she agreed to visit another psychiatrist, went through months of electro-shock treatment and returned to me unchanged.

I saw the husband periodically only to be subject to a barrage of questions. Why was she so indifferent, why so unappreciative of all he did for her? He was doing most of the cooking and taking care of the apartment. All she wanted to do was drive around in her car—and recklessly at that. Why had therapy not helped her? He was discouraged and became increasingly angry. What had I been doing all those years? Did I need the money that badly? I tried not to be defensive. I reviewed in detail the whole story of Angie's background and my work with her. I shared with him my declining feelings of optimism. I urged him to get other opinions. We talked on a number of occasions when Angie refused to see anyone further. I tried to help him understand the situation, specifically, that Angie's illness or character disturbance or whatever name we gave it, might not be responsive to any kind of therapy.

I didn't question his devotion, I simply tried to explain that my therapy might not have the power to heal. He kept insisting, more out of his own frustration than anything else, that Angie continue her visits with me. Perhaps, as a result, she refused to see me anymore. Finally, at the husband's insistence I did call her asking her to stop by. I encountered an icy and negative response. I never heard from her again.

Years passed. I heard once that the opera singer had moved to Europe but nothing further. It all had receded into some corner of my mind when some years later—after a phone call out of the blue from the singer and a visit to the office I found out what had happened. The singer's career had taken them to Europe but the marriage had not improved. Angie had become pregnant but over his tears and protests had gotten an abortion. In Salzburg where he had just finished singing in a music festival he had been waiting for her to drive down from Munich to meet him only to hear that she had been involved in a serious accident on the Autobahn and had died on the way to the hospital. He shook his head slowly and shrugged, palms outstretched. Eight years had gone by. He had married again, had two children and was living in Germany. As he got up to go he thanked me and said that he remembered how much I had tried to do. He looked at me. Could it have been suicide, he asked? I nodded. We shook hands and said good bye.

Chapter Four
SIBLINGS, PLAYMATES, CLASSMATES:
The Search for Friends

As most doctors will tell a young person thinking about going to medical school, it's not for the fainthearted. Not that it is a marathon of memorizing—it is that—but it also sets up several psychological hurdles which, as autobiographies of young doctors routinely describe, can trigger emotional crises. The experience of dissection in the anatomy laboratory is the first of these—the one most written about—and usually next on the list is the emergency room with severe bleeding, wounds, pain and the deaths on arrival, the DOA's. Once students have met the shock of suffering and death of other humans and can accept the truth of it without a trembling hand and heart, each is on the way to becoming—the roads are many for those with talent—a true healer. Two more hurdles remain, first, the many and tragic failures to cure that true healers must face, and second, the possibility that these may be the result of their own negligence or incompetence.

The psychiatrist has, in addition to the above, a few that are peculiar to the chosen pathway. One is the unexpected and the irrational whether of thought or deed. Often these deviations are harmless and are dismissed as human or amusing; at other times they call for serious thought and immediate attention. Rarely there are behaviors so unexpected or violent as to leave one numb. Suicide is one example and any psychiatrist if he practices long enough will have a number of such tragedies. Procedures to prevent suicide cannot be relied upon. Insisting on another course of anti-depressant medication or on shock treatment, or telling the family of the risk so that they can keep watch, or extracting a promise from the patient or other standard methods, all can fail. Insisting that the patient accept hospitalization can be particularly threatening. More than one patient has circumvented that recommendation by moving suicide to the top of the agenda. Getting a patient into the hospital by ruse or trickery is equally bad; a clever patient can outwit any hospital system. With every suicide, most psychiatrists undertake a period of self-questioning and cross examination which goes on for a long time. Finally, in the interest of self preservation, one has to come up with some kind of acceptance. Psychiatrists, who have spent their adult lives acquiring the skills necessary to help people, do not react well to demonstrations of their own ineffectiveness. It is hard for them to accept the fact that all humans have the "ace of spades" up their sleeves, that they can play it whenever they want to, and that no power on earth, including psychiatrists, can prevent it if they so decide.

Thinking about Angie's possible suicide reminded me again of my failure to help her and the deep puzzlement and frustration I had felt at the time. In her case I had gotten a detailed story of her infancy from the time of her birth. The facts could be presented almost like a documentary film to Angie and to her mother as well, both of whom possessed clarity of mind and high intelligence. Uncover the trouble between mother and infant and healing will follow. I had felt certain that, when patients had the real truth, insight would follow. The eventual outcome would be recovery, the restitution of health, and the healing of family wounds. Perplexity over the failure with Angie persisted. Finally however, a break-through led to an understanding of what may have happened.

While reviewing Harlow's research on the motherless monkeys, I was re-reading the descriptions of how monkeys could be healed, even after severe damage as a result of disturbances of mothering. The description was as follows:

The age-mate or peer affectional system (which directly follows the maternal-infant affectional system) has been relatively neglected in the study of both human and non-human animals, and its full factual and theoretical importance has not been appreciated. This system, doubtless, continues to operate, even after the monkeys have become adults, and then takes the form primarily of affection between adult females, between adult males and between specific heterosexual pairs.

There was something important here. I sat, mulling it over. The article, on maternal deprivation in Rhesus monkeys, further described Harlow's observations. The deprived infant could, if introduced to age-mates even if the damage was severe, recover psychological health and be restored to normal growth. Sociable little monkey playmates were able to help the infant overcome fear and agitation, coax it out of apathy to become an active participant in the give and take of play behavior until it acquired full group membership. Harlow mentioned that some monkeys were so patient and skilled in overcoming distrust and helping socialize the deprived young one that they were nicknamed, "therapist monkeys."

Here was a missing piece of the puzzle. The peer or play group was the key. Angie had been forbidden to play with her age-mates, the students at the exclusive school where her parents taught and this separation from others had continued throughout life. Angie's profound despair which began with the troubled nursing experience had been reinforced by the continued experience of isolation and absence of healing from age-mates that she had been unable to overcome. Her problem was a demonstration of the crucial importance of the peer group.

The experience with one's age-mates is that phase of social growth when the young individual learns what is important in the social group, what unwritten rules exist, how his or her parents differ from other parents, and how to relate to or "handle" parents and other adults as well. In the peer group, one practices meeting the challenges of daily existence, one practices and prepares for a variety of social roles—career, courtship, leadership for instance—and one learns to determine and assess the appropriate social situation for such roles. While all this is going on, the peer group usually functions with joy and carefree play. Angie had missed all of this. She had missed the greatest reward the peer group has to offer, a true friend. She had missed the healing power of friendship.

I had never practiced group therapy. During my psychiatric residency, I had led groups but not for extended periods. Hospital patients who were usually severely disturbed or in crisis situations were, I had thought, poor candidates for working in a group. They would come and go every few weeks, and one got no sense of progress or even of continuity.

Now, convinced of its importance, I began to do group therapy in the office and, to acquire experience, led groups at several hospitals, nursing homes and retirement residences. Within a few years, the many and often remarkable ways the group could stimulate growth, heal a person who had experienced deprivation, or repair the damage after one or another of life's misfortunes had been manifest time and again.

Group therapists in those days were looked down upon by psychiatrists in general and psychoanalysts in particular. According to the prevailing dogma, keeping track of the communications of a single patient was difficult enough; to monitor the communications of six or eight patients was unscientific and was courting chaos. I couldn't agree. Indeed, it seemed to me that individuals who had ostensibly completed psychoanalysis were often lacking in relaxed peer skills.

Belief in group therapy's benefits provided motivation but mastering the art didn't come easily. It was quite different from individual therapy. Remaining unruffled when confusion and emotions ran high could be difficult. Bringing in new patients to group therapy was a ticklish business; regardless of how carefully one had worked with patients on an individual basis their behavior in a group was not always predictable. Emotional adjustments following the introduction of a new member could be stormy, or a new member could be shy and frightened and very much in doubt as to whether to continue. In the latter case it was important for me to provide a little security, to let them hold on to that terry-cloth covered psychiatrist for a while. Usually, after a few weeks, they moved into full participation in the group and, often, demonstrated assertiveness and leadership. They began to feel better and function better, even those who had had serious difficulties in living.

Doing group therapy became a source of pleasure and satisfaction, and I wondered why some therapists complained of the strain and tension of it all. A few quit altogether. I had visited a number of other groups and, clearly, some leaders were tense, over vigilant, and gave no sign that they either enjoyed the group or thought it was important. Without realizing it, they were setting the tone of the group and many patients became discouraged and quit. I felt lucky that I enjoyed and seemed to have an aptitude for group therapy. I assumed it was because I'd learned from the research on monkeys how important it was. Second only to mothering, groups of friends were necessary for growth.

Years later, a more likely reason for my belief in and enjoyment of group therapy occurred to me. I was one of a large family. Counting my mother and father we were a family of ten and it became clear that group therapy is, in some ways, like a family gathering. My recollection mellowed by time perhaps was that dinner time consisted of a great deal of general confusion, punctuated with occasional miscommunication, disharmony and squabbling, but seasoned with a fair amount of joyous banter, humor and affection. Like a therapy group, whatever was going on had much to do with caring, growth and learning. Like a therapy group, the one with the biggest problem often dominated the situation, or, at least, controlled the agenda.

As the years went by the peer group became a dependable resource for helping patients. At the suggestion of a patient who was struggling with a drinking problem I attended an open meeting of Alcoholics Anonymous, a grass-roots organization that had been founded a dozen or so years previously. Impressed by the remarkable power of this peer group to heal I visited many open meetings although Alcoholics Anonymous was dismissed out of hand by colleagues at the time as well as being the target of many a joke or wisecrack. Every few years, new groups came into being modeled on the twelve-step program of Alcoholics Anonymous, and, having patients who were wrestling with the corresponding problems, I visited these groups, too.

Over the course of the years, I visited Gamblers Anonymous, Pills Anonymous, Drugs Anonymous, Pot Smokers Anonymous, Narcotics Anonymous, Neurotics Anonymous, Debtors Anonymous, Overeaters Anonymous and a number of other community self-help fellowships. From them I continued to receive some of the better parts of my continuing psychiatric education. I attended so many meetings that it was assumed, I think, that I was an alcoholic plus one or more of the above. I learned, nevertheless, not only about the vast range of human problems—including a few more of my own—but also the many ways that humans managed to solve them. Guiding patients to the appropriate self-help group added greatly to the help I was able to give.

Mothering behavior was still the crucial area of inquiry but, of comparable importance was the experience with playmates going back as far as patients could remember, searching out the hurts and rewards of games, of joy, of friendship. As Professor Harlow had predicted from his observation of young monkeys, studying the peer/age-mate phase of growth could be rewarding.

Mothering and the peer group taken together are the alpha and omega of human development. Mothering offered a vast and varied field for study. It transcended species, it covered millions of years and thousands of different societies and cultures. It embraced wide variations of experience yet retained an unwavering constant of nurturing and care. Similar statements could be made for peer experience. Its role in individual development, its role in educating and organizing the social group was, like mothering, a constant and a key to understanding human growth.

Mothering and friendship are the two pillars that support the arch of society. They are magical forces, the first providing for the beginning of life's journey, the second taking up where the first leaves off. A mother's care plus caring friendships are powerful, positive influences, their effects lasting a lifetime.

In my work with patients I was acquiring some skill at spotting the failures of either the mothering experience or the experience with peers. How did these failures happen and how could the damage be undone? The search ahead was challenging.

Chapter Five
SEX: NATURE'S MANDATE

Mothering. Friendship. What of sexuality?

Every psychiatrist, sometime during his training, has had to consider whether sexuality is or is not the main motivating force of existence. Freud and the twentieth century brought the question of sex out into the open. Few people today appreciate the hypocrisy and inhibition that once surrounded the subject. It was still hush-hush during the 20s, through the years of the Great Depression, and even after World War II, until the sexual revolution of the 60s.

Freud was the spokesman for the doctrine that sex is the single most powerful basic and central driving force of life. We are born with it, he insisted; it is an instinct. Freud's conclusions came from his practice of psychiatry, analyzing and making notes of the spontaneous, uninhibited outpourings of the patients who stretched out on the couch in his office in Vienna for one hour, day after day, and, obedient to his instructions, said whatever came into their minds.

Jung and Adler, both of whom had for some years worked closely with Freud, were the first to differ and became spokesmen for alternative views. Thousands of psychiatrists since have lined up on one side or the other. Now, one hundred years after it began, the debate continues.

Visiting Austria, thirty years ago, I decided to look for Freud's office, hoping to get a feeling of the Vienna of one hundred years ago and the origins of psychoanalysis. I spent half a day trying to find the place; the tourist information center had no information and a call to several historical societies yielded nothing. Finally when I had about decided that it must have been destroyed during the bombings of

Vienna in World War II, I learned where it was from a doctor at the local chess club, took a cab to 19 Bergasse, found the place all right but the building had been converted into a plastics factory. Some years later a commemorative plaque was placed on the door. I felt that Freud deserved a little better. Even though his theories have been greatly modified—some say, superseded—he is one of the founders of modern psychiatry. By this time, I, too, knew what it was like to listen to patients for eight, ten or even twelve hours straight with only a few minutes between appointments.

Freud had established the pattern, the rules, of listening. Hour after hour, day after day, year after year, he had listened and made notes of the verbal productions of a daily parade of human beings. Hundreds of patients, male and female, poured forth their life stories in the presence of a detached but interested doctor who assured his patients that he would remain non-judgmental and uncritical.

The Victorian years, prissy and proper, provided the background for Freud's visits with these troubled humans. Encouraged to drop social constraints and inhibitions, what they thought about and what they talked about, not surprisingly, concerned sex. As their dreams and long buried memories unfolded, the sexual themes stretched all the way back to the earliest years of childhood. Freud's critics asserted that normal people didn't have these thoughts. Freud's patient's, according to them, were mostly hysterical women suffering the repressions of the Victorian era. The debate went on and on.

Freud's discoveries overturned forever the myth of childhood innocence. Children could no longer be pictured as little angels spared from and oblivious of carnal knowledge; they were bright and perceptive investigators, hiding their interest and secret motivations from parents, teachers and the adult world. Often Freud's patients reported sexual seduction in childhood and Freud at first felt that this was the cause of adult neuroses. Later on he began to distrust the reports and concluded they were based on imagination, sexual fantasies that, as children, they had secretly wished would happen.

The studies of behavior of infant monkeys agreed with Freud's observations that sexual behavior begins in infancy. Baby monkeys in the early months of play exhibit sexual behavior of a toddling nature, and at first there isn't much difference between the behaviors of male or female. Baby males and baby females have baby erections of penis and clitoris, both sexes clumsily mount and thrust, both sexes present or accept being mounted.

These behaviors support Jung's views which assert that all species, including humans, have male and female characteristics inherited from parents. With monkeys, as time passes, the baby males present less and the females mount less until each develops behaviors characteristic of their gender. Sex play continues right through puberty as adult sexual behavior develops. The sexual urge shows individual variation and choice; a few, for no apparent reason, appear to have little or no sex drive at all.

Generally, sex is a powerful urge. The hectic, turbulent seasonal rituals of breeding in fish, birds, and mammals are well known. The competition for mates is ceaseless and intense. Violence and death is not unknown. Nature equips its millions of creatures with this powerful urge, and, for a high percentage of individuals, nature demands that they respond even at great risk. In many species—insects, fish—the sexual act means death for the individual of one or both sexes, nature's Liebestodt.

While each creature has resources for survival, the imperative to breed and continue the species seems to be given top priority. The strength of the sexual urge of male baboons was tested by starving them for weeks and then admitting them to an enclosure where food was presented along with a receptive female. They all by-passed the food to attend the more powerful drive. Nature has designed the system to perpetuate the species, not the individual. Individuals must take their chances.

Freud incorporated these facts of nature into his descriptions of human behavior. His theory states that a powerful biological energy, sexual in nature, is present at birth and follows a pathway of development from infancy to maturity. He called this energy "libido." In infants the libido is concentrated around the mouth; its object is the breast. Never one to inhibit speculation—or imagination—Freud said that the infant, sated with mother's milk after feeding, resembled an adult after an orgasm. The first developmental step he called the oral stage of development. The libido migrates from the mouth to the bowel during the anal stage of development and parents can find themselves embroiled with a stubborn infant in the battle of the potty. After a few years, the libido becomes concentrated on the genital area and the individual can then grow to full sexual maturity.

Sexual difficulties were seen as failures of the libido to follow the developmental pathway. If a portion of the libido failed to migrate from the oral area—oral fixation, Freudian psychiatrists call it—the patient developed an oral character. Oral characters were of two kinds, the passive and the active. The passive were dependent individuals with a character symbolized by sucking. The active were aggressive individuals with a character symbolized by grabbing, biting and devouring; in short, a life driven by acquisitiveness. Oral characters also become chatterboxes.

Anal characters were described as compulsively clean, orderly, stubborn, obsessive and miserly, their lives centered in the bathroom and dominated by constipation and hoarding. Like the oral types, these also had sexual difficulties. Only the genital character could reach full maturity. Society, according to Freud, isn't helpful to the individual; on the contrary it is a frustrating force, opposing nature's powerful instinctive urges.

Instincts, located in the central nervous system, Freud labeled the Id. Society's repressive forces, which were transmitted by the parents, he labeled the Superego, best thought of as the conscience. The struggle between child and parent occurs because the child wants to follow its instincts and the parents must train it to accept society's restrictions. Within the Ego of each child, a battle takes place between the demands of the Id and the equally powerful demands of the Superego. This is everybody's seesaw battle between what I want to do, Id, and what I ought to do, Superego, and finally, what I decide to do, Ego.

Freud's views created enormous controversy, much of it due to the shock wave felt by the Victorian world at any mention of sex. Doctors were as prudish and hypocritical as everyone else. Freud presented a paper to the Medical Society of Vienna suggesting that the cause of hysteria was sexual repression. It produced such outrage and unpleasantness that he never spoke to a medical audience again.

Half a century went by before the hue and cry simmered down, and a few still accuse Freud of introducing wide open attitudes toward sex which then led to degeneracy and decay. Other critics, aware of the reality and frequency of child abuse, claim that Freud turned against his own discoveries for an assortment of reasons, some of them opportunistic and political. They accused him of blaming the victim. Others claim he faked results and altered his cases.

Much criticism of Freud today is irrelevant. Freud was a pioneer investigator groping for insights into human nature that would free us from our repressed and restrictive selves although he was, perhaps, overly insistent that his work was not only scientifically valid but verifiable. His emphasis on an unconscious mental life that influences our behavior, on the fact of infantile sexuality and on transference phenomena are fundamentals of modern psychiatry. He opened vast new areas of inquiry and started psychiatrists on a road that transformed them from being custodians of the insane to becoming specialists in solving the problems of living that confront most of us. His followers, not Freud, were responsible for turning psychoanalysis into a cult, a mythology and a monopoly—now in decline. The search for the facts of mental life continues. Truth and clarity lie somewhere in the future.

For all psychiatrists, it was necessary to know something about sex and why people seemed to have so much difficulty. Most patients had sexual conflicts of one kind or another. Having become interested in primate behavior it occurred to me that if one were a non-human primate, a monkey or an ape, the whole business would be rather straight forward. As a self-respecting monkey, you gradually understood more and more about sex as you grew up, it was a natural part of play and learning and preparation for adult sexual behavior was a function of the peer group. It all worked out well; females were often subject to male domination—after all, the male was much bigger—but not brutalized. Males adapted to female rhythms and stratagems without becoming unduly enraged or frustrated.

Puzzling over why humans made sex so complicated was being simplistic. Monkeys and apes didn't have to understand such complex issues as private property, the role of the father, marriage vows and contracts, family networks, religious and other institutions. Still, I wondered why instead of sex being joyous and satisfying, it got mixed up with the whole spectrum of emotions: shame, fear, anger, anxiety, guilt, panic, jealousy, and often, particularly when alcohol or drugs were added, violence and injury.

Estelle A. was a patient of Dr. Jane B., a psychiatrist and good friend of many years. Estelle had come for therapy because she felt certain she would ruin every chance for a happy relationship with a man. She was thirty-five years of age, dynamic, attractive, and had successfully launched her own business. Dr. B. consulted me because Estelle had been in therapy with her for over a year, had just managed to wreck another relationship and was becoming seriously depressed. She had gotten what history she could, and although Estelle seemed to be open and cooperative with her, she felt Estelle was holding back. Worried because some comments about suicide had come up in recent sessions, she wondered if I might be able to help.

Estelle had grown up on the West Coast, was the third of three children, with one brother ten years older and another brother five years older. Her well-educated parents had a two career marriage, the father in the defense industry and the mother in the electronics industry. Their combined incomes provided the family with ample material comforts. They lived in a well-to-do neighborhood. The grandparents had lived with them when Estelle was a baby but the grandmother had moved back east after the grandfather died.

The trouble, according to my colleague, had begun when the younger brother began sexually molesting Estelle about the time she started school. Efforts to get additional facts were unavailing, Estelle would not or could not reveal fully what had happened. More out of a favor to a colleague rather than willingness to take on a suicidal patient, I agreed to try Estelle in group therapy.

At the time, I was doing a lot of group therapy and had nine or ten groups meeting weekly for two hour sessions. Having this many groups gave me a fairly wide choice in selecting which patients for which group. Too wide an age span tended to inhibit free expression, and, once or twice, the censorious and inhibiting atmosphere set up by opinionated oldsters interfered with the progress of younger members. Organizing groups around shared interests worked best.

Over the years I had "true" peer groups, groups of retirees, of young people, of married couples, of alcoholics. Estelle agreed to join a group more out of obedience to her therapist than out of hope for relief. She participated, but in a somewhat reserved and measured way, and deftly deflected questions from other group members if they came close to tender subjects. As the months passed, she showed no signs of sharing or opening up in any areas of pain or hurt but it was clear that she enjoyed the openness and honesty of the group. My colleague reported to me that suicidal ideas had stopped and that her general attitude was one of resolve, if not optimism.

It had become routine at that time for groups to hold weekly alternate meetings without the leader being present, the theory being that much can be learned from the way people behave in the absence of an authority figure. For some, the alternate meeting without my presence made no particular difference, but, for others, their change in behavior was so noticeable that it often led to uncovering and eventually clearing up their distrust or fear of authority.

The combination of individual and group therapy finally began to reach Estelle. The freedom and openness exhibited by the group was communicated to Estelle who became relaxed both with me and her peers. Encouraged and accepted by the group, Estelle began to hint at some deep hurts. One day, one of the female members shared an early memory of having been sexually molested by an uncle and, then, being blamed and punished by her parents. The group members responded with sympathy—and considerable anger toward the uncle and the parents.

"I wish my parents had punished me," Estelle said. "It at least would have given me the feeling that they cared."

Estelle had not been punished by her parents, indeed, they seemed to have been oblivious of the sexual abuse. Their indifference was worse than punishment, she explained, as she felt certain that she could never turn to them for help. Now, with group support, Estelle could at last share the story of her childhood with people who had demonstrated their ability to care, people who could listen. The group sat in total silence and stillness, a tear visible here and there on a male or a female cheek, while Estelle poured out the whole history, one painful word at a time.

"I don't even remember when it began. I don't remember exactly how I felt at the beginning, maybe just a sense that he was doing something wrong."

Frightened, she obeyed his orders to keep their behavior a secret even from the older brother. With the parents away from home during the day and no discovery by the housekeeper the behavior continued.

Estelle began to sob. "Then he brought in boys from the neighborhood," she blurted out, half choking.

In fits and starts, she continued the story. She hated the shame of the experience which had become brutal and sadistic. She began to hate her brother but she was threatened by him and by his friends with dire punishment and revenge if she violated the secrets of their "Sex Club." When she made faint attempts to stop further sexual behavior the brother threatened to tell her parents about her promiscuous sexual behavior with the others. Over the years, the behavior tapered off but ended only with the brother's going away to college.

In her social life, and in her school and career life, she continued to behave "as though nothing had happened" which is the way she had been ordered to behave. Being attractive she was generally liked and she was also a good student. However, she never had close friends and feared any kind of confidences. She dated because she didn't want to appear strange and, in college, responding to peer pressure she tentatively tried once or twice to have a relationship. Scarcely had she begun an affair before she would have intense waves of revulsion and anger that would force her to break things off even though she neither castigated the man nor explained her behavior.

After college she returned home to California but a desire to make a clean break and to start over brought her to New York. The same feeling made her avoid working closely with others, particularly men. With limited capital she started a secretary and executive placement agency where she spent most of her time on the phone or alone in an office, and within a few years, as a result of her energy and enterprise, the business became profitable. Her deep inward conflict continued to interfere with the possibility that sex could be joyous, wholesome and part of a creative and productive relationship. The relationship that had just broken up was, according to her therapist, the last straw. She wasn't going to try any more.

When Estelle had finished telling her story little more was said for the rest of the session, but the group understood why Estelle had developed a rigid and unshakable conviction that if you trusted or worked closely with a man you would eventually be used and brutalized. They understood why Estelle had felt that no friend could accept a person with such an unmentionable history. They understood why attempts at closeness and intimacy made her sick, made her physically ill. And their understanding healed her: often, care is cure.

Estelle did well in the years that followed. With the group's support and tutelage, she joined in the fun of having both male and female friends and eventually understood the playful side of sex, too. Estelle once confessed to the group that she had absolute terror of the male organ. She hadn't yet acquired the courage to use the word penis. In her long buried fears, the penis was conceptualized as some kind of instrument of torture, a powerful spear or other variety of weapon.

The group, with its easy sense of empathy and fun, was able to reassure Estelle even in this sensitive area. The girls in the group, in the spirit of wholesome earthiness, convinced Estelle that she possessed the ultimate mechanism for rendering male power and weaponry harmless, and, unlike Delilah, she didn't have to go through the rigmarole of giving the male a hair-cut.

Estelle did very well. She married and had several children. Some years later, I learned from a group member that Estelle's parents met annually with all their children and grandchildren and that Estelle harbored no bitterness, even toward the brother whose victim she had been. The "peer-play" group had succeeded in overcoming a very severe sexual problem.

A case like Estelle's was not an isolated one. Time and again, I found that patients who had been deprived, for whatever reason, of healthy peer relationships often had a difficult time when they entered the period of courtship and sexual behavior. In our culture, the peer group is the primary source of sex education; the family and the school have, if not abdicated, accepted secondary and often non-contributory roles. Peer groups can, I was discovering, often solve sexual problems when individual therapy has failed.

Chapter Six
TRANSFERENCE: FUNNY BUSINESS IN THERAPY

Freud's discoveries in the field of human sexuality were extended and made even more valuable by his descriptions of the psychological phenomenon that he labeled, transference. A few case summaries make this clear.

Anna O. was a young woman patient of Dr. Joseph Breuer, an older colleague of the young Sigmund Freud. Anna O. suffered from paralysis of her limbs and partial loss of vision which would get better every time she was able to recollect and tell Dr. Breuer about painful memories from long ago, before the illness began. Anna called Dr. Breuer's treatment "the talking cure" and her case contributed to Freud's idea of catharsis or directing a patient to say whatever came to mind.

A second case, Dora, was a young woman afflicted with a paralyzed arm whom Dr. Freud treated with this newly discovered method of free-association. Freud had studied in Paris and had watched Dr. Charcot, the great French hypnotist, produce or induce a paralysis in subjects under hypnosis. Charcot would tell a patient that when he or she came out of the trance they would, for instance, be unable to move an arm or leg. The patient in the drowsy, relaxed and suggestible state which characterizes the hypnotic trance would—coming out of the trance—be totally compliant, paralyzed, and have no memory of the cause. Hypnotic suggestion, likewise, would remove the paralysis.

Freud reasoned that repressed sexual desires functioned like a hypnotist's suggestion. Dora's hysterical paralysis was suggested by herself as punishment for having forbidden thoughts of a sexual nature. Anxiety neuroses were also caused by repression of some painful conflict. Dora's case was the cornerstone of Freud's theory which stated that mental illness could be caused by buried memories.

An interesting aspect of Anna O's case, the case mentioned first, was that she developed an intense attraction to Dr. Breuer, which so upset him—and Mrs. Breuer, as well—deep in the grip of Victorian proprieties, that Dr. Breuer immediately terminated his relationship with the patient. Freud wasn't so shaken by this kind of event, even when a young lady patient unexpectedly enveloped him in an amorous embrace. He knew that this could happen in hypnosis and had seen it demonstrated repeatedly by Dr. Charcot.

A woman after coming out of a trance will, in response to a suggestion made during hypnosis, throw her arms around the neck of the hypnotist no matter how old or ugly he might be. Freud understood that the behavior of his patient wasn't due to any seductive activity on his part. The patient, on uncovering buried memories of a long lost love or yearning, found herself in the grip of powerful feelings. Automatically transferring these to her doctor and convinced she had fallen head over heels in love with him, she threw herself around his neck.

This was the first example of what Freud labeled, understandably, transference. He had the objectivity and the courage not to take the attitudes of patients personally, to remain detached during demonstrations—sometimes dramatic—of irrational love or irrational hate. Freud, eventually, wrote extensively on the phenomenon. Therapists were cautioned to watch not only the patient's reactions, but their own reactions as well. The therapist's reaction was called the counter-transference and could, like the patient's, be distorted. It works both ways. Psychiatrists occasionally "fall in love" with their patients, or think they have, which, as someone has commented, makes for good movie scenarios but bad malpractice suits. Freud's theories provoked much controversy and still do. Nevertheless, his discoveries were of great help to psychiatrists, particularly inexperienced ones.

Early in practice I had my first encounter with this matter of transference.

Norma L. was a prominent actress who was admitted to the hospital with a diagnosis of acute alcoholism. Her physician had checked her over physically and wanted me to follow her through de-toxification and help her work out some plan of recovery. I observed her for several visits as she slowly sobered up while the sedation to prevent convulsions was gradually withdrawn. She stared at me with some confusion at first and I couldn't be sure she realized that I was a doctor sent to care for her.

As her appetite for food returned along with her ability to converse I suggested that a long talk might be in order and told her I'd stop by the next day. The following morning I made some friendly introductory remarks to the effect that it was time to do a little thinking about her life and what alcohol was doing to it.

She listened for a minute or so, then, said, "I'm sorry to interrupt you, Doctor, but I've fallen madly in love with you."

For a split second I thought she was playing a game but could see that she was deadly serious. I said something to the effect that, regardless of what feelings we had about each other, we had a very important problem to discuss and that we should not let anything interfere.

"I know that, Doctor, I know about the problem, but I also know that I am in love with you," she went on, "I've read about love at first sight and all that, but it's never happened to me before and it's very important that we decide what to do about it."

After the first shock, a number of thoughts flashed through my mind. "Everything I've been reading about transference is really true. This is it." Finally, as my confusion lessened, the kind of questions one might expect, "Did I do something to cause this? Something inadvertent?" I couldn't think of anything. All I had done was stand by the bedside for a few minutes daily for two days, and I couldn't have uttered more than a dozen sentences.

Once again, I made an effort to get the patient to deal with the problem. I told her that she had to do something about her health, that it was a matter of life or death. She was absolutely certain that she had fallen in love with me, and that was the only important item on the agenda; all other problems would take care of themselves. Finally, I patted the back of her hand and told her I'd stop around the next day. She gave me a most benign and condescending smile as I left. She had accepted the reality of our love, the smile said, and I would, in time, accept it, too.

I spent the afternoon in the library reviewing material on transference and whatever I could find on the behavior of the alcoholic. The thought occurred to me that this lady alcoholic was going after me with the determination of an alcoholic going after a drink. I continued the hospital visits and listened patiently to her assertions as I tried to get things back on track. Yes, she'd be attentive to nutrition and would take her vitamins. Yes, she'd begin to go back to her AA meetings when she had time.

The puzzling aspect in this case was that the transference never went away. The patient did take up her AA program again but periodic binges continued for years. Every few months there would be an emergency call, usually late at night. I got to know her husband over the course of the years through the phone calls and the hospital visits. We reluctantly put up with Norma's unshakable obsession that she was in love with me.

Years passed and I would get a call from Hollywood at any time, day or night. I never refused the calls; Norma and I had become friends. I accepted her along with her addiction, her attachment to me and her apparent helplessness to do anything about it. Finally, having accepted my own failure to alter her way of thinking, I could feel only warmth and compassion.

Years later, an almost identical repeat of the case of Norma occurred, not an actress this time but a charming and beautiful woman, Lois N., the ex-wife of a wealthy Wall Street financial consultant. Her attachment, or more specifically, her transference, took place when I was called to the hospital to take charge of her acute alcoholism. She, like Norma, was a binge drinker and would have periods of sobriety lasting from weeks to months. Having had the experience of Norma and having found that attentiveness and a sympathetic attitude did no good, I was a little less supportive this time.

I told her it was inappropriate, that it was irrational and took our minds off the job we had to do. She had little reaction to anything I said or suggested. No matter how much I remonstrated she would just toss her head and laugh heartily. She loved me. I was trying to wiggle out of it and she knew it couldn't be done. She attended a few AA meetings, she entered a de-toxification and rehabilitation program at a sanatarium but signed out after a few days. Although she wandered from one amorous adventure to another she claimed I was her only love. For years the late night calls would come every few months even though I urged her to seek other professional help. Eventually, she remarried and, I learned, moved to the south of France.

Freud had discussed at length the sexual nature of the transference. Somehow that didn't seem to be the crucial factor in the case of either Norma or Lois. True, there was something sexual in their actions and attitude toward me but devoid of any kind of maturity; in its innocence and grim seriousness, it was more like the first school girl crush of adolescence. More important were the early experiences with mother. The two cases were remarkably similar and both patients seemed to have been casualties of early experience. Both had had mothers who were unreachable or unavailable because of varying degrees of abandonment or indifference. Both patients turned to their fathers for protection and nurturing and, when this failed, to a series of other men from childhood on. Both had great appeal in charm and seductiveness but were isolated from their peers either by haughtiness or competitiveness. Neither had ever had a close friendship and neither could muster the courage or determination to make a commitment to peers in the fellowship of AA. Both were plagued by a deep inward sense of worthlessness. Both had the unshakable conviction that, although they were irresistible to men, they were, basically, defective and unlovable.

Once again, humans, desperately struggling, revealed the basic requirements for growth. Mothering and the peer group. Good mothering, good friendships. Mothering was provided for us without choice, friendships we had to seek out but both were needed to develop the capacity for mature courtship behavior and its mellowing into grown-up love and sexuality.

The peer group is a powerful social instrument for good, although—unfortunately, as with gang phenomena—for bad as well. Even where mothering or "parenting" has been deficient, the peer group can be effective, solving seemingly hopeless problems in living, loving and working. Just how it did so was intriguing and challenging, its mysterious power second only to mothering in its creative impact on the individual's growth. Main stream psychiatry had at that time largely overlooked the great healing power of the peer group. With the passing years more and more therapists, including psychiatrists, learned how to use group therapy with its collective healing powers of sensitivity, understanding and friendship.

Mothering was needed by the individual to reach a stage of development where he or she was ready for peer relationships, but it took good peer relationships to reach the stage where the individual was ready for mature sexuality. Mothering. Peership. Courtship. These three were fundamental phases and processes of growth.

What other processes were necessary for the individual to mature, to thrive? What pieces of the puzzle were still missing? What else was needed to complete the picture?

Chapter Seven
TERRITORIALITY IN ANIMALS: HUMANS, TOO?

The world of mother and child. The world of playmates and friends. The world of courtship and lovers. Separate worlds. Three different languages. Three sets of views and values. Three distinct cultures, each with its own satisfactions, its own risks, its own hurts and its own joys.

While they vary widely from culture to culture and from individual to individual, these three stages of social growth provide, for all of us, the scripts and the roles for act one, act two and the opening of act three of life's unfolding drama. In growing up we slide back and forth from one stage to the other easily and innocently; we run back and forth between mother and our playmates unaware of the pendulum swing between being a dependent child and practicing for grown-up roles. We do the same between the immaturity of our teen-age behavior and courtship. In adult life the three stages of growth become interwoven—the three primary colors of living blend together— and the sequential nature of how we grew up is largely lost to memory. Patients, day after day, called up memories from these repeated phases of individual growth—often seeing them in a new light.

Perhaps—so my thinking went—the inventive side of humans had been exaggerated. Rather than being unique discoverers and innovators humans—in some areas of existence at least—merely displayed variations of behaviors encountered in the rest of the animal kingdom. The more I learned about these fundamental phases of existence the more I wondered if they were nourished by roots that extended deep into our evolutionary heritage. The study of animal behavior had been a good place to begin but other fields were important, too. Such subjects as physical anthropology, to find out about fossils and ancient humans, and social anthropology, to learn about "stone age" and other human cultures would have to be studied if the evolutionary beginnings of human behavior were to be revealed.

A medical education leaves one quite ignorant of animal behavior. Students are drilled in endless facts about muscles, nerves, blood vessels, livers, spleens, kidneys, hearts, lungs, glands, cells, nuclei, and so on. They also pick up miscellaneous lore about tape worms, ticks, bacteria, viruses, dogs that carry rabies, rabbits that carry tularemia, parrots that carry psittacosis, and mosquitoes that cause epidemics. Busy learning, they routinely vivisect or experiment on animals of one kind or another.

Finally, they study how all these things interact to produce various diseases as well as what remedies or cures are available to counteract them. A medical education, goes the wry comment, is the development of the memory at the sacrifice of the imagination. Still innocent and naive, aglow with relief on being graduated, young doctors tend to feel that the knowledge they have acquired is more extensive than it actually is.

It was sobering, even bewildering, to read of the vast animal world, species beyond counting, their origins and lives intertwined and complex. Living creatures are everywhere; their habitats, the jungles, forests, savannas, deserts, rivers, lakes and oceans amounting to the sum of the world's geography. Naturalists spend a lifetime studying the evolution and behavior of a single species. Not only animals, but plants, too, are part of the warp and woof of nature's wondrous tapestry. Plants have evolved an intricate relationship with animals, using colors and scents and flavors to entice animals to eat their fruits and spread and sow their seeds. Setting limits, they protect themselves by producing repellent toxins, and other chemicals that guide and control the appetites of plant eating animals. The diversity and variations of plant-insect relationships had only begun to be appreciated.

This was a world of which humans were once a part, a world they left millions of years ago. To learn about that world, even the fundamentals, was a forbidding challenge, a journey without end, yet fascinating to the point of being addictive. It was a meandering journey, too, replete with intriguing miscellany. The female of the gypsy moth can signal for a mate over a distance of several miles, the male navigates in on a molecular beam of her sexual perfume. The song of the humpback whale is fifteen minutes long without a repeated phrase and can be heard by another whale over hundreds, some claim thousands of miles.

When my journey had first begun, just after World War II, information was hard to come by. In these days of information glut that may be hard to appreciate. Then, however, the search could be frustrating although, fortunately, for not too many years. The United States was the only major power with an industrial plant not in shambles. The accumulated needs of the people, after years of rationing, stimulated demand, many things began to happen, and the years were charged with energy and restlessness—the dawn of the electronic age, of television, of computers. The Cold War and the arms build-up began, the Russians launched Sputnik and triggered the space race. Economically, politically, socially; these were turbulent years, years that triggered the information explosion. Research expanded on a vast scale, not limited to military goals but extending in many directions. Naturalists from a variety of fields, including ecologists and conservationists, studied animals in the wild. Anthropologists observed primitive cultures in remote regions. The number of scientific journals doubled in ten years, would double again in the next ten, and then, a third time. The flood of scientific papers became unwieldy.

It was hard to know what to look for and where to look.

Studying went on with no end in sight. After office hours I would go here and there, nights, week-ends and vacations, textbook or notebook in hand, taking courses, attending seminars, alternately haunting laboratory, library and lecture. Embarking on the journey by reviewing the theory of evolution was easy enough; much of it was familiar from medical student days. All forms of complex life, Darwin had written, are descended from simpler forms. Life on earth began billions of years ago as a bit of protoplasm, a submicroscopic bit of living stuff. Over time animals evolved from single celled forms through such simple creatures as jelly fish and worms on up through fish, frogs, reptiles, birds, mammals and, finally, primates, the highest form of mammalian life, the monkeys and apes—and us.

Centuries earlier, naturalists beginning with Aristotle had described the animal kingdom in an ascending ladder of complexity and by Darwin's time classifications were extensive, detailed and in Latin. They were based not only on living animals but on thousands of fossils uncovered wherever humans constructed canals, mines, buildings or just dug into the earth while farming. Fossils revealed many forms that no longer existed; periodic extinctions involving many species had occurred and explanations other than the Biblical flood were needed. Further, geologists had known that the world was older by billions of years than the 4,004 years Biblical authorities asserted. Scholars such as Cuvier, Goethe and Lamarck had speculated on the possibility of an evolutionary process wherein complex forms came from simple antecedents but none had offered satisfactory explanations of how it could come about.

For that matter Darwin himself, did not know what we know today about the intricate mechanisms of evolution; Mendel's work on genetics and the discovery of DNA were years in the future. Darwin's formulations were necessarily generalizations. In simple terms his theory stated that the offspring differs from its parents and that competition between offspring for food and mates determines which individuals will produce the next generation. The qualities of the successful competitors are passed on, in turn, to their offspring. The changes from parent to offspring might be very small but operating over millions of years they eventually result in a new species. Darwin labeled this process *natural selection*, popularly known as *survival of the fittest*. Today, with the vast new field of gene research, evolution is still the cornerstone of biologic thought.

The initial thesis of evolution that the offspring differs from its parents goes without saying. We all know, too, that animal breeders are able, within a few generations, to bring about remarkable changes in a particular breed. Over years, dog breeders have produced a Saint Bernard and a toy poodle from similar stock, but an elephant from an amoeba or a man from a monkey is a different story. One problem most of us have in understanding evolution is our difficulty in conceptualizing time. While we seem to grasp what we mean by a minute, or a day or a year the concept of a million years is beyond our grasp. Unless one is a geologist or an astronomer, a million years or a billion years have no more significance than a string of zeros. Our world, the planet Earth, say these scientists, is roughly five billion years old.

Biology professors have a clever way of helping first year students understand the complex natural world and the vast reaches of evolutionary time. Every known human society, goes the lecture, has its "creation myth," the story of where its people came from. There are thousands of such myths. The Bible offers a Christian version which differs from the others but shares episodes with a number of them. The story of the first man and woman, the story of a paradise and the story of a great flood, for instance, occur in many of them.

Science, explains the professor, has its own "creation myth".

Borrowing an idea from time-lapse photography where we watch the growth of a plant from seedling to full blossom in less than a minute, the scientific myth collapses the five billion years of the Earth's age into a single calendar year.

According to this metaphorical history there are no traces of life in the early months. The Earth is a dead world, more closely resembling a planet such as Venus, its atmosphere without carbon-dioxide or oxygen, the chemicals which identify and support the plants and animals of today's world. Billions of years passed while chemical reactions and, later, primitive anaerobic organisms liberated oxygen from the rocks and lava to create the ozone layer protecting living organisms from lethal solar radiation and, eventually, produce the atmosphere we know today. By early summer primitive life forms appeared then all through summer and fall evolved into variant protozoa, bacteria, slime molds and algae and other single-celled varieties.

Suddenly—in evolutionary time, five million years or so—with the advent of the Cambrian age, late November, the first multicellular creatures such as Hydra and jelly-fish evolve, then round worms and flat worms, then insects in strange shapes and colors. By early December the Jurassic ages bring amphibians and primitive reptiles and by mid-December the Age of Dinosaurs. During the Cretaceous age they reach their zenith and begin to die out. By December twenty-fourth the dinosaurs, like millions of species before them, are extinct. Primitive mammals appear and many species continue to evolve but no monkeys or apes until December 28th or 29th.

There are still no humans. Our most primitive ancestors, creatures four or five feet tall but walking upright, possibly carrying a digger stick, finally make their appearance in late afternoon on the last day of the year. On New Years eve humans with bigger brains, stone tools and fire finally arrive. Ten minutes before midnight, modern humans that look like us make a furtive entrance on the stage of history. Cities have been in existence for a minute, more or less, and all modern tools, inventions, weapons and high-tech just a few seconds before the end of the year and the first chord of Auld Lang Syne. It's so humbling that many folks don't like to think about it—some won't.

What can be said in general about the creatures of Earth? How do they live? How do they behave?

Every animal has nine fundamental behaviors. Some, the obvious—one, two, three, four—come to mind immediately; food, shelter, sex, fighting. Behaviors less obvious are care-soliciting and care-giving. Three others; exploratory behavior, mimicking behavior and eliminative behavior complete the list of nine. Whether one studies insects, elephants or presidents of the United States, the behavior of any living creature is limited to these nine items.

Terms vary. Mimicry is called allelomimetic behavior and includes things like flocking in birds, schooling in fish, herding in cattle and, countless activities of humans who are, according to Aristotle, "the Most Mimick of all Animals." Fighting behavior is called "agonistic" by the scientist; it includes struggling to escape as well as to subdue. Exploratory behavior has several alternative terms; ruminative, investigative and a few others. Eating is called ingestive behavior since it includes both eating and drinking.

Learning what I did of the behaviors of the solitary animal was perplexing; I wondered, as a psychiatrist, if any animal, even the lowly single-cell amoeba, is truly solitary. Eventually, sexual drives or other circumstances must bring living creatures together. Paramecia, commonly studied single-celled animals, routinely reproduce by fission or cloning but, periodically, two individuals come together (or conjugate)—whether out of loneliness as the poet might say or in the process of exchanging bits of DNA, the conventional scientific explanation.

The classification into nine individual behaviors was telling only part of the story. To study any creature in isolation—

especially a human—is to miss the very essence of existence; while not all animals live in social groups, all animals are social, even the most defiantly independent of us. Freud, and other pioneers of psychiatry, did study the isolated individual but, in after years, psychiatrists began to take a more inclusive approach. Understanding human problems meant broadening the view to include, not only what were labeled our instinctual drives or complexes, but our social nature, that is, our ability to modify instinctual drives, to communicate effectively in our relationships with others.

Humans with their social skills—as the scientific myth pointed out—are late arrivals, recent products of evolution, but the roots of those skills in the behavior of non-human primates are millions of years old. The monkeys and apes represent the highest branches of the evolutionary tree but their humble origins can be traced all the way back to the world of the giant reptiles, the time of the dinosaurs, and to a tiny animal about the size of a small rodent, the forerunner of all mammals. Theorists have suggested that the extinction of the dinosaurs, one of five known extinctions, was brought about by the earth's collision with a large meteor. Meteor showers, they assert, occur periodically—perhaps every twenty-five, perhaps every sixty-five million years—with catastrophic effects on the atmosphere, the climate, the plants and animals.

Although theories remain locked in controversy, most experts agree that the earth at the time of the dinosaur extinction was undergoing major geologic changes with profound impact on climate and vegetation. The dinosaur's warm, watery, treeless world of swamps and ferns was vanishing, replaced with rivers and valleys and plains with flowering shrubs and trees. Vast forests appeared and spread around the globe. Evolving birds and insects moved into and flourished in the forest canopy, busily ferrying seeds and pollen and aiding the wind in the spread of plants and blossoms.

One of the animals that Nature picked to fill the niche vacated by the dinosaurs was a tiny, four-legged, shrew-like creature eking out a precarious existence scrounging for insects on the forest floor. This unlikely candidate to carry the banner of evolution toward humankind possessed the primitive reptilian brain but had acquired a crucial addition the dinosaur brain lacked, namely, control of body temperature. The creature was warm-blooded. Cold-blooded creatures become immobilized and moribund in cold weather but this little insectivore had its own thermostat. It could maintain a steady body temperature and go on about the business of living in spite of the swings of the thermometer although it paid for this improvement by having a very busy and hectic existence. Needing to find, consume and digest more than its own weight of food every twenty-four hours it no longer had the privilege of dining in a leisurely manner like a browsing dinosaur.

Some theorists have suggested that even the fierce dinosaur, Tyrannosaurs rex, became a big frozen steak for these tiny creatures when the temperature dropped toward zero. The scenarios of paleontologists must, of necessity, be speculative and fanciful. Paleontologists now question such simple explanations and challenge every item in the dinosaur scenario, asserting that the metabolism and nervous system of dinosaurs resembled that of birds rather than lizards. New fossil finds and new studies hint that—unlike snakes or turtles—they were not cold-blooded and that they cared for their young.

Most scholars agree, however, that a rodent-sized insectivore was the earliest ancestor, the forerunner of all mammals, creatures that beside being warm blooded, give birth to their young and nurse them with milk produced by mammary glands. Hatching the egg inside the mother's body was another great evolutionary advance in protecting offspring; the eggs of reptiles, birds and fish are vulnerable to accidents, weather and predation.

In the next thirty or forty million years evolution exploded to create a vast multicolored web of plants and animals, including nineteen major divisions of mammals from the tiniest mouse to the biggest whale. One of these divisions or orders was the Primates. The ground-dwelling shrew climbed into the trees. From limbs with claws they evolved hands and feet with fingers and toes that could grip and hold. Eyes which had been in the side of the head evolved toward the front giving primates stereoscopic vision, crucial in judging distance. They began to rely more on vision than smell for getting food; as the nose got smaller the face flattened out. These adaptive changes went along with tree-dwelling in the vast new forests. It was a change from a nose to the ground type of existence to the more familiar one of hand to mouth. Unlimited new foods rewarded resourcefulness; leaves, fruits, nuts, berries, buds, flowers, bark, resins, birds' eggs, nestlings and lizards made insects an optional food source.

Creatures such as these, equipped with hands that could grip and manipulate objects, possessed of curiosity and an investigative brain, inclined to be social and, cooperative, providing extended nurturing to newborn and extended learning to the young, could only continue to evolve, diversify and flourish. Exploiting countless variations of climate and food supply, exploring every ecological niche, they evolved into hundreds of species and spread to every part of the globe where trees offered welcome. Taxonomists, the specialists who classify things—overlooking the fact that the church fathers had initially claimed the term—named these creatures Primates, from the Latin Primus or first, because they were the most evolved of all mammals.

Observation of primates, specifically of infant Rhesus monkeys, was what had alerted me to the crucial importance of social behaviors (in contrast to individual behavior), at first mother-infant, and, later, the importance of playmates and, finally, courtship-sexual behaviors. I learned about three additional—also basic—forms of social behavior from other animal studies. These were territorial behavior, dominance behavior and spacing behavior. At first, I could not see how they functioned in human society. Humans are so skilled at concealing their motives that it is not always possible to determine just what they are up to and sometimes they themselves don't know. Gradually, I became aware of how pervasive these behavior patterns are and began to understand how they operate. Who owns what? Territory. Turf. Who is socially important? Status. Dominance. Whom can I trust? Closeness. Distance. Much of the time these forms of behavior—like our thoughts—are covert, hidden, and unconscious. No wonder we get confused.

In animals, whose skills at deception are less evolved, these behavioral patterns are, comparatively, straight-forward and easily recognized by a trained observer. Back in 1920, an English naturalist, Henry Eliot Howard, had published his observations on territorial behavior in English song-birds, and straightened out some time-worn misconceptions. The ceaseless, melodious bird song heard in the spring when the birds returned from their annual migration wasn't, primarily, a love song incident to ardent wooing. The males, singing, were staking out a bush or other greenery and defending it against all comers. The females, in fact, delay their return from the winter migration until males have settled their territorial disputes and the chorus of song has toned down. Female singing isn't all love songs either, some females do not sing at all; the brain centers for singing die out before maturity. The female specializes in listening, her safety and the safety of her fledglings increased by silence. Of course, the matter hasn't been settled. Experts in animal communication still argue about many aspects of bird song. They haven't, in fact, come up with any satisfactory explanation for the mocking bird who mimics everything from babies' cries to traffic noises, apparently for the fun of it.

Isolated observations of territorial behavior had been made before Howard's work. Way back in 1678, an Englishman, named Willoughby, wrote in a letter to a friend, "It is proper for the Nightingale at his first coming in spring, to occupy or seize upon one place as its Freehold into which it will not admit any other nightingale but its mate."

After Howard's publication of his observations of territorial behavior, its occurrence in other creatures was confirmed by numerous observers. Like the nightingale, the male of various species, whether fish, fowl or mammal, stakes out his turf before he undertakes to find a mate. Territorial behavior, however, has many forms, varies with seasons and circumstances, and is a subject of much investigation and debate by naturalists. Territorial behavior is, of course, not restricted to the male. Lizard or lynx, the female, in setting up a nest or defending her young, may drive off an invader twice her size.

As I began reading scientific accounts of territorial behavior I became aware of how deeply rooted it is and how often it operated in humans. With patients, examples came up constantly; the drive to acquire or control "turf" or its equivalent in money or material goods is characteristic in varying degrees of humans everywhere. I came home from a lecture on territorial behavior one evening to observe two of my own children drawing a chalk line down the middle of their bedroom floor to settle a territorial dispute.

The universality of territorial behavior across the animal kingdom did not escape the media. Popular articles described its operation and its many variables in a wide variety of species. A book, *The Territorial Imperative*, quickly became popular. Its author, Robert Ardrey, asserted that territoriality was the root cause of war, of poverty, of cruelty, indeed, of most of humankind's ills.

The extent to which humans with their big brain cleverness cover their motives and camouflage, expand, and elaborate upon territoriality—as they have on all the other animal behaviors—seems unlimited. The human capacity to scheme can outdistance one's imagination.

Once the importance of learning and social experience in determining behavior was recognized, based on the work of Howard and others, instinct, once the standard explanation of behavior, was replaced by such terms as "unlearned," in contrast with "learned," behavior. The nature versus nurture controversy developed and the search for other social behaviors important in the regulation of animal relationships followed.

Chapter Eight
DOMINANCE: WHO PUSHES WHO AROUND?

A few years after Howard described territorial behavior, Thorlief Schjelderup-Ebbe, a Scandinavian, described dominance behavior. For a naturalist of genius, nature can reveal her secrets anywhere. Thorlief's discoveries were based on watching ordinary barnyard hens. Out of his work came the term "pecking order" after he had demonstrated that in a flock of, say, twenty hens there will be a dominance order which is consistent over time. Number one in the pecking order is deferred to by all. She gets pecked by nobody. Number two hen defers to and gets pecked only by number one, and so on down the line to number twenty, who, as you would have guessed, defers to and gets pecked by all the other nineteen.

Another scientist, part prankster perhaps, demonstrated that if you gave an injection of testosterone to number twenty she promptly became number one, and the others, with some ruffling of feathers, moved a notch down the status ladder. For males, dominance is a primary preoccupation, often visible; for females it operates in more subtle ways.

Dominance behavior, like territoriality, can be observed up and down the evolutionary scale. Its forms are many and varied depending on the species. The question of who dominates whom in human society and how they do so is an important question for all of us. What role dominance played in the lives of my patients became an important aspect of therapy. In many situations how it operated was obvious; in others it could be so subtle as to elude the most sensitive observer.

Mr. H. was a top corporate executive with a Fortune 500 company. He was referred to me by one of his vice-presidents who had consulted me a few years previously. His appointment, it turned out, was not to talk to me about himself but about his teen-age daughter. I recalled what I had heard about Mr. H. He was a powerhouse at the corporation, a perfectionist, master of detail, issuing crisp and clear orders and following them up tenaciously. The staff had given him a time-worn label, The Bull of the Woods. He entered my office, introduced himself, looked me up and down slowly and deliberately, sat down in the proffered chair and proceeded to outline briefly the problem he thought I might be able to solve. His daughter, Peggy, the eldest of four children, was about to graduate from private school, had been accepted at Vassar and had suddenly announced that she was not going. She had decided to stay in New York City, to attend a local university, and live at home.

It's a disappointment to her mother and me," said Mr. H., "Frankly, I had been looking forward to her leaving."

According to him, she had been extremely difficult for the past several years. She would defy parental orders or suggestions and would challenge or contradict opinions voiced by either her mother or her father. The three younger children were beginning to follow her example. Things had reached crisis proportions. Having listened for the full hour I suggested that it might be helpful to see his wife and then, if both he and she were in agreement, to see Peggy. He did not conceal his disappointment.

"I assumed that you might be able to offer a solution without involving them. I would expect a psychiatrist to solve problems that are beyond the scope of the parents," he went on.

"I appreciate the compliment," I said, with a smile, "but your wife's information and, if feasible, your daughter's would be helpful."

"I hadn't expected this," he said, as he got up to leave. "I will, however, mention it to my wife." With a curt nod he was gone.

"That's the end of that," I thought.

Weeks had passed when the receptionist told me that a Mrs. H. had made an appointment. Her visit turned out to be as empty, incomplete and unsatisfactory as was the visit with her husband. She contributed very little information about herself, about the marriage and about the family.

"I really don't understand why he doesn't let Peggy run her own life." she concluded.

This came as a surprise. I had, of course, assumed that she was upset, as was her husband, by Peggy's decision not to leave home.

A remark toward the end of our visit was equally puzzling. I had said something to the effect that permissive parenting had limits, that parents really had to be in charge until children had demonstrated that they could run their own lives.

"Since when has he been in charge of anything." she said, half under her breath.

This added to the puzzle. "Well, I think the next step would be to chat with Peggy," I suggested, not knowing what else to do.

"She won't come. She's never asked for help in her life."

Once again I said good-bye with the feeling that this would be the end of it. It wasn't. Peggy made an appointment the next day. She lost no time in getting to the point.

"Will you get my parents off my back?" she said, clearly giving an order in the form of a question.

Peggy was an attractive and very determined teenager. I relaxed, looked at her for a moment. "I'm always happy to help when I can, but you look like a very capable young woman to me. How does it happen that you haven't been able to handle this yourself?"

She sat, staring at nothing. Her jaw tightened. "Because if I do something, one of them always undoes it."

"Hmm." I may have smiled.

"It's not funny."

"Not funny, strange."

Pause. "Oh."

"Could you tell me a little more about it?"

Peggy launched into a summary of family life that, edited for strong language, could have fit nicely into a text book. In a short time she cleared up the myth and mystery of her father's dominance behavior. I had been trying to fit a concept of an authoritative type individual into the family setting and had asked why she seemed to resent her father's leadership.

"Leadership! What leadership? The only leadership I ever saw around there was him saying, yes, darling."

It seemed to be true. Not only did he not make decisions, he didn't participate in anything of importance in the family.

"But he decided you should go to Vassar?"

"He never decides anything. He just whines if you do something he doesn't like. He has never told me I could or couldn't do anything in my whole life. My mother used to tell me to ask my father but that didn't work. Finally, she quit telling me what to do."

"Who does make the family decisions?"

"Nobody." Pause. "Maybe I do."

The more I questioned and the more she shared, the more I became certain she was right. She not only made her own decisions but had become advisor to her two brothers and her sister. She made decisions about where her brother and sisters should go to school, as well as vacation plans, plays, restaurants, and other activities for the whole family.

I was beginning to understand why her mother, secretly, didn't want Peggy to leave. Tired of trying to get the father to assume leadership she, too, had abdicated. Mr. H., the Bull of the Woods at corporate headquarters, simply hung up both his hat and his leadership when he came home.

"He's like a child. Always hoping she'll be nice to him."

"She isn't a loving wife, then?"

"Who wants to be married to a child?"

It was a strange story but Peggy seemed to have gotten the family problem into clear focus.

"She gets a head start on their Martini ritual, and has one or two before he gets home. Then she gets angry with him and then they have some kind of an argument and then he feels guilty, so he goes into the Yes, Darling routine all over again."

"If that's a true picture it could be pretty discouraging."

"You said it."

"Vassar will get you away from all this."

"And leave my kid sister and my brothers? I'm not going to go."

We talked about this at length. She had, indeed, taken over leadership of the children. She advised them on dress, on behavior, on their studies. I suggested that Peggy try to get the parents to come back and see me. They never did but Peggy returned a number of times.

We were able to talk together, and we agreed that leadership in her family was a responsibility of her parents and not of hers. It was enough to assume leadership for herself. Her parents, I suggested, were unlikely to pick up their responsibilities as long as she was around. Furthermore, going on with her education did not mean abandoning her sister or brothers. Increasing her own wisdom and understanding would help them. She could still be friend and advisor without living under the same roof.

The problem of Peggy and her family illustrated how complex dominance behavior and the related issues of leadership could be. Male dominance of the family, the standard for centuries, was undergoing some changes and who pecked whom in human society wasn't always easy to figure out. Unlike barnyard hens it wasn't always a straight line. Although it is called a pecking order there is little order. Humans often take turns pecking each other. And human pecks can draw blood, too.

I never heard from Peggy or from either of her parents again but the experience had taught me that a single behavior—in this case dominance behavior—can operate and control a family and yet remain almost completely outside of awareness. Years would pass before experts would focus on the dysfunctional family and the widely variant disturbances it could manifest.

Chapter Nine
SPACING: HOLD ME TIGHT BUT DON'T FENCE ME IN

A third social behavior, as basic as territorial and dominance behaviors, is spacing behavior, much studied in animals. Most of us are vaguely aware that spacing isn't random. We keep an appropriate distance between ourselves and other people; we huddle, scatter or cuddle or find a comfortable intermediate spot depending on the circumstances, but it is usually automatic and we don't think about it unless we're rudely bumped into, caught in a crowd that restricts our movement, or find ourselves to be a stranger at a party. Animals attend meticulously and literally to matters of proper spacing. Not to do so is to risk a nip from a neighbor. A scientist who had observed a number of langur monkey groups in India said that if she had a snap-shot taken from a helicopter of one of her observed groups raiding a farmer's field she could identify every member of the group—even though the image of each was little more than a dot—simply by taking a ruler and measuring the distance between each monkey. Humans, like their primate cousins, observe spacing literally in moving away from or toward one another in business, on civic or social occasions. Humans, however, also handle spacing problems metaphorically as is reflected in the many forms of our language. We say, "I feel close to so and so," or, "I wouldn't touch him with a ten foot pole," to express our sense of trust of others on the one hand or our sense of distrust on the other. We hear such phrases repeatedly; often, they exist as unconscious thoughts that influence daily life. We humans, in fact, can stand quietly right next to someone we hate—something no self-respecting, unhypocritical monkey can do. Perhaps this made human society possible.

Research on spacing in animals has included such things as the amount of space between one-celled paramecia in a drop of water, between geese of a flock on a migratory journey, or between monkeys feeding in a grove of fig trees. Each of these examples illustrates a different method for regulating spacing, the first is chemical, the second visual and the third auditory. As a survival mechanism the importance of spacing can be appreciated. Depending on the particular species and the situation, an animal can, in effect, say, "if I can touch him he's too close, if I can smell him he's too close, if I can see him he's too close, or if I can hear him he's too close." These factors operate in humans as well but the calculations are made in a trice and we're usually unaware of the subtlety of the operations involved.

Overpopulation, the result of permanent overcrowding is, obviously, a disturbance of spacing behavior and has, with the passing years, assumed increasing urgency. The problem, however, had challenged science for more than a century. Darwin's theory of natural selection which stated that only the "fittest" survive was based on Malthus's theory of population control. Malthus stated that since the food supply increases arithmetically, i.e., 1,2,3,4,5, and the animal population increases geometrically, i.e., 1,2,4,8,16,32, animals will always outgrow the food supply. The result, went this theory, is unbridled competition, murder, famine, war, disease, and epidemics; mechanisms that limit overcrowding and unrestricted population growth. The weak perish, the strong survive.

Darwin's original scenario presenting such a dismal outlook has, through the years, been much modified. Professor Wynne-Edwards of Aberdeen University, one authority on spacing behavior, effectively challenged Malthus's views. He asserted that animals do not breed indiscriminately without reference to available space, but regulate their numbers depending on the food supply, crowding and other factors. Cooperation exists side by side with competition. Animals have evolved various methods of birth control, stopping or slowing breeding, in maintaining an appropriate population and balance of nature. Humans, not other creatures, upset Nature's balance.

The study of territoriality, dominance and spacing was adding new depth to understanding patients. Listening to the patient's stories of their experience of mothering, of friendship and of courtship had, long since, filled up the hours. Now, three other kinds of life experience extended the listening list to six. Territoriality—how driven were patients to acquire material possessions? Dominance—did patients strive for power and control over others; how did they behave with people above and below them on the social ladder? Finally, spacing— who did the patient feel close to or uneasy with or repelled by?

In the early years, what the patient talked about could, on occasion, be so confusing as to sound like babble. Patients' behaviors—territorial behavior, dominance behavior and spacing behavior so easily observed in animals—could be difficult to identify as patients constantly changed the subject, bouncing from one subject to another. In the course of a single session what the patient talked about could include references to nurturing, friendship, and courtship as well as dominance, territoriality and spacing, a mix of all six of the fundamental social behaviors that guide the lives of humans and animals alike.

With the passing years, listening became easier and remembering became automatic. Recognizing the variants of nurturing, of give and take, of sexual yearning, the many manifestations of mothering, friendship and courtship—became a part of the daily routine. Examples of territoriality and dominance came up repeatedly as patients shared their secret cravings for possessions and striving for status or recognition.

The poignancy of loneliness for a loved one or for someone to love was routinely expressed in terms of closeness or spacing—or, as with anger and hate, the opposite, wanting distance or revenge. All six items bobbed in and out, flowing along with the patient's story.

Woven on the loom of their daily lives, patients revealed patterns that were both consistent and persistent. As the twig is bent so grows the tree. An experience with mothering that included protection, nurturing and acceptance made it easy to move on to one's age group with the capacity for playfulness and for making friends. The experience of give and take in the peer group provided on-going rehearsals for later successful courtship. A happy courtship, in turn, could set the tone for the rest of life's journey and a balanced attitude toward status and material possessions, toward trust and working with others, as well as toward the responsibilities and stresses of living.

The converse was true. If the experience of mothering— often through no fault of the mother—had been one of fear, confusion and suffering, life thereafter could be a desperate exercise in regaining or maintaining function and balance. Recurrent patterns could be recognized. A patient might seem to be dominated and accept subservience in every significant relationship in life but then react periodically with outbreaks of anger and irrational behavior which made things worse. The patient would then beg forgiveness and return to being dominated. Another patient would be very much the opposite, would insist on dominating and control only to be overwhelmed periodically by guilt and depression. The loneliness of withdrawal could then be relieved only by returning to the dominating role. A third unrewarding life style was simply to remain detached from other humans, using one's busy career or other obsessive activity as an excuse. Periodic attempts to establish closeness would cause such confusion and anxiety that the person would quickly retreat to a rigid schedule of allegedly important priorities. Occasionally a patient would conform exclusively to one of these patterns but more often a patient would exhibit mixtures of two or all three.

While these generalizations about behavior were helpful, there were no easy answers. Human feelings resisted mathematical or mechanical definitions. About the time one's explanation of the cause of a patient's problems was in order it would all fall apart. The unexpected kept one alert. I was constantly amazed at human resilience, the power to heal, to recover, to grow, to overcome misfortune. The life scenarios I listened to daily began to take on new vitality and new meaning. Bringing their behaviors into awareness helped patients clarify problems in living. Patients, in reviewing their own stories with detachment and objectivity, began to make discoveries about themselves leading to new ways of getting well, getting on well with others and getting on with living—sometimes releasing unknown stores of energy and creativity.

Chapter Ten
WHOSE INVENTION IS FATHERING?

"Good afternoon, Mr. H.," I said. The patient sitting opposite me, although at most in his early sixties, was bent, wrinkled and tired. He was also having difficulty breathing. Each exhalation was accompanied by a prolonged high-pitched wheeze.

"Take your time," I said, slowing the rate of our conversation to a leisurely, one word at a time approach, "we've got plenty of time, we can take it easy."

He managed a wheezy laugh. "Bronchial asthma," he took several breaths, "had it for years."

At least, I thought, he's not in heart failure. "Used to have hay fever myself. When it was bad I'd wheeze. It's no fun".

"Dr. B. wants me to go to the hospital on Monday. Wants to do some tests and try some new treatments. Over the past few months I haven't been able to get much relief."

"Well, take it a little easy if you can. Did Dr. B. ask you to see me, or did you come on your own?"

"He thought I might be depressed."

"What about you? Do you think so? It's depressing enough to have asthma."

"I'm not depressed. It's my children. I told Dr. B. That's the only problem I have."

"When your breathing is a little easier, I'd like to hear about them. How many do you have?"

He held up three fingers. I nodded. He was beginning to settle down. His breathing eased and the intense wheezing lessened. I commented on the fact that, by relaxing, he seemed to have some control over the wheezing and the shortness of breath. He gave me a surprised look as though the thought had never occurred to him.

"Well, I bought this furniture store for my oldest son and ...."
He paused then started off on a new tack. "I've never had
anything against California. That's really not the reason that I
was upset. Maybe it's something else. I didn't want to be angry
with either of them."

His confusion and distress relating to the children was
obvious. Concerned that he might precipitate another attack of
wheezing if we pursued it, I casually changed the subject.

"Could you begin at the beginning and tell me a little about
yourself?"

Noting that he had an accent I asked him when he had
come to this country and from where. For the next hour his
story slowly unfolded. I suggested that we break for a cup of tea
which the receptionist brought. His was the last appointment of
the day so we continued on. It was a long and complex story.

"If you get tired we could finish this tomorrow," I suggested.

"Oh, no, I'm not tired. I'll be all right."

He seemed relieved at having the chance to share what
was on his mind.

"We got out in '39. Just managed. I'd had businesses in Bel-
gium and Amsterdam. Metals. When we saw what was hap-
pening I turned everything over to my partners. They weren't
Jewish. Very few of us got out. None of my wife's family. I lost
two brothers. My sister, Sophia, did get here. When my wife
died two years after we got here Sophia helped with the
children."

He went on to describe a tragedy like so many stories that
we heard during those years, replete with desperate resourcefulness, chance events, hairbreadth escapes, and the awful
hollow feelings and guilt related to those left behind. We
talked for two hours before I again suggested that we stop, that
I would find the time to see him the next day. He was reluctant
to leave but I insisted that he not tire himself further.

When he returned the following morning he was feeling much better and he continued to pour out more of the story. He had been fortunate in one area, business. His partners returned his full share of the business after the war. Having learned much about the United States, he made a great deal of money importing a pure form of liquid white lead which was in great demand.

He was a devoted, if somewhat strict and demanding father. He played a dominant and guiding role in raising the three children after the death of their mother when the boys were seven and six and the daughter was three. Aunt Sophia was a loving presence but had only minimal influence. The three children had been given a good education and all cultural opportunities to develop intellectual, recreational and social skills. They thrived, had many friends and seemed to grow away from the tragedy of their early years, something that neither their father nor their aunt were able to do.

The father continued to be protective and controlling. He resented the number of non-Jewish friends they had made and felt that all of them were drifting away from their religious training. He had played a major role in helping the children select their careers and he continued to participate in every decision. The eldest son had graduated with a degree in business administration and was interested in retailing. The father arranged for the purchase of a furniture store, the successful growth of the enterprise led to the purchase of two more stores and the possibility of setting up a chain. The second son became a lawyer and finished high in his class at an Ivy league law school. He had recently passed the state bar examination. The daughter was still in college.

The trouble began about five or six months ago the father told me. The eldest son had announced that he was selling the stores and moving to Vermont. As the story unfolded it was clear that the announcement should not have been unexpected. The son had always been interested in crafts of all kinds, had studied in depth the history of handicrafts in this country and his interest in antiques rather than profit had played an important role in his selection of the furniture business.

He had married his college sweetheart, equally drawn to crafts, who besides being a talented painter was interested in weaving. They had presented Mr. H. with his first grandchild and another was on the way. Their dream, which they had often shared with him, was to get away from the city and move to where they could do what they had always wanted to do including raising children closer to nature than living in New York City permitted.

The second son, on the threshold of a New York law career, announced, also out of the clear blue according to the father, that he was moving to California. Careful questioning revealed that it was not out of the clear blue, the son had visited friends in California repeatedly during his growing up years and often expressed his desire to go there. Furthermore, the girl from New England he was in love with also wanted to move there.

At first, the father felt that neither son would follow through on their decisions. He had dismissed both projects as impractical and illogical, and thought that both sons would come to their senses. Within the past few weeks he had found out that they were implementing their plans and were both preparing to move. The father insisted that he had never wanted to dominate them, that he had always told them to follow any course that they felt was truly what they wanted. He denied that he felt bitter. When I asked questions about the daughter his silence was obvious.

"Has your daughter told you that she too was planning to leave New York," I asked?

"Oh, no," came the answer. "She's wants a career in fashion. Plans to go to Parson's School of Design next year."

"She, at least, hasn't been a disappointment."

Silence.

"Is there some difficulty you haven't shared?"

"I don't think it's important."

"Daughters can sometimes be the cause of worry."

"She's made an appointment with a surgeon."

"Oh? Anything serious?"

"A plastic surgeon, she's going to have her nose operated on."

"Cosmetic surgery? Par for the course these days."

"She didn't even consult me. That's what upset me."

"What would you have advised if she had?"

Silence.

"That's probably why she didn't."

Mr. H.'s hopes and feelings were becoming clear. He felt certain that the children were growing away from him or from his religion or both. I doubted it. Many things I had heard directly from him indicated that they all held him in affection and deep regard. He felt very much alone, his sister, Sophia, had died a few years previously, and he clearly wanted his children and grandchildren within daily reach. He had sacrificed much for the children and it was clear that he had certain expectations.

Our second session was over. He said that it had done him a lot of good to get the full story out. He was scheduled to go to the hospital the following Monday so I told him to call me after he got out and we'd decide where to go from there. I was gratified that he had felt some relief as the result of our talks but I realized I had offered nothing in the way of an answer to his distress. What he had done in stepping into the mothering role was nothing short of remarkable. Could any person, male or female, have done much better? I was groping in the dark.

Mr. H. had mentioned that his main hobby was reading and that he took much pride in the extent of his library. From somewhere inside of me came a recollection: if you can influence a man's reading you can influence his thought. I asked him

if, among the classics, he had the works of Shakespeare. When
he assured me that he had, I asked him how much he'd read of it.

"A few of them years ago. *Hamlet, MacBeth, Romeo and
Juliet, The Merchant of Venice.*"

"*King Lear,*" I asked?

"So? I should have?"

"Well, lots of people seem not to enjoy it but as long as you
have it at home and have a week-end before you go to the
hospital try to read it. I'd be interested in what you think."

Mr. H. had a puzzled expression but thanked me again for
listening to his long story.

"Good-bye, I'll call you."

On Monday morning Mr. H. phoned. He wanted to thank
me, he said, for suggesting that he read King Lear. He finished
reading it on Saturday and had experienced ease of breathing
greater than at any time in recent years. He had decided to call
Dr. B. and cancel going to the hospital. I urged him not to. "The
improvement in your acute attack of asthma," I told him, "may
have happened because you've resolved some problems but
you'd better let Dr. B. try to find out why you have asthma in
the first place."

I saw Mr. H. for several visits after he left the hospital
where Dr. B. had found important contributory causes for the
asthmatic attacks. In the years that followed he remained
virtually asthma free. He would drop in for a visit, show me
pictures of the grandchildren and tell me about the children
and how basically loving they all were. He had remarried.

Mr. H. felt that I was responsible for the happy development in his life, crediting me with pointing out that children
should not be forced to prove or declare their love. I told him
that we both had to thank Mr. Shakespeare. I didn't mention
that I really wasn't clear on what fathering was either. All I
knew was that King Lear had made some mistakes.

How many ways were there to raise a child? In the case of
Mr. H., a male, the father, had been forced through circum-

stance to take over mothering. His was the first example I had encountered although he had not been a complete replacement for the mother. The children had had their own mother for the early formative years, and, after her death, Aunt Sophia, who lived next door, and household servants supplied considerable physical assistance. Nevertheless, throughout the years of childhood the father had supplied a full measure of nurturing, protection and guidance and had done so with dedication and affection. He had done a creditable job. I wanted to find other examples.

In the course of staff or committee meetings at the hospital, I often had an opportunity to speak to obstetricians or pediatricians who dealt with parents and children on a daily basis. I asked them what experience they had had of fathers assuming conventional mothering chores. The question was met at first with raised eyebrows. One colleague wondered if I was collecting cases where the male wanted to push the wife aside and take over. I told him that might make an interesting subject at some future date but that I was interested in cases where the male chose because of death of the wife or some other circumstance to step into the mothering role.

Of a dozen or so physicians, many of whom had been in practice for many years, none could come up with a single instance of a male taking over the mothering duties. In cases of an unexpected death of a young mother the fathers had had immediate access to a grandmother or other female relative from one or both sides of the family or had opted to hire nannies or housekeepers. My colleagues had many examples of male domination in the management of the children which was variously explained as necessary or unnecessary but they could offer no examples of the mother being replaced by the father.

Over the years, I had slowly gotten a deeper understanding of mothering. More specifically, I had begun to realize that mothering behavior has been a fundamental and dynamic process through millions of years of evolution; the roots of mothering behavior are traceable back, long before the dinosaurs to earlier forms of life on Earth. Mothering behavior has been described in insects. More elaborate forms of mothering behavior are encountered in reptiles and birds, increasingly complex but still largely genetically determined programs of protection, nurturing and guidance.

In mammals, diversifying over the past sixty or seventy million years, the female evolved an anatomy, a nervous system, a glandular and endocrine system and a behavioral repertoire designed—beyond giving birth—for furthering growth. At the higher reaches of evolution, monkeys for instance, mothering behavior comes to be defined as care given with satisfaction—and joy—not smothering but an artful blend of acceptance and rejection, leading to growth and maturity in the one receiving the care. Care is understood as every nuance of giving from nursing to support, protection and teaching, a broad definition but well supported by observations of nonhuman primates. This had reached a high degree of subtlety and complexity in the mothering behavior of monkeys and apes millions of years before evolution gave rise to humans, millions of years before a spoken language.

But what about fathers and fathering? Male anatomy, glandular and endocrine systems evolved over millions of years prepare for siring but not for fathering. In the higher primates, those closest to humans on the evolutionary scale, no fathering is observed. Rarely a young male—lonely?—will adopt an orphaned youngster. In general, no male gorilla or chimpanzee, although tolerant of toddlers and protective of the group, helps the mother raise her little one. The male orangutan plays even less of a protective role, leading a solitary existence apart from females and young.

Every time I thought I had gotten a grip on some aspect of human behavior a new set of questions erupted. Is fathering a human invention, recent, imperfect, unfinished? How does it help—or hinder—mothering?

Chapter Eleven
THE FAMILY: ANOTHER RIDDLE

The first patient of the day was a tall, athletic, blonde-headed young fellow. I glanced at the chart the receptionist put on my desk. Name, Brian N., age 27. He looked directly at me, serious and without the trace of a smile. I motioned toward the chair and he sat down slowly and guardedly.

"Did my friend, Mel J., call you about me?" he asked.

I didn't respond immediately, searching my memory.

"You know Mel J., don't you?" he continued with just the slightest increase in tension.

"Sure, sure," I paused. Mel J. and his wife had been patients. Mel had called me some time before to tell me he was referring a friend who was having some kind of difficulty with his psychiatrist but, as the days passed, I had forgotten about it. "Now I remember, that was several weeks ago. He said you'd probably be making an appointment."

A long pause followed.

"Did he tell you I was a homosexual?"

The remark surprised me. Back then homosexuality was still listed by official psychiatry as a character disorder, the result of nurture, not nature but fewer and fewer psychiatrists believed it and only a poorly trained or unwise psychiatrist would judge or would meddle in the matter of a patient's sexual orientation. Could Brian, I wondered, possibly be thinking that I disapproved?

"No, he didn't mention that," I said, slowly.

Another pause.

"Well, I am."

Another pause.

"Yes. Well. So, how is it?"

A long pause.

"It's terrible."

We sat in silence, just looking at one another. I turned up the palms of my hands and shrugged in a gesture of both sympathy and puzzlement.

"Yeh, you're right," he said.

I laughed. Then we both laughed. Finally, I suggested that maybe both of us should try to figure this one out. Brian was agreeable and we spent the rest of the visit chatting about his family and background.

That visit, as it turned out, was the end of his homosexuality. Psychiatry is full of surprises. Brian's was another one of those human stories where an unexpected change of behavior establishes psychiatry for what it is—perplexing, intriguing, challenging. Another aspect of the case was that Brian had been seeing a psychoanalyst for seven years. A week or so before seeing me he had finally decided to quit.

"He's supposed to be a good analyst."

"Oh. And he didn't help you?"—"No."—"Did you make a real effort?"

"I never missed an appointment in seven years."

"What do you think happened?"

"I don't know. The only time he ever listened to me was when I was talking about some crazy sexual encounter. Then he'd perk up. Otherwise I think he was mostly asleep."

"Sounds like something was wrong. Maybe, for now, we could skip some of the sex talk and talk more about you."

Over the next few weeks Brian shared the whole family story. Brian's father was a successful Boston business man having founded his own electronics firm. He had married a Back Bay debutante and they had four children. Brian, who was the second child, had an older brother, James. The two younger were girls, Patty and Belle.

"I really don't know what happened; it never came up with my therapist. My father favored James because he was the eldest and, besides, he was so bright. My father was forever quarreling with my mother so she just pulled away with my two sisters. I don't think mother ever got up before noon. Mother and my sisters had their half of the house. All I know is that I didn't have anybody, just a few Irish maids and they weren't particularly nice."

Brian described the father as a grim disciplinarian, insistent upon achievement and with a violent temper. The older brother, James, was a super-achiever, acceptable to and praised by the father, and was given the job of supervising Brian, seeing that he got to school on time, that he got home from school promptly and completed his lessons. Brian dug in his heels and resisted his brother every step of the way. Morning after morning it would be an argument from the time he got out of bed to get dressed, to eat breakfast and to get to school on time. Brian did poorly in his studies and was always near the bottom of the class.

"I spent most of the time just staring out the window daydreaming or counting the minutes till school let out."

His attempts, he recalled, to get any help or attention from his mother were fruitless. She would be with her bridge-playing friends or going some place with his sisters. Brian felt she was impatient with him because his father blamed her for Brian's poor performance. She seemed to give Brian the brush off as quickly as she could. By the time his sisters were eight or nine years old, the mother would take them off every summer to the south of France, leaving Brian at home at the mercy of his brother and father or banished to summer camp.

At camp Brian excelled at tennis and swimming and kept at it for hours at a time because it was the only thing that helped him take his mind off himself. He also agreed, at the urging of a camp counselor, to try boxing and quickly discovered unusual talent. Fast reflexes, quick foot work, and a powerful punch made it easy to win the camp boxing medal at a very young age. He brought home his medals for tennis, swimming and boxing and gave them to his father. His father took them from him, opened the drawer of his desk, dropped them in, closed the drawer, and told Brian that he now expected him to win medals in school work.

As he told me this Brian shook his head slowly. "They wouldn't give you credit for a thing. Not James, not my father. They wouldn't give you a point, not a point."

A recollection popped into my mind. "Your friend, Mel, did mention something about you I just recalled. Didn't you knock out the school bully or somebody like that? Mel said he never forgot it."

"Oh, that guy. He weighed about 190, I don't think I was 140 then. He'd been lording it over me and the athletic coach heard us arguing. The coach, just joking, laughed and suggested that maybe I wanted to put on the gloves with the guy. He didn't think I'd do it. They all laughed when I said, OK."

". . . and?"

"I knocked him cold in the first round, he was a sucker for a right hook."

"Sounds as if you learned to make your own points. But who were you really hitting?"

"Yeh, right. I was hitting my father. Or my brother. Probably both."

"You catch on fast."

At prep school—the same one his father had attended—it was the same old story. He was last in his class, remained in school only as a result of constant tutoring insisted upon by his father. He felt lonely and isolated. One holiday he was kept after school to make up an exam, and missed the last bus to town where he would get a train to his home town. He decided to hitch-hike and was picked up by a truck driver in a big trailer truck. The guy was nice to him, bought him a big lunch at a truck stop, encouraged him to talk about his family and school, told him he was bright and capable and introduced him to homosexual experience.

"I hardly knew what was going on." Brian reported.

After two years of college, he quit, became apprenticed to a stock broker, and, eventually, did well on his own. His good looks and, perhaps, even his aloofness seemed to be a magnet for girls. On many occasions they would invite him out and he would go along although he thought they just felt sorry for him because they could see how lonely and miserable he was. He could never believe that they truly cared about him; deep down he was sure that they were like his sisters and his mother and, in spite of their invitations and willingness, he would avoid becoming intimate or attempting an affair. He remained alone and aloof and would have periodic homosexual encounters with kindly older men, total strangers.

"I don't know what I want," said Brian some months later, "but it's not that."

"Well, you get some kind of sexual relief but it sounds like you want something more."

Whether Brian saw me as a father or as a less threatening older brother or just a friend didn't make any difference. It was enough that he trusted me and that he had no doubt that I believed he was a human being worth respecting, worth cherishing and worth loving.

Step by step he began to see things in a new light. As it turned out, there was really no evidence of maternal deprivation. Brian's mother may have shown occasional indifference but she had never abused or neglected him, and, generally, had been thoughtful and attentive. His mother hadn't really rejected him as much as she had distanced herself from his father. The perception of maternal neglect, however, was difficult to modify. While his father had been central to his misery, no one had, in his view, ever truly helped him; the logic of Brian's pain colored everything and tarred everyone with the same brush.

Eventually, he did understand. He developed more detachment and objectivity, resentment drained away. He realized that the hurts administered by the family were extra painful because he had become dependent and needy. He admitted that his father and brother had, in a crude and ineffective way, been trying to help him.

With the passing months he became friendly and warm toward his father and his mother and sisters, too. Although we discussed it at some length he was never able to feel comfortable with his brother. The Cain and Abel story is a powerful one; intense sibling rivalry—dominance interaction—is encountered repeatedly in the practice of psychiatry, quite as tenacious as the rivalry of son and father, Freud's Oedipus complex with mother's love as the prize.

Brian's father felt much gratitude toward me, apparently crediting me with returning a son he loved and thought he had lost. He asked Brian if he could come to New York to meet me. He never did; a few weeks later, he had a heart attack and soon after recovery and convalescence had another and died shortly thereafter. It was good to learn from Brian that the bitterness had been dissolved before his father died. A year or so later Brian married an attractive young woman, a gifted artist, and they had several children. I would hear from time to time that things had continued to go well as the years passed.

The complexities of Brian's family life, the various tensions, between the father and mother, between brothers and sisters had made Brian's problem particularly difficult to understand. There had been a happy outcome, fortunately, but it left me wondering.

What is the effect on the child of stress and tensions between parents? What is the effect on the child of the father's taking charge of mothering or dominating the mother or otherwise influencing mothering behavior? What happens to the single-parent child? This led to more of those questions.

How did families evolve? How long have families been around? What is a family?

Chapter Twelve
HUMAN BEGINNINGS

Increased possibilities to learn first hand about primates
came along in the 1950s. Private laboratories, universities,
armed services and other governmental agencies expanded
research. Funded by government grants, primate centers sprang
up in a dozen or more regions of the country. The research
projects covered a wide range of subjects—studies of disease,
of stress, of hormone function, of drugs, studies of learning, of
conditioned reflex, of injury, of brain damage. Unfortunately
few of the projects dealt directly with behavior. The projects
that were classified as behavioral research such as reactions to
stress or drugs offered little; usually they were conducted on
individual animals. Even large numbers of animals in roomy
cages with attached runways were far from constituting a
natural free-ranging group. Human or non-human, how much
could one learn about behavior by studying prisoners—especially those kept in solitary confinement?

Better possibilities to observe behavior of free-ranging primates existed at Almagardo, New Mexico, where the armed
services maintained a large colony of chimpanzees. They were
kept on a big patch of desert surrounded by a moat where they
were permitted to roam free. One of them would be the country's first astronaut and many were undergoing preparatory
training for the role. Their capacity to learn was remarkable. In
exchange for little more than a dried banana pellet and a pat on
the head they would master a set of dials, gauges, pedals and
levers that would challenge a bright human. Indeed, one story
of their intelligence going around was about a chimpanzee
who was unbeatable at tick-tack-toe played on an electronic
keyboard. She could not get another chimpanzee to play against
her since she won every game along with the reward of a

banana pellet, automatically delivered for each victory. Her opponents became discouraged and would quit playing. Soon enough, however, she solved this problem by purposely losing—throwing—a game every once in a while to keep her opponents interested. A sequel to the story held that a visiting army general got beaten three games in a row and, like the losing chimpanzees, avoided a rematch. And—as someone added—quit eating bananas.

Although the government research scientists were cooperative and friendly, their work, too, was of limited interest. The equipment was a marvel of technology but most of the projects were of a highly specialized nature. The reaction of animals to centrifugal stress or acceleration-deceleration revealed little about behavior. Just watching the free ranging chimpanzees offered more than experiments on captive and restricted animals. Observing the interactions of forty or more chimpanzees romping, feeding, exploring and occasionally fighting on the enclosed expanse of desert provided the illusion of animals roaming free. After hours of watching, it became clear that this was a poor approximation of life in the chimpanzee's natural surroundings. There were no pregnant females, no infants, no juveniles. There were no trees. Food was supplied. The chimpanzee methods of foraging and other adaptive behavior of their natural environment were eliminated. Individuals were removed periodically for experiments and a social structure of any meaningful kind could not be established. Restricted by this kind of research the opportunity to learn about the natural behavior of these remarkable creatures was extremely limited.

By now I had spent a good many years in acquiring a general understanding of animal behavior. The field was vast, time limited, the opportunities to learn random and I often regretted the superficiality and unevenness of my knowledge. Curiosity had to be reined in; a limiting of scope was necessary. I remained interested, even fascinated, by primates such as Rhesus monkeys, baboons, langurs and other species but my main focus of interest narrowed down to the primates that most resemble us, the greater apes.

In the early nineteen-sixties, George Schaller's reports of his months spent with the mountain gorilla began to appear soon followed by Jane Goodall's studies of chimpanzees, and, later, studies of the orangutan by Barbara Harrison and others. Such studies set the standards for increasingly detailed observations of these creatures in their natural surroundings. Naturalists from many countries have continued the work; the results are a monument to dedication, determination and the powers of human observation. Their struggles with the heat, insects, tropical diseases and twisting trails through seemingly impassable terrain were compounded by such obstacles as limited funds, language barriers, and political turmoil in Africa, Asia and Latin America. The praise they have received is well deserved. Jane Goodall's pioneering studies have received wide acclaim but many others are continuing such work and furthering discovery. That the creatures they study would accept human observers, become indifferent—or the technical term, habituate—to them, and go on with routines of living unchanged in millions of years provided a great step forward in the study of animal behavior.

I had the pleasure of talking with Ms. Goodall, by then Dr. Goodall, on one of her visits to the United States. She was the guest of Dr. William Lemmon, a professor of psychology at the University of Oklahoma, and had come to give a series of talks to the students. Dr. Lemmon maintained a large chimpanzee colony a few miles from Norman, Oklahoma and I had visited him several times over the years. Bill, as I had gotten to know him, sponsored and supervised chimpanzee study projects of considerable variety. Roger Fouts, who had taught sign language to a chimpanzee named Washoe, was continuing his teaching with Washoe and other chimpanzees. Washoe had been the research subject of the Gardners, a husband and wife team of psychologists, and the reports of the talking chimp had precipitated heated discussion throughout the scientific world. Dr. Maurice and Jane Temerlin had raised a chimpanzee, Lucy, from infancy and had made detailed notes of her growth and progress. For another project, Bill made rounds periodically to visit adopted chimpanzees he had placed in a dozen or so homes around Tulsa and Oklahoma City and he took me along on several occasions. The adopted chimpanzees were treated the same as their human sisters and brothers, were dressed like them and ate the same food with some semblance of table manners. The human youngsters appeared to make no distinctions whatsoever between human and non-human and made valiant if futile efforts to match the chimpanzees' gymnastic abilities. Anecdotes about these chimpanzees raised with human siblings of similar age were hilarious and intriguing.

Dr. Goodall gave several easy and informal lectures on her observations of chimpanzees at Gombe in Africa to halls packed with fascinated and enthusiastic students. Dining that weekend with a small group of the faculty she was most gracious in her behavior and answered our questions with thoughtfulness and precision but it was not difficult to determine what her basic attitude was toward any work having to do with captive chimpanzees. Dr. Lemmon and I, both psychotherapists, were focussed on groping for and searching out that mysterious, impalpable and unfathomed bridge between human and chimpanzee and were, perhaps, less sensitive to the fact that our bouncy, mischievous, seemingly happy subjects were, nevertheless, fugitives and captives removed from their true home. Dr. Goodall was well aware, as were we, that it is not possible to keep an uncaged chimpanzee much beyond five or six years of age. They are powerful, impulsive, impetuous; chimpanzee handlers frequently have less than ten fingers. By the time they are mature it is too late to return them to the wild although several projects are dedicated to the endeavor. Dr. Goodall's priorities, clearly, were those of a dedicated conservationist and lover of animals, only secondarily those of a behavioral theorist or therapist.

Today, over seven hundred and fifty different kinds of primates, grouped in some two hundred species survive and have adapted to a wide range of habitats and diets. Some are exclusively leaf-eaters, others live largely on fruit, others on grasses and seeds. Marmosets of South America rely on the sap and resin from trees, macaques of South East Asia include crabs as a staple of their diets, Japanese snow monkeys subsist on the bark of trees in the winter. Half of the species are on the endangered species list. Ninety percent live in the tropical forests of Africa, Asia, South and Central America. Seventy-five percent live in just five countries, Cameroon, Zaire, Madagascar, Brazil and Indonesia, all areas of the highest human birth rates.

The destruction of habitats to provide farmland for exploding human populations is the beginning of the end for many species. Natives for generations have felt that to survive they are entitled to kill or capture for food, fur or barter all the monkeys that live on their lands. The imperatives of conservation spread slowly. Some species of primates, stressed by the encroachment on their forest homes, may, like the panda, simply stop breeding. In-depth studies of these creatures in their natural environments have been conducted on at most a few dozen species and many species may become extinct even before such studies can be conducted. Game preserves, breeding farms and zoos may be the fate of those species that escape extinction. If the tragedy of destruction of our wild heritage is avoided, much credit must flow to Dr. Goodall for her remarkable work with the chimpanzees at Gombe.

As the world-wide interest in Dr. Goodall's work bears out, the similarity of humans and apes evokes, as it has always evoked, a special curiosity, a curiosity tinged with wonderment—we can sometimes see it on the faces of children as they watch monkeys or apes at the zoo. It was once believed, and natives of certain African tribes still believe, that apes are a deteriorated race of humans too ignorant to hunt and too lazy to plant grain; religious explanations suggested that apes were humans turned into beasts as punishment for sin, serving as examples for other humans.

Beginning with the Renaissance, anatomists and naturalists began systematic studies and detailed comparisons but puzzlement continued. In 1789 C. E. Groppius wrote: ". . . so near are some . . . as to structure of body: face, ears, mouth, teeth, hands, breasts, food, imitation, and gestures...that distinguishing marks separating them from Man are found with great difficulty."

The first satisfactory explanations came with Charles Darwin's, *The Origin of the Species,* but were obscured by the controversies which followed. In 1859 the publication of his theory of evolution evoked stormy opposition from religious fundamentalists who insisted that the Bible is a source book of facts, not a spiritual guide. Even the clergy accepted the scientific description that each human develops in the womb from a single-celled, fertilized egg comparable to the lowly microscopic amoeba, a process that appeared to model—scientists say recapitulate—the evolutionary process. However, the reaction was of another sort when, in effect, the headlines read, DARWIN ASSERTS MAN IS DESCENDED FROM A MONKEY. The conclusion was inflammatory. The first human was not divinely created in the image of God—a white male, perfect, flawless—but a product of nature, the final flowering of evolution. Today we are more sophisticated. Religious thinkers see no conflict between religion and evolution. God has many methods and miracles, say enlightened theologians, evolution is just one of them. Hysteria and headlines sell newspapers and Victorian England reacted vigorously to any questioning of its belief system.

In spite of the ever increasing evidence to support evolution, little change in attitudes as a result of Darwin's theory has occurred in the last one hundred years. Queen Victoria may have been less hysterical and resistant to the theory of evolution than the clergy. On hearing about Mr. Darwin's theory, the little grey-haired symbol of the Victorian age is reported to have said, "Oh, dear, let us hope it will not become generally known." In one sense, time has respected the Queen's wish. Darwin's revolutionary theory and all the intricate scientific proof of our kinship with other living creatures have not convinced many of us that we are related to an ape or, indeed, need change our attitude toward animals in any way.

Still fascination and incredulity persist and may account for the feeling any contemplative human has upon watching one of the greater apes: the gorilla, the orangutan or the chimpanzee. These three are the sole survivors of twenty or more species of apes that evolved over the millions of years before humans. Isolated and unauthenticated sightings of massive creatures like Big-foot or the abominable snowman account for continuing interest in a ten-foot ape, Gigantipithecus, whose fossil remains establish that it once roved the forests of Southeast Asia.

All of the great apes exhibit behavior, gestures, facial expressions and sounds or calls that are hauntingly human but the diets, the social organization, and details of the behavioral repertoire of the three leave little doubt as to which one is closest in evolution to humans. The solitary, fruit eating orangutan, and the plant eating, unexuberant gorilla reveal their distance from us when compared with the omnivorous, mischievous, unquenchably sociable chimpanzee.

What is this creature like, some of whose ancestors four—or five or six—million years ago took the decisive turn on the evolutionary pathway that led to Homo sapiens? Chimpanzees can walk on two feet and frequently do. They waddle, however, and are not truly bipedal; they are knuckle walkers. Their brain volume averages 450 cubic centimeters, less than half that of the human. Size alone, it should be noted, does not determine intelligence; some humans famous for intelligence had small brains. Chimpanzees are intelligent. Although they lack the proper machinery—a coordinated larynx, vocal chords and diaphragm—to form the sounds necessary for speech, their communication skills are remarkable. Scientists' efforts to teach them sign language were, if inconclusive, not unreasonable. Both Washoe and Lucy behaved, at least in my presence, as interesting but limited—and somewhat restless—conversationalists. However, they communicated as well and used fewer gestures than two excited human beings arguing in different languages.

Chimpanzees make tools. From a twig they strip leaves and fashion a probe to extract termites from a termite mound. From wadded leaves they make a sponge with which to soak up rain water from a tree crotch or rock crevice to drink or to clean up a messy infant. To crack nuts they select appropriately shaped rocks both to get a proper anvil and to provide a hammer. They break off branches to embellish a threat display or to use as missiles against a predator although their aim is poor.

Steady progress marked the studies as the years unfolded. Research in immunology and molecular biology would reveal—even more than Darwin could have guessed—the remarkable closeness of chimpanzee and human. Studies included saliva, tissues, organs, blood and blood proteins and, within recent years, the near identity in structure of DNA itself. We are, these findings assert, 99% chimpanzee. Surprisingly, tests reveal that we are closer to the chimpanzee than the chimpanzee is to the gorilla. The similarity in appearance of gorilla and chimpanzee, mainly hairiness and stooped gait, is misleading. Millions of years ago evolutionary pathways diverged. Creatures taking the gorilla path went one way. Creatures taking a line of development which would lead to both chimpanzee and human went another. In everyday language chimp and human are siblings, gorillas are cousins. Millions of years after chimp and human had parted from the gorilla, human and chimpanzee pathways also diverged. At first the differences were not great; increased ability for upright walking and some increase in brain size are not radical evolutionary developments—as, for instance, are the evolvement of amphibians from fish and birds from lizards. In five million years, however, these minor variations led to such striking differences in appearance and cultural accumulation—while the chimpanzee remained closer to the original—that the awareness of our origins was lost.

In spite of the increase in our knowledge of the similarity of human and chimpanzee the Darwinian revolution was and, essentially, has remained an intellectual, academic event. Darwin's theory did, however, trigger a renewed search for fossils of early humans, a search which began about the same year as the California gold rush and continues to this day without signs of let-up. Darwin had predicted that the remains of our most primitive ancestor, the so-called "missing link," would be found in Africa simply because of the large number of anthropoid apes still surviving there. The squabble this precipitated among paleontologists reached its height with the Piltdown hoax. One or more pranksters or embittered scientists planted a human skull along with an ape's jaw in a quarry near Piltdown in the English countryside. Its discovery along with subsequent finds proclaimed that an ape with a human-sized brain once roamed English soil, that not only the Empire but human origins as well were British. Paleontologists argued for half a century before modern chemical tests uncovered the fraud.

Eventually, the continuing stockpiling of fossils and facts seemed to confirm Darwin's guess that the earliest human-like fossils would be found in Africa. Paleontologists can now take us back in time some ten or fifteen million years ago to eastern equatorial Africa, can reconstitute and model the terrain, the climate, the plants and animals, and, assisted by primatology and other disciplines, provide a convincing scenario of human origins.

The climate of the earth was changing, becoming cooler, less humid. The lush tropical vegetation which had once extended well up into what is now the temperate zone had receded to become a broad band of equatorial rain forest. Over the next six or seven million years the dryer climate gave rise to wide stretches of grassland, bush and occasional tree interrupted by forests and tree-edged rivers in some areas and semi-desert in others. Meteorites, volcanoes, earthquakes and shifts of the earth's tectonic plates periodically re-routed rivers and changed the terrain. Here, in east Africa, the formation of the Rift valley, the mountains, hills, lakes and rivers further altered the landscape of forest and savanna. Only animal eyes beheld this scene, the ancestors of the animals that today have survived to become the herds and other creatures of Africa's shrinking plains—now facing the same threat the American buffalo faced a century ago.

Here, in a forest area surrounded by savanna, lived a group or groups of apes ancestral to humans. Averaging between fifteen and thirty members their tree-based life resembled that of present day chimpanzees. Foraging, feeding, and browsing filled three quarters of their waking time; their diet consisting mostly of fruit and leaves supplemented by blossoms, nuts, seeds, insects and, periodically, meat of small animals. While they confined their daily migrations to a five or ten square mile territory, there was no permanent camp or home base. They slept in trees at night or during a noonday siesta wherever they stopped feeding, building a new nest daily. The food supply was rarely concentrated sufficiently to supply the whole group; the members separated in twos and threes for hours of foraging. Gatherings of large groups happened from time to time and members related to each other excitedly with much play, affection and grooming.

Males, a third again larger, dominated the smaller females, tended to travel together in male groups and engaged from time to time in struggles, occasionally violent, for dominance. Periodically a group of males would stealthily patrol the borders of their territory and would attack any smaller group they encountered, killing whatever individuals were unable to escape. The alternating rhythms of peace and violence, affection and hostility were even more volatile than in humans.

Breeding, dependent on the availability of a receptive female, was communistic and promiscuous; males, usually without antagonism, took turns in sharing females. Courtship, consisting largely of checking female readiness, followed by brief copulation, not an on-going association, was the characteristic encounter of male and female. Males exhibited little interest in non-estrus females. On occasion a single male might coax a receptive female into separating from the others and, foraging and courting, go off alone for several days or more.

Individuals foraged for themselves; food sharing was not routine. On occasion, when a hunt for monkeys or other small game had been successful, the lucky male hunter might share the kill. Not always. If the kill were small he might not share or if he had eaten his fill, and if begging from female or juvenile was persistent, he might grudgingly share a piece of the carcass. Customs varied between groups—the beginnings of a culture. Males would accept grooming, a routine peace-making and emotion-soothing behavior, from a female and would usually reciprocate. Males provided females and young with a measure of security and protection.

Females raised one offspring at a time, the attention, tenderness, nurturance, protection and guidance continuing for five years or so. Food sharing between mother and infant was routine. The mother, permissive and tolerant, allowed the infant to take food from her mouth or her hand, a system of learning by experience that enabled the young to master the extended list of edible foods. This privilege tended to taper off with weaning but varied from mother to mother.

Years of friendly closeness continued to surround the mother as the young matured and might include infants and juveniles from a daughter's pregnancy; in effect, a single parent extended family. Males, who as juveniles had left maternal protection to tag along after the adult males, usually retained a friendly and protective attitude in their contacts with mother and siblings in the years that followed.

At some point, perhaps four to six million years ago, triggered by competition from other species, the opportunity arose to leave the safety of trees and increase the food supply by exploiting the resources of the savanna. A wide assortment of foods became available: various plants, grasses, grains, seeds, tubers, tender roots and shoots, grubs, insects and new kinds of small game. Our ancient primate ancestors, surveying the vast plains from trees at the edge of the forest, came down to earth, a move that most agree was the single most crucial step in human evolution. The new and rewarding environment was also more dangerous and called for many adaptive changes, the details of which are extremely difficult to reconstruct. The brightest survived. Facts being so sparse, discussions of this period are highly speculative. Alternative views exist.

A minority challenge the view of the crucial role of the savanna with some evidence that forest-dwelling chimpanzees exhibit more advanced tool use and cooperative hunting techniques than chimpanzees living on the edge of the savanna. A Dutch naturalist testing such a hypothesis set up a specimen of a stuffed leopard with a motorized head that rotated from side to side. Chimpanzees living on the edge of the savanna mounted an elaborate defense, jumping up and down, creating great commotion, alternately charging, breaking branches and hurling them, periodically strengthening their cooperation by mutual hugging, stroking and other forms of social reinforcement. When the specimen leopard was presented to forest-dwelling chimpanzees they simply scattered and disappeared into the trees. Less social cooperation was his conclusion.

Our chimpanzee-like ancestors were not the first primates to exploit the savanna; several species of monkeys had already done so. Baboons with their huge fangs and tight defensive organization, patas monkeys with their great speed, and vervet monkeys with their small size, stealth and vigilance had all been successful. Our ancestors were, however, the first of the greater apes to do so.

Paleontologists strive to unravel the mystery of what happened next in human evolution. Finding fossils of creatures intermediate between chimpanzee and human is, of course, the dream of every paleontologist. One such discovery was a revolutionary find, a "missing link," unearthed in south Africa in 1924. Named Australopithecus or southern ape by its discoverer, Dr. Raymond Dart, the fossil skull was of a creature estimated to have been about five feet tall with a brain close in size to that of apes. The position of the skull's foramen magnum, the outlet for the spinal chord, indicated that the creature had probably walked upright. Years later, the fossilized footprints discovered by the Leakeys in Tanzania provided direct evidence of upright walking three and one-half million years ago. Many fossils of Australopithecus have since been found, particularly in eastern equatorial Africa or further north at Lake Turkana and Hadar in Ethiopia.

Finding fossils is always an event of great good luck even in fossil-rich areas by canny and tenacious fossil hunters but no hominid fossils are available for that crucial period four or more million years ago when our ancestors first ventured out onto the savanna. The oldest Australopithecine fossils consist of little more than a tooth or a bone fragment. The one or two fairly complete skeletons found in the last twenty years or so are less than four million years old. Experts suggest that Australopithicines were bipedal but probably walked with a somewhat stooped gate and retained much tree climbing ability. From the early A afarensis they evolved into three or more species on the basis of diet, including herbivores like A. robustus with powerful jaws for masticating grains and grasses and lighter-jawed omnivores like A.africanus and A.ethiopicus subsisting on softer diets, fruits and possibly scavenged flesh. Whether humankind evolved directly from A. afarensis, as a recent finding of a fairly complete skull suggests, or from a latter A. gracilis form still evokes controversy among paleontologists who seem all too ready to engage in petty squabbles. Mysteries abound, enough to go around: the evolutionary challenges presented by periods of dramatic climatic and other ecologic changes, leading, finally, to the earliest humans, Homo rudolfensis, Homo habilis (the first toolmaker)—two million plus years ago—and Homo erectus a million years later.

Volumes have been written about the changes in both anatomy and behavior that occurred as the group spread out onto the grasslands. Discussions have centered on brain size, upright walking, and mechanisms of controlling body temperature. Brain temperature under conditions of direct tropical sun is a particularly crucial adaptation since a few degrees above normal limits could be fatal. Chimpanzees and humans show important differences in methods of regulating body temperature: namely, the adaptations related to upright posture, loss of body hair, and loss of skin pigment. Differences in brain circulatory systems are particularly important and A.gracilis, findings hint, had the human type of brain circulatory system.

Experts can, at best, guess what the creature was like from fossil fragments. Behavior leaves no fossils. Our best source of information on human-like behavior—other than that suggested by fossil finders—must come from studies of the greater apes, particularly the chimpanzee. Gaps in knowledge, supplied on the one hand by paleontologists and on the other by primatologists, have had to be filled in by speculation.

There has been, however, no shortage of speculators.

Chapter Thirteen
SOME FEMININE INPUT

Paleontology has been a male monopoly and is still male dominated so it is not surprising that the speculations about the origins of human society have, until recently, reflected the male viewpoint. Various scenarios about human origins have featured male domination, male inventiveness in tools and weapons, male hunting skills and male proclivity for territoriality, fierce and violent if necessary. Books of a few decades back like *The Naked Ape, The Territorial Imperative* and *The Imperial Animal* not only popularized these views but hinted that male behavior, so deeply rooted in biology, is basically immutable. Such writings provided an appropriately depressing obligato to world events of the day. All made the best seller book lists.

Formulations starring male protagonists generated images that had romantic, even heroic dimensions: a naked savage with a spear facing a charging lion, for instance. The role of the female is seldom mentioned except for her fulfilling male needs, sexual and otherwise. Big game hunting and male largesse in gratitude for her sexual favors met female needs for food and protection. Such scenarios are not, however, well supported by fact. Big game hunting and weapons for defense against large animals are not supported by studies of early humans, indeed, were millions of years in the future. Until evolution had moved much further along, the female would continue to feed herself and her infant and impart food-gathering skills to the young.

Studies—particularly those conducted or assisted by women over the past few decades—have begun to correct the imbalance. Steadily accumulating fossil evidence with accurate methods for time dating has provided ever more data with which to work. Fossils of plants and seeds contribute to knowledge of the climate and reveal what foods were available. The size and shape of fossil teeth, the thickness of tooth enamel and microscopic scratches on its surface indicate whether a diet consisted of soft fruits and leaves or tough grains and roots mixed with sand or grit. Fossils of carnivores provide evidence of predator pressures; fossils of small animals indicate available prey. Environmental models of the times of our ancient ancestors could be drawn with increasing detail and reliability.

More importantly, female naturalists, both in numbers and significance of contributions, have contributed and continue to contribute much to understanding primate behaviors under natural conditions. Female academics have labored to correct the record and submit alternative views of human origins. Their formulations of the earliest events of human evolution have given attention to an active and crucial role played by the female.

Venturing out onto the savanna brought new pressures. Grasses, grains and seeds required different and more challenging ways of foraging than fruits and leaves. Digging tubers and roots called for sturdier tools than the flimsy twig adequate to probe a termite mound. The diet continued to be largely of vegetable origin; the small amount of animal protein came from grubs, birds' eggs, capture of small game and scavenging. Hunting large and dangerous animals would require another million years and the invention of weapons—spears, bow and arrows—a considerable advance over simple stone tools. Hunting and gathering would prevail for the millions of years until the domestication of plants and animals. The stage was set for the development of civilization. For millions of years, however, mothers continued to gather food for themselves and their infants. Older daughters tagged along, helping with infant-tending chores and developing new food gathering skills. Males continued to forage on their own, the foraging areas and the distances traversed steadily increasing.

Females would continue to spend more time foraging than the males. Mothers having to provide for two would be the major food gatherers, as they are in chimpanzee society and in the hunting-gathering tribes of the African grasslands today. Females would be motivated to develop new ways of food gathering as demonstrated in studies of Japanese macaques where females introduced softening of dried sweet potatoes—by soaking them in water—and separating grain from sand—by floating it on pools of water. Females and young, not adult males, were the channel for the dissemination of the discoveries.

Ability to assume and maintain an erect and vigilant posture would aid in guarding against predators in open grass country and would favor both sexes but increased walking skill, which freed the arms and hands would be crucial for the female for carrying food and infant to the safety of a tree or a nearby cliff. Chimpanzees can thread a needle, not, however, when they are standing up. Bipedal balance, free hands and nimble, experienced female fingers would favor a variety of manual skills whether picking berries from high branches of tree and bush or digging roots and tubers.

The premium on intelligence would become ever greater in this novel and more dangerous environment. Selection would favor the brightest with the bigger brain. With increasing brain size gestation lengthens but the central nervous system is still only partially developed. The infant is born in a helpless state requiring an extended period of dependency—and risk. Female inventiveness and skill would increase, the female role in nurturing and teaching the young would steadily lengthen. The improved social skills of succeeding generations, made possible by increasing brain size, would largely be the result of the extended learning time with the mothers. These trends would continue for perhaps millions of years before any alteration in the independent patterns in the daily life of adult male and female could occur. It is likely that at this most crucial period in evolution—the spaces of the savanna considered—not more but rather less of the female's time was spent within the range of male protection or attention.

It may be speculated that the first significant change in male-female relationships might have occurred with a revolutionary behavioral change related to the setting up of a home base safe from predators. This, too, was in all likelihood a female invention based on female necessity. Readily available trees were a crucial resource and savanna offerings were spotty. Needing a protected place where the young might be safe to eat food gathered by the mother, a base camp, however temporary, was a likely solution. Food storage and a more permanent home base would have followed. The pressure of necessity to set up a home base would never have affected forest-dwelling chimpanzees to the same extent as our savanna-dwelling ancestors. No longer the den, the lair, or the nests of lesser beasts, the evolved female invented "the dwelling" and, in the years to follow, raised it—after enlisting male help—to an art form. Improved bipedalism, invention of a sling or crude basket for carrying infant or large quantities of food, and the spread of food-sharing behavior from mothers to the entire social group would have developed along with the fact of a home base.

A home base would bring about closer association of the sexes which in turn would favor an increase in sociability, cooperation and communication skills already begun by the extended association with the mother. This process covered millions of years and embraced many changes in climate and food supply. Even with the appearance of humans, including the Neanderthal of 100,000 years ago, the female—some studies suggest—gathered most of the food for herself and her offspring which they consumed on the spot. Fossil findings reveal that the home base was still rudimentary and primitive compared with that of our immediate ancestors, the Cromagnon of 35,000 years ago.

The inconclusive evidence for establishing complete as opposed to a rudimentary home base makes it difficult to be certain about the origins of pair-bonding although male theorists tend to place this at an earlier date than facts would substantiate. Pair-bonding, the life long association of a male and female, has in the institution of marriage become a sacred and a civil rite but pair-bonding had its counterpart in animals long before the advent of humans. It appears in evolution with vertebrates and is encountered in bats, birds and others across the evolutionary spectrum. It seems to occur where the raising of an offspring requires unusual parental investment in protection and feeding during a prolonged period of dependency. Nature films of penguins, albatross and other species depict touching scenes of parental dedication and cooperation.

Pair-bonding is encountered in a few species of primates, for example gibbons and marmosets, both tree dwellers, but paradoxically, pair-bonding is not observed in the higher apes, the most evolved and intelligent primates. It is a social behavior that humans have developed for which chimpanzees, our closest animal ancestor, provide no solid clues.

Speculation, however, has been extensive. Having played the active role in establishing the home base, the female would no longer restrict her sexual activity to the period of estrus but would extend receptivity to the full menstrual cycle enabling her to reward an appealing male whenever she chose. This, indeed, does occur in one subspecies of chimpanzee, P. paniscus, or bonobus. In addition she would introduce a new way of copulating, the face to face position—which, incidentally, occurs in the bonobus or pygmy chimpanzee. Food sharing would begin. The female chimpanzee has been observed slyly taking food from a male happily engaged in copulating with her. In the setting of a home base with new dimensions in courtship and sexual behavior the beginnings of pair bonding would logically occur.

Speculations on the later events of evolution aside, the chimpanzee mother is a single parent. She raises her infant without assistance from the male and the period of dependency calling for constant attention to the infant continues for years. The survival of the chimpanzee species is evidence enough that the female has been able to do an adequate job. That these skills were the solid foundation leading to increased intelligence, increased social skills and to the evolution of the human species seems reasonable if not obvious.

The mothering behavior of the chimpanzee has been the subject of thousands of hours of observation by experts in animal behavior both in the natural environment and under captive conditions. The intelligence, the capacity for caring, nurturing, tenderness and teaching as revealed in these studies should give pause to anyone who insists upon an unbridgeable conceptual gap between human and chimpanzee. Mankind's vaunted linguistic and technological accumulations, however remarkable, are secondary phenomena. Indeed, they are trivial when viewed in the light of the chimpanzee mother's gift of dedication, sensitivity, and loving care for her infant.

To watch a chimpanzee mother and not realize that one is witnessing a transcendent behavior representing the best of one's self or the best of human behavior is to miss an elementary truth. Humans may conduct endless discussions—which they do—of duty, discipline, sacrifice, justice and dedication but the behavioral manifestations of all of them are clearly visible here. Mothering, as observed in primates, particularly the higher primates, is a clear statement from creature A, that the life of creature B is as important or more so than the life of creature A. While her focus is primarily on her own offspring—as with human mothers—it is not exclusively so but spreads outward toward others in need, the faint beginnings of dissemination of caring and altruism. If one wants to discover and contemplate what wondrous miracle is, in essence, responsible for one's own capacity to love and care for another human one need look no further. To attempt to derive such qualities from the male, from his dominance, protection and generosity toward the group is to stretch credulity to absurd lengths.

Like verbal communication and advanced technology, pair-bonding is not observed in the higher apes. Mother love is millions of years older. Human societies manifest one form or another of pair-bonding and history indicates that it has always been so. Less accepted is the role of the female in that achievement, especially the likelihood that it is a female invention. So accustomed have we become to the idea of male inventiveness and domination, not only in human society but in species at all levels of evolution, that it is difficult for most people to understand that pair-bonding has, as logic indicates, been a female idea from the beginning. Reluctance to embrace that idea has an enduring masculine quality.

The female achievement is doubly remarkable in view of the dominance of the big and powerful males, a significant feature of the chimpanzee-like society that led to human origins. Although the presence of the dominant males offered protection, their self-oriented behavior, readiness for conflict and their persistent insistence on sexual gratification made it a mixed blessing. The chimpanzee mother, like the human mother, manages to find safety and sanctuary for self and infant by skilled negotiation between self and others in a society balanced precariously between peace and violence.

Darwin formulated, in addition to natural selection, another important process, 'sexual selection'. He knew, as animal breeders have long known, that one of Nature's methods of producing fit offspring was by bringing the right male and female together. To illustrate sexual selection Darwin cited Nature's many methods of equipping the male to win the female—the plumage, the dances, the mating calls and the contests of strength. Such a process, Darwin stated, brought about the human race. Starting with an ape-like ancestor millions of years ago, an increasingly intelligent and highly social creature evolved which we have modestly labeled Homo sapiens, the wise one.

Although Darwin was well aware that in human society the female plays an active and definitive role as the architect of mating and marriage, his writings emphasize the male role for the rest of the animal kingdom. Unknown to Darwin was the skill and initiative of the non-human primate female in selecting the friendlier, more socially skilled male as a sexual partner. Her skill, which has been well documented, requires ability for subtle discrimination as well as a surprising talent for dissembling. A male with qualities of assertiveness and the capacity for dominance would be of value to the female. The female faced a double task. Select a male both strong and gentle, dominant yet cooperative, basically an ideal combination of strength and intelligence, then manipulate circumstances to consummate such a selection.

Those males selected by females had superior capacity for pair-bonding and loyalty to a single female. Gentleness and interest in infants and young, willingness to assist in food gathering and sharing along with the ability to defend female and young against aggressive males and intercurrent predators rounded out the picture. With the successful introduction of pair-bonding the female had succeeded in organizing for primate society the first mothering team, subsequently labeled "the family."

Team forming, in general, was an early evolutionary advance preceding advances such as specialization for production of tools and weapons. Teams were a natural development from the cooperative mother-child duo, that is, a female creation. Over thousands of generations intelligent males would improve on their social skills along with skill in tool and weapon making. On the basis of the affiliative skills learned, so to speak, at his mother's knee, the male would develop alliances with other males for hunting, for defense and for other group projects. Recognizing the female as originating cooperation and alliance skills, of inventing the home base, of initiating pair-bonding, leading the male toward participation in a mothering team—family formation—is to recognize the female, not as the passive follower of the male, but as the true creator and founder of the human race. With this revolutionary new arrangement for reciprocated experience and learning, the female triggered an evolutionary break-through that lifted the species out of the animal world to a state of being that we label human.

Chapter Fourteen
THE CASE OF GREGG C.

The need for new definitions emerged.—Fathering, for instance, is best defined as mothering behavior, learned from the female and practiced by a male. The family is best defined, simply, as a mothering team. Our constant and daily use of the linked label, father and mother, obscures the source and traditions of caring. In its implication of a natural and firm bond it deflects inquiry into the truth, the unevenness of fathering behavior and the vulnerability of the human family.

With the development of language, writing, culture and civilization, the family as a mothering team evolved new functions and variations. In addition to the new member, the father, the team included siblings—possibly the first members—as well as grandparents, aunts and uncles or other members of the extended family who participated in raising the young. Eventually, it expanded to include non-blood-related participants such as nannies, teachers, trainers, nurses and physicians who contribute to the care or growth of the dependent ones. They are all functional members of the mothering team, increasingly important in today's complex society.

Looked upon as the product of a mothering team a child can be seen and appreciated from new perspectives. One child may be raised by a stressed, struggling, ill and impoverished single female virtually without assistance. A second child may be raised by a mother and father whose relationship is characterized by dominance, violence and alcohol. A third may be raised by a healthy, happy and harmonious couple with a rich network of relatives, friends and helpers. The full picture is obtained so seldom that children are often evaluated or judged without awareness of the profound differences in the mothering teams.

The functioning of the mothering team is the least understood and the least appreciated of any major issue facing human society. While there are random descriptions there is only limited comprehension of the widely varied circumstances that the infant and child encounters in our society primarily because males have always set up the rules and fielded the teams. A baseball team with two on one side and ten on the other would be unthinkable—to a male. Such teams occur routinely in mothering. The plight of a female heading a mothering team abandoned or intermittently dominated by a male in a male-dominated society—while of minor interest to males—offers a challenge to anyone seeking to understand the interaction between child and community. The impact of this bland unawareness on the educational system is, of course, obvious.

My interest in primates, particularly the primate mother, had led me to a somewhat unexpected but increased awareness of my own behavior as a therapist and, perforce, a new view of the psychiatrist. The qualities that I had seen operating in the chimpanzee mother, namely, dedication, intelligence, devotion and according one's own needs secondary status were the very qualities I had sought for in my role as psychiatrist. Most certainly, I was a full member of the mothering team helping patients grow to maturity or get over an illness.

One more definition needed to be added. The psychiatrist, clearly, is best defined as society's specialist in corrective foster mothering. To say "corrective foster fathering" is redundant. The definition of fathering, more specifically, the operative description of fathering, is, to repeat, simply mothering behavior learned and practiced by a male—whatever "masculine" touches he chooses to bring to the role. That I was anatomically a male—and, happily, enjoyed being so— was a secondary matter. That I was capable of various technical skills was also secondary. Mothering is characterized by all sorts of specialized skills from extracting sharp splinters from fingers or sharp specks from eyes to sharp observations on where one's behavior is amiss by doing absolutely nothing when to do so would be meddling. Male colleagues, it occurred to me, were not likely to take readily to my definition of a psychiatrist—or to the definition of fathering—or to the concept of the "mothering male."

The years of inquiry into the workings and wonders of mothering now broadened to include that strange human invention, the family. Its structure and membership varied from one century to another, from one culture to another and varied widely even within a single society. It was many things in one, a defensive and sheltering unit, a productive and economic unit, an educational and political unit. Interest in the family opened a new chapter— sometimes confusing—but looking at it as a "mothering team" helped.

Seeing myself as a member of the mothering team began to influence the way I worked with patients. Although I had no particular wish to alter established patterns of practice, a kind of informality was insinuating itself into my behavior; several patients, in fact, commented that I was changing before I became aware of it myself. Apparently, having theorized about it for so long, I was behaving less like a professional guided by psychoanalytic theory and more, perhaps, like a friendly old uncle. No longer relying primarily on logical deduction or other forms of precise reasoning I was using resources characteristic of friends—intuition, empathy, concern.

The practice of psychiatry was still influenced by Freud and was to a large extent proscribed. Orthodoxy decreed that only the individual patient could be seen, that to see another member of the family was taboo. Patients were scheduled strictly on a hourly basis, appointments were set weeks in advance and the psychiatrist remained silent much of the time. I had, long since, given up the couch as not helpful in therapy. Freud himself had said that he had employed the couch because he did not want to be stared at all day long.

Practice inched further and further away from the old model. How often patients chose to see me was often left to them, the schedule could be changed if need be. Sessions were not rigidly segmented into hourly slices of time and ran over if my schedule permitted. Patients could come alone or could bring anyone they chose if it would advance the project of understanding and discovery. Patients need not announce in advance who they were bringing, and sometimes I had to bring in a few more chairs. Occasionally, it was productive to make a house call, to visit the patient at home. How family members arranged themselves, who said what and in what sequence could give clues to how the family communications operated. Clearly, psychiatric illness was not an individual illness: it was a family illness—even when the family had long since disbanded or disappeared—the patient being the indicator and usually exhibiting most of the signs and symptoms.

While I had begun to do away with professional rigidity, the time tested basics of psychiatric practice still held. The new informality did not permit invasion of privacy. Familiarity breeds contempt and in therapy even more so. It can damage the sensitive patient. Patients were asked to reveal only what they wished to share, setting the pace and direction of work was by mutual consent; rapport, empathy and respect still dictated the dimensions and limits of therapy.

Over the course of years I talked—again, only with the patient's permission—quite frequently with family members but there was no reason to set up limitations of any kind. On occasion, I have talked to friends and lovers of patients, ex-wives and ex-husbands, grandparents, aunts, uncles and cousins as well as war buddies and drinking buddies, partners and classmates, lawyers and clergymen—anyone who in the patient's view cared and could contribute. Collectively they brought much helpful information to bear on patients' problems. The atmosphere of an easy open house, not unlike that of an informal and pleasant family, predominated in the office over the formal, the restrained, and the professional—which, on occasion, is necessary. Mothering and psychiatry are both family therapy.

Greg C. was a partner in a Wall Street investment firm. He came from a banking family in the Midwest. Both his father and grandfather had been president and major stockholders in a large bank with branches in Iowa and Nebraska. I saw him the first time in an emergency consultation. A lawyer, Barney L., a former patient of mine, called me. He had been a class-mate of Greg's at Yale and he begged me to see Greg that day if possible. No, he was not suicidal. No, he was in no danger of harming someone. But it was an emergency. I agreed to see Greg after regular office hours.

As I let the last patient out— the receptionist had already left—I noticed Greg in a far corner of the reception room. I came over to him, offered my hand and said, "Hi." He did reach out his hand but said nothing and he followed along as I went back to my office. Beckoning to a chair I sat down opposite him, smiled, and tried to add up what I saw. He was tall, thinning blonde hair, early forties, good looking. He was pale, his skin had a grayish tint, he was expressionless, his face frozen but with a hint of fear he was unable to repress.

"No hurry." I began, "there's plenty of time. I don't have to go anyplace."

He finally managed a mumbling kind of statement. "The partners had a meeting this morning."

"And?"

"They want to fire me."

"Fire a partner? They can't fire a partner, can they?"

"Well, they haven't put any kind of a time on it. They just think I should begin looking around."

On the surface of it, it didn't make sense. As we went into it further it didn't make sense either. That Greg, a successful partner and managing director, could feel that his position was so insecure, so tentative, was puzzling. I asked him if he recalled being this disturbed by any other disappointment or defeat in life. He thought for a minute or so but his answer was, no, he could recall no time when he had been so shattered. He went on to suggest that perhaps there might be something physically wrong. He hadn't slept for several nights and hadn't been feeling well over the past few weeks. He had seen his regular doctor the previous week who reassured him that everything was perfectly normal. It was late in the day and he, clearly, was exhausted.

Buying time seemed practical. "Look, it's clear that you've drained out a lot of energy. Whether it's psychological or whether its physical or both is hard to say. Today is Friday. If you just go home and get as much sleep as you can I'll see you the first of the week. If you develop a fever, cough, pain or get in a panic or can't get through the week-end, call me. I'll be available and I'll get right back to you."

He seemed agreeable. "I'm not sure I'll be able to sleep. I haven't had a decent night's sleep for weeks."

"Do you have some kind of sleeping pill at home?"

"My wife does but I don't like to take pills."

"Better let me give you enough for a few nights." I wrote out a prescription. "Take one, they're mild. If you can't get to sleep take another. I'm not enthusiastic about sleeping pills but it's the lesser of two evils." I handed it to him as he left the office.

He called me on Saturday afternoon. He reported that he had gone to bed early Friday evening and slept until an hour before he phoned.

"I slept for over fourteen hours without moving. What was in that sleeping pill?"

I laughed. "I told you it was a mild sleeping medication. I rarely give a sleeping pill of any kind. You finally gave yourself permission to sleep. How do you feel?"

"Well, I guess I feel rested."

"That's a good beginning. Do you need to see me today or can it wait till Monday?"

"Monday should be all right."

I gave him the appointment. When he appeared on Monday he looked much better, looked, in fact, like Wall Street molds people to look. Significantly rested, he was able to sit down, relax and talk in a coherent, straight-forward manner. He apologized for causing so much trouble.

"I'd like to thank you for . . ." he paused.

"Well, I haven't done much of anything to be thanked for . . . except maybe helping you discover that you're healthier than you think."

As I had suspected he had many more worries and concerns than being displaced from his partnership. That, in fact, was more or less the last straw. His marriage had been breaking up for months. Two of his three sons were in trouble, one had been caught by the headmaster at his New England prep school for distributing marijuana, LSD and some other drugs as well. The other had run up a credit card debt of several thousand dollars. Things, it seemed, were pretty much of a mess.

I listened to him jump from one subject to another as he seemed to be desperately searching for a single answer that would miraculously solve all the problems at once. I began to sense that he might think I was the source of that hoped for miracle.

"Silvia and I have been going to a marriage counselor for several years. We spend hour after hour listing the advantages of marriage versus separation and divorce. We couldn't even find out why we got married in the first place. We both got so sick of it that we decided last month to just go ahead and separate. The marriage counselor was somebody a friend suggested. Barney finally persuaded me that I should get some real expertise if I wanted some proper answers."

"Where do you think we ought to start?"

"I don't know. Nothing seems to be working."

"Well, it's clear that this qualifies as an emergency. The usual label is "crisis intervention"."

"You can say that again."

"Then, first things first, now what do you think we should tackle?"

I could almost see Greg begin to writhe as he struggled for a response. He became pale and sweat was visible on his forehead. "I don't . . ." His answer was lost in an inaudible mumble.

It was difficult for me to grasp this kind of paralysis and equally difficult to understand how my simple question had precipitated it. Here was the partner in a top brokerage house in Wall Street, used to making split second decisions involving millions of dollars and, now, unable to suggest a simple agenda. It occurred to me that he might have misinterpreted my question as saying that I couldn't or wouldn't help him. I decided to test the thought.

"It should be pretty simple for us to set up priorities."

"Yeh, I guess it ought to be." He was visibly relieved, he looked as though he had been given a reprieve. "Us" had apparently been the magic word.

"You told me that there's no emergency about the firm. Couldn't we put that one on the back burner."

"Yes, I think so."

"Well, couldn't we say the same thing for any immediate action on the question of separation and divorce? I'm not saying that your career and your marriage aren't important. Only that there's no immediate emergency."

"Yeh, sure."

This was no time to undertake a search for why his paralysis of volition was so profound. In the days when my focus had been on the individual and not the family I might well have pursued such an inquiry. Now it was clear that something had to be done to pull this family through a crisis. Later we could explore why a rescue had become necessary.

"The problem of that son of yours. Now that does sound like an emergency."

"It sure is."

"Then let's put the problem of you and your career and your marriage on the back burner and work on this one."

"I don't know what to do."

"Neither do I. All I want us to agree on is that it's important. Right now, it's the most important."

"Yes, that's true, isn't it?" Greg looked at me as though I possessed some special wisdom.

We'd been talking for nearly two hours. I leaned forward in my chair and stretched out a hand. "Let's shake on it. We can take this up again after lunch."

Thus developed another case dealing, not with a "patient" but with a family. Seen in an individual photo most everybody looks different than in the family portrait. It's the same with an individual's problems.

Chapter Fifteen
PSYCHIATRIC PROBLEMS ARE FAMILY PROBLEMS

"First of all, I'd like to meet that son of yours."

"Would that help?"

"I don't know but I'd like to talk to him."

"I don't know what the school is going to do."

"Never mind about that. I don't either."

"I thought I might need a lawyer so I called Barney. He advised me to wait and see what they were going to do, then negotiate."

I felt certain that I should show him that I was going to stick with him. "We might have to do that later. Right now speak to the headmaster. Concoct some kind of story. Tell him you want your son in New York immediately. Tell him you want the boy seen by a doctor. Tell him you've picked out a New York specialist."

"I dread calling him."

"Don't make it a "call," no discussion, just tell him. Tell the headmaster what you want. If he says, no, call me and I'll talk to him."

Half-frightened and half-relieved he agreed. The head-master was, apparently, also relieved that a next step had been suggested to him. John, aged fifteen, appeared at the office the following day.

"Hey," I said, sizing him up as he came in my consulting room, "I'm glad you could get here."

Sizing up was an apt phrase. I had expected a tall slim blonde, he was short and black haired. Later on I learned that his mother, Silvia, was black-haired and Italian. He was scared. I told him that I was here to help. I explained that his father had given me permission to try.

"That is," I added, "if you can think of some way I could help." With that remark the fear left his face, his head turned slightly and his eyes looked off into space. I gave him time.

"I don't know what they're going to do."

"Why worry about that? The question is, what are we going to do? Could you explain how this whole thing came about?"

"I don't know exactly what . . ."

I interrupted. "I'm not here to judge. Try to remember that. What you tell me is absolutely confidential. I will tell your parents only what you and I agree I can tell them."

I was certain that I could get his permission to tell them something. John went on to tell me that except for possession of drugs the school had made no other charges. No one had been caught while using them. No one had been hurt in accidents or any other drug-induced behavior.

"Well, I'm not going to rat on anybody."

"A guy who won't rat on his friends must be pretty strong. Don't you know any way of getting a message through to them?"

John thought a moment. "Well. there's one way. The brother of one of my friends lives near the school. He could probably get a message through to the guys."

"Sounds like a good idea. You can call from here when we're finished if you want to." In an off-hand non-questioning tone I went on. "Where did you manage to get all the drugs?"

"From a guy I met in Central Park."

"Wow. You could get hold of some bad stuff if you don't know your sources."

"This guy sold stuff to my older brother and his friends. They know what they're doing."

The story went on. John was several years younger than the oldest brother, Henry, and it was apparent that he felt inferior in many ways—shorter, not as smart, not as popular. Life for John was a desperate striving to keep up with Henry and with everything else.

The story became somewhat convoluted as teen-age stories often do. John, it turned out, had been supplying drugs of all varieties to his classmates and upper classmen for nearly two years. He, himself, didn't enjoy taking drugs, he would pretend to use them and would share a joint only when he had to behave like the others. The only reasonable clue to such behavior seemed to be that John craved the acceptance and popularity that his older brother seemed to have.

"All those drugs must have cost a fair amount of money?"

"Yeh."

"Do you have that kind of money?"

"No."

"So?"

"Well, there was a lot of old silver stuff stored in the attic."

"You took it?"

"Well, the guy helped me find a place where I could pawn it."

His grandmother, of Italian parentage, had been a Newport belle. The silver, priceless and antique, had been her family's.

"I'll tell you what. I'll work on this problem with the headmaster if you tell your father and mother about the silver. Otherwise, we'll have to let the school authorities handle the matter and that could be very harmful to both you and your friends."

It was a tough choice and he didn't like it but he agreed to do so.

"Tell them tonight and come in and see me tomorrow." He left. I called the headmaster at the school, told him that I had begun my examination of the boy and would call him the following day. I advised him not to make any rash moves such as talking to the police or members of the Board of Directors until we had more of the facts.

"We've never had an experience like this. I'd heard of troubles at other schools but never here at ___."

I thought I detected a note less of reverence than fear in his use of the school name.

Feeling a twinge of guilt at using facts to manipulate, I casually remarked, "Well, let's just hope that such a record can continue unblemished. I'll call you tomorrow."

The parents, Greg and Silvia, with John in tow were both in my office the following day. They were shocked and numb. A rough estimate of the value of the lost antique silver was between fifty and one-hundred thousand dollars. John could not recall how much cash he had received because on most occasions the drug dealer had been with him when they disposed of the various pieces and John had often not even handled the money. At most, they guessed, he had received the drugs and a few thousand dollars.

We talked for another hour or so while John cooled his heels in the reception room. "I can appreciate your confusion and your feelings of guilt. We always search for something or someone to blame. Right now we'd better focus on what to do about the school. The headmaster stated flatly that John would have to leave the school and I see no alternative to that. We could, perhaps, endeavor to bring in all the boys who used drugs and threaten the school with scandal but I don't see how John or the boys would benefit from that."

Both parents were agreeable to my continuing discussions with the headmaster. Both were agreeable to continuing our meetings as long as necessary to get things straightened out. Over the next week an acceptable deal was worked out with the headmaster. John would withdraw from school but would be permitted, with the help of tutors, to finish the year's work and to take the final examinations. If he passed successfully, the headmaster would credit him with the school year and provide him with recommendations for transfer to another school.

The headmaster was relieved. We talked at length about his setting up a good program in drug education and in setting up standards for maintaining a drug-free school. I agreed with him that conducting interviews with all pupils who might have participated in drug use would be a good idea if it was used for education and not punishment. Little did either of us know at the time that the country was on the threshold of a drug abuse epidemic which would in another ten years reach proportions in the United States comparable to the disastrous period of Prohibition with world-wide dimensions as well.

John lived at home for the rest of the year and I saw him once or twice a week and, less frequently, Henry and the youngest brother, Paul. I saw Greg and Silvia on a continuing basis. John and Silvia were an early experience in 'family therapy,' informal and unrehearsed.

Several thinkers, years before, had said that mental illness takes place, not in a vacuum, but in families. They were ignored. Other therapists arrived at treating families along different pathways. Within twenty-five years there would be a specialty of family therapy, many theories, even schools and institutes. Some years late, self-help groups and a nation-wide network would spring up with memberships composed of 'adult children of alcoholics' or 'adult children of dysfunctional families.'

Chapter Sixteen
GREGG AND SYLVIA: HAPPY ENDING

With the family crisis resolved we could get to the problem of Greg and Silvia. They were a remarkable couple. I had sensed that about Greg from our first meeting and Silvia made a similar impression. I could not get hold of what it was about them, some deep sadness or sense of loneliness, perhaps. They were both bright, very quick and, of course, well educated. Greg had been raised in Iowa in a city where his had been the leading family for generations. His grandfather had founded the bank, a great uncle had been governor of the state. While Greg's father was strict and religious, his mother was, perhaps out of competitiveness, even more so. Greg's descriptions made me think of Grant Wood's painting, American Gothic, with surroundings, props and dress changed to those of wealth and privilege. Wealthy or not, the family was frugal and every effort was made to conceal their wealth and status.

Silvia's parents were Italian. For a number of years in childhood she had spent her summers in Newport with her parents and her winters at a boarding school in Italy with occasional visits to her maternal grandmother's villa in the hills outside Florence. It was difficult for her to remember the details of her education because there were so many changes. Until ten, she was educated at convents in Rome and Florence. Later on she was sent to a girl's school in Switzerland, except for a year in New York and another year when the family traveled around the world. She was enrolled in Smith for one or two years, and at Sarah Lawrence for another. She described the main 'friends' of her childhood with a kind of shrug as Solitude, Reading and Writing. Gifted in writing and considering it as a career she found herself in a writer's workshop at the

University of Iowa where, during a holiday, she met Greg at a party.

The problem of son John and his ill-feted project to win friends by dispensing free drugs was being resolved. He was doing well in his school work and in his work with me, gratifying to me because I did not work with many teenagers. At the cost of a few thousand dollars plus the help of the police much of the antique silver was recovered. Greg and Silvia's visits could, finally, address the problem of their relationship.

"What was it," I asked during an early visit, "that you two saw in one another? Please, take your time but I do want to know." Neither had answers. Each waited for the other to say something but the silence continued until it was clear that it was up to me.

"Let's just make guesses," I suggested.

Silence.

"Well, you're both attractive. Way above average, I'd say. Was that it?"

The movement of their heads answered, no.

"Status? An arrangement? Socially speaking it was a good marriage. Was that it?"

"Not that. I wouldn't have married for that. I don't think Greg would either." Greg nodded.

More silence.

"How about loneliness?"

Greg responded. "Maybe, but I don't think so. We were both very busy with careers, fairly active social life. We didn't seem very lonely."

"Well, we humans are very good at covering up what hurts us including loneliness."

"Not exactly loneliness," said Silvia, "more like shyness."

"I never thought of myself as shy, maybe not as aggressive as I could be."

"You are shy," said Silvia, glancing at Greg.

"You two may be on to something. See if you can straighten it out a little. You are two very bright people yet you didn't know why you wanted a divorce and you didn't know why you got married and now you tell me you don't know what drew you to one another in the first place. For two people of your sensitivity it doesn't make sense. See if you can help me."

Greg was called out of town on business for several weeks which gave me a chance to have five or six visits with Silvia. She was attractive to look at, responsive and cooperative. She felt that she had genuinely loved Greg, felt that he had truly loved her. There had been three children within the space of six years, Greg was struggling at the firm and there was little time for either of them to consider whether they were happy or not. Things had seemed slowly to deteriorate, neither could say just when and why. There were few open quarrels. Although Greg had never been very affectionate, what little affection there was had withered away and sex had become infrequent and unsatisfactory. Silvia had been away from her writing during these years but with the deterioration of the marriage had gotten back to it and had had several feature articles published in women's magazines.

"All those years. How about affairs?"

"Never did. My religious background, I guess. In childhood I had seriously thought of becoming a nun." She chuckled. "Considering how well I've been able to manage without much of a sex life I guess I could have done quite well."

"How about Greg?"

"Why don't you ask him?" she said, throwing me a gentle curve. "He always told the marriage counselor that he had never played around. I believe him. No matter what he might say, he's shy. And he's really shy around women."

"Do you still love him?

"I've given up. It can't go on. I did everything I could. Honestly, I did. Except that family of his. That I could not handle. That mother. I really tried. I had told her that I wasn't devout but had to agree to give up Catholicism. She demanded it. She insisted that the children be raised as Protestants. Greg wouldn't have cared one way or the other. I finally gave up. Those Christmases. They were unbearable. His father died two years ago so we don't talk about it anymore but I dread the thought of seeing her or having her visit."

"Has this upset Greg? Did he want you to care for her or something?"

"He can't stand her, or his older sister either—who's just like the mother. I don't know what it is but their unhappiness just seems to spread out over him like a mist."

What I was able to learn reinforced my growing conviction that these two had never really wanted to get divorced. They had simply been conducting a marriage with considerable determination and courage which was, for some unknown reason, lacking in easy warmth and friendship, in affection and in joyous and free sexuality. They were left with a few common interests which had grown stale and lifeless.

With the boys away at school, what remained of the satisfactions and duties of parenthood was not enough to keep the relationship alive. The marriage had deteriorated to an arrangement and a dull one at that. Two unusually bright people had become, as far as their marriage was concerned, numb and bewildered. Something was wrong. Something was amiss and the answer wasn't forthcoming. There was nothing to do but keep going. For months visits with Greg or Silvia or both continued.

Finding the pieces of the jigsaw puzzle of Silvia's life and putting them together continued along smoothly. One could not help but be drawn to her. She was open, honest and unguarded. She admitted that she had felt like an unwanted and unattractive little ragamuffin in the presence of her mother who, like the grandmother, had been an acknowledged beauty. Changing from country to country and school to school, she had never had a chance to have friends or be part of anything. She, nevertheless, had not become bitter and withdrawn. She accepted her isolation, had made a virtue of solitude. Her comments about herself and the world, however, had a piercing and poignant quality.

She had accepted the failure of the marriage almost as though she expected it, as though life had been successful training in accepting disappointment—or even failure. Growing up, she had not experienced a loving, caring family. She accepted it. She had a mother who was far more beautiful and charming than she could ever hope to be. She accepted it. In spite of her Catholic upbringing she had hoped to become, perhaps with her husband's help, an exciting and appealing wife, including she asserted, freedom and joy in her sexuality. When Greg had shown little appreciation and even doubted the sincerity of her love making, she accepted that, too.

Her attitude of acceptance did not really cover her sadness. She made no effort to cover a kind of witty and bemused cynicism. In spite of my failure to untangle the marital problem the sessions with Silvia were gratifying. In addition to her openness she was unusually well read in three or four languages. Intelligent conversation whether of art, politics, philosophy or psychology flowed freely from Silvia. I was surprised to hear her say that Greg had never considered her very intelligent.

"Whatever happens between you and Greg it is very clear that you will do very well. You will continue, I'm sure, to search for fulfillment the way you always have. Meanwhile, let's go on with our talks."

While Silvia's discussion of her early life flowed easily it was exactly the opposite with Greg. I once asked him if there was some kind of family taboo against discussing family history. While he denied that there were any barriers to sharing biographical data he somehow managed to skirt or avoid it. He insisted on focussing on the unfairness of his firm and his conviction that they would continue to push for his resignation. He claimed that in his early years he had made a great deal of money for the firm and that their pointing to his lack of production during the past year or so was outright discrimination. He wasn't worried about loss of income: with his investments and inheritance he could retire if and when he chose. It was the lack of appreciation, the indifference and, often enough, the veiled hostility of his partners that were the source of his resentment and anger.

For weeks my attempts to nudge him to discuss his mother, his father, his sister, his early years were met with deft evasion, superficial descriptions and rationalization. What complaints could he possibly have had? As long as he did well in school, which meant being at the top of his class, and as long as there were no complaints from teachers involving discipline, no reasonable material requests were refused.

While ostentation was forbidden he could have most anything he wanted. He was permitted to have a horse at one of their farms since this seemed appropriate. He had been given a Tennessee hunter at an early age and had become a proficient rider by the time he was eight or nine. He was sent to the best camps and, later, to the prep school his sons now attended. The smooth surface of his presentation remained unruffled. Yes, his family had been strict. But that was true of all religious families in Iowa. There didn't seem to be much affection or open expression of joy. His parents entertained a great deal and when that happened everyone seemed to have a good time. We seemed to have hit a brick wall.

Off and on over the past weeks we had discussed his relationship to friends. He seemed to be well liked, perhaps, he thought, because of his family he was catered to. His parents always saw to it that he was given a birthday party including a large number of friends. He remembered being embarrassed by the number of presents that the friends brought but by the time he was a teenager it occurred to him that the fathers of many of them had loans at the family bank.

What did come out was that during the teen years when his buddies began to talk about girls and scheme to be with them, his whole network of friends disappeared. He would go through all kinds of dodges and excuses to avoid anything to do with asking for dates or discussing the subject. His relationship with girls was limited to the school activities that brought boys and girls together. He was relieved when, at fifteen, he was sent away to prep school, which made his isolation from the adolescent courtship scramble less noticeable.

Paradoxically, he could recall no antipathy toward girls. He confessed, in fact, that there had been no time during his growing up years that he had not held in fantasy a favorite girl he had chosen from among his classmates. He would dream and fantasize incessantly but would neither approach nor speak to the girl of his choice. During one year the girl chosen for his fantasy turned out to be a new and young teacher who taught French. He was so paralyzed by being in her class that he arranged on the ground of competing interests to postpone the study of language.

This was the first hint of the shyness around girls that Silvia had mentioned months before and which Greg had denied. I decided to confront Greg in any way I could.

"The more I think about it the more I have the feeling that you are covering or concealing something that is important."

"I've tried to answer every question as honestly as I could. I certainly have tried to share everything I could remember."

"Then you must be forgetting. Why a healthy guy like you wouldn't be just as girl crazy as the rest of the guys in Iowa is a mystery to me."

"I don't know. Maybe it had something to do with my parents. At prep school I sat around in all the bull sessions when we were talking about girls."

"What about your parents?"

"I don't know, I really don't. It seems like they watched everything I did. I know it sounds crazy but I almost had the feeling they knew or could see things I did even when they weren't anywhere near."

"That does sound spooky."

"Well, you've got to remember that they could get information about me from anybody they chose. They'd get first hand reports from the teachers and the principal. I never knew all their sources of information."

"Like every time you cussed or masturbated?"

"Oh, god."

"So?"

"I just thought of something. I haven't thought about in years. My mother and my sister got down on their hands and knees and prayed for me outside my bedroom door. Every morning. I don't know for how long. It seemed like weeks and weeks."

"That must have been some big sin, what had you done?"

"I can't remember. All I remember is that when I asked them to stop they told me that I would have to confess to my father what I'd been doing."

"Stealing money from the bank?"

'Oh, no, not that. I was only five or six."

"So what was it?"

Greg burst out almost with a yell. "Playing with my penis. My god. That was it. I know that's what it was. My mother caught me."

"So? She punished you?"

"No, no. She let out a scream and then she fainted."

"Fainted?"

"She fainted. My god I was scared. I thought she was dead. It was awful. My sister came in and she started yelling at me. I didn't know what I'd done."

"That's some story. Sounds like something out of the nineteenth century. Did she ever tell you what you'd done?"

"Sinned or broken God's commandment or something like that. I could hear them praying outside my door every morning."

"Didn't it make you angry?"

"I was too scared. I do remember having a horrible thought. I used to listen to scary programs on the radio. Maybe it was Inner Sanctum or some program like that. There was this story about a man in England who had some kind of a store and when a person came in he didn't like he would press a button and they would fall through a trap door. Then they were killed and ground up into sausage meat and then he sold the sausages to boarding houses in London."

"One of those gory stories. Like Sweeney Todd. I think he was a barber."

"Maybe I wished my mother and sister would fall through a trap door and be ground up into sausages."

"That sounds pretty much like a kid who's really angry."

"God, I hadn't thought of this in forty years."

"You couldn't be blamed for trying to forget that kind of experience."

The release of that memory opened the gates to a flood of associations and recollections that filled visits for weeks. Greg felt that life after that became an experience of unrelieved fear and shame. He had done something horrible that had no name. On top of that he had had thoughts of murder. He was not an acceptable member of the human race. All he could do was go through the motions of good manners with his mother and sister and everybody else. Feelings of warmth and closeness and trust were never to be part of living.

The only positive relationships of his life were with his teachers. His efforts to please them and become liked by them seemed to be the only real purpose that remained. In becoming a good student he became a bookworm and spent most of his time reading. Because of his inner shame he felt distant and apart from his classmates. Eventually, they ignored him assuming that because he was rich he was snobbish.

"Things got a little better when I went away to prep school. I felt relieved to be away from the family and I wasn't a rich kid anymore. Most of the guy's families had more money than mine."

"Did you finally discover that masturbation was part of growing up?"

"I guess I learned about everything there was to learn in prep school. I even joined the guys when they went to New York on a free week-end, getting drunk and chasing after hookers."

"Sounds preferable to isolation in Iowa."

"I was pretty scared but I went along. God, I just thought of something else. It must have been the first or maybe the second summer after I went to prep school. I wrote a letter to one of my friends and told him about a week-end I had in New York on my way home. I told him about bumping into some call girls and going to their place and how I went to bed with two of them at the same time and gave him all the details on what they did and how great it was."

"Teen-age exploits."

"Actually, I made most of it up."

"Standard."

"I put the letter in the pocket of my jacket and I was going to mail it the next day but my mother found it."

"And read it, of course."

"Oh, God. She showed it to my father. He made me read it aloud."

"He what?"

"He made me read it aloud at the dinner table."

"I don't get it."

"Every night before he said grace he would have me read

it from start to finish. Then he would say grace and then we would eat dinner."

"Now I've heard everything." It dawned on me that he had never felt he could turn to his father. No wonder he had been frightened by the thought that I would not or could not help him. "I wonder how dinner tasted." I said, quietly.

"I was kinda sick the whole summer. I got over it, finally. But the feeling that I was abnormal and unacceptable never went away. I really didn't think anybody could like me. Not a girl, anyway."

I summoned up a tone of derision. "Yeh, who could possibly love you?"

Greg chuckled, a nervous chuckle, but quickly became grimly serious.

"What goes on with families?"

"I wish I had answers to that one."

"If I was so repulsive . . ." he paused.

"Not you. Masturbation. Sin. That sort of thing. How can we ever know what was in their mind? Some old nineteenth century attitudes, probably. The important thing is what you think of yourself."

"Honest to God, I don't think I ever asked myself that question. I just wanted to scream that they were wrong." His voice took on a screaming quality. "Wrong. Wrong. Wrong."

Neither of us said anything for a few minutes. "O.K., you've made your point. Could we try to find out what you think about yourself?"

"I guess I don't really know what I am."

"You mentioned being 'unacceptable'"

"That can't be right."

"Unlovable?"

"I don't know."

"Pretty fundamental questions. Worth meditating on, I'd say."

Greg got up from his chair, walked slowly to the door, shaking his head slowly back and forth.

Lost in thought with a wave of his hand he left. "See you Monday."

I continued to see Greg and Silvia over the course of the ensuing months. Once they discovered the poor regard in which they had held themselves, once they discovered how they had insidiously put down not only themselves but also one another, once they had discovered how much pain it had caused, changes became sweeping. Their view of themselves began to be wholesome and realistic and they began to see life as an on-going process of self discovery. In so doing it awakened new interest in and the enjoyment of others. Family life, social life, their careers and the careers of the three boys took an upward swing. Best of all, however, was that Greg and Silvia quite simply fell in love. The "family" approach to therapy works.

Chapter Seventeen
THE POWER OF THE GROUP

"Turbulent" has become the descriptive label for the nine-teen-sixties. Early in the decade the assassination of a president, late in the decade the assassination of his brother and, in the years between, crisis after crisis—the threat of the H-bomb, the Cuban missile crisis, the struggles over civil rights and the assassination of the leader, Martin Luther King, the Vietnam War, the epidemic of drugs—marijuana, LSD, heroine and other chemicals—riots at a national political convention, the student protests, campus sit-ins and culminating in the massacre of four college students at Kent State. Such widespread cultural and social upheavals had profound and repeated impact on the practice of psychiatry.

Conventional orthodoxies were challenged. Psychoanalysis as the standard of therapy was pushed from center stage, rejected as patriarchal, overly intellectual, authoritative, anti-female, intolerably long, boring and only for the rich. Who really knew about the human mind, anyhow, reflected the prevailing attitude. Group therapy spread and new forms of therapy—some revolutionary and radical—emerged. The pharmaceutical industry introduced a wide variety of new chemicals for emotional troubles—anti-anxiety and anti-depressive drugs—particularly for patients hospitalized with serious mental illness. Tranquillized patients became quiet and manageable, psychiatric hospitals were no longer Bedlam, thousands of patients were discharged and returned to communities unprepared to accept them. Mental patients joined the homeless and wandered the streets. New kinds of sedatives and minor tranquilizers found their way into general use. Lightly referred to as aspirin for the psyche, misuse and abuse were common. Many patients became addicted.

It was a decade of change and instability. Encounter groups, marathon groups and communes sprang up around the country. Psychedelics and hallucinogens—pot, acid, speed, mushrooms—were widely used by the young who claimed that they led to insight and higher goals for the "beat" generation. Many young people took off for the far east—India, Tibet, Burma—where gurus of various persuasions offered emancipation from intolerable establishment strictures. No social institution—government, education, church, the family—escaped criticism.

Families were split with dissension. A father who had served in World War II had little tolerance for a son who became a conscientious objector or escaped to Canada to avoid Vietnam. Families lost their young to drugs, communes and new religions. Some theorists suggested that the usefulness of the family in raising young was finished, that new systems such as the kibbutz which was thriving in Israel would be the wave of the future and endorsed the actions of young people who turned to sects and cults. Many parents blamed psychiatrists for participating in or founding communes, for turning children against parents, for destroying families and for condoning promiscuity and psychedelics. Other parents, however, turned to psychiatrists for counsel and help with the problems of young people.

Families fortunate enough to have a durable and loving mother, particularly if a father possessing the same qualities were around, seemed better able to weather these social stresses but nothing was certain. Tragedies of overdose from drugs, teen-age suicide, accidents from reckless behavior struck families in seeming unpredictable patterns. The family—not the commune or religious sect—still was the best available model for group therapy. Some of the newer innovations were acceptable but not others. I was unenthusiastic about psychedelics even when their popularity reached tidal wave proportions accompanied by claims that they cured alcoholism and schizophrenia. As chemical intoxicants they were simply mood changing drugs having all the dangers of intoxicants in general; the line between use and abuse not always easy to determine, particularly to those—I told patients about the Indians, Eskimos and alcohol—ignorant of their effects. Watch Out became the guideline. Experiment with caution; drugs may provide a quick "high" and temporary relief from stress but they are an uncertain pathway to ecstacy or bliss.

The encounter group was another psychological fad which had spread across the country. Challenging what was felt to be Establishment hypocrisy including conventional group therapy, the encounter movement waved its banner proclaiming, "Let It All Hang Out." No more dishonesty, tell the other person what you think. Sanctioned and encouraged by therapists, the groups became shouting matches for denunciation and hatred. That this would drain deep and chronic abscesses of the psyche as proclaimed was, I felt, without foundation. It was a misuse of peer experience and, instead of being curative, served as a rehearsal for the next hateful encounter.

The movement included behavior, too. Clothes were a form of hypocrisy and nude encounter groups—along with "pot" and "acid"—became symbols of freedom. Whimsical and impulsive sexual encounters, billed as recreational sex, were included as proof of emancipation. All this, it seemed to me, had nothing to do with people seeking understanding, sensitivity and concern for self and others—important guidelines for everyone. If the family is accepted as a model for group therapy it follows that sex within the group is, metaphorically, incest. Not all group members accepted this view, asserting that the beginnings of play and sexuality occur in the family, and many courtships were launched in the course of group therapy. Never, however, were the groups, although forthright and open in their discussions of sexuality, a ticket for promiscuity.

Creativity, inventiveness, and innovation flow from the young—whether the observations are of monkey, ape or human—I welcomed suggestions and avoided the veto. My rejection of the encounter group, for instance, was not because it sanctioned impulsiveness or because it was noisy but because it endorsed expressing hatred. Groups do get pretty noisy at times and group members felt that the occasional feeling of wanting to scream is common to most humans. They agreed that shouting or a scream of pain should not be discouraged—scream therapy had become popular on the West coast. I had a sound-proof room constructed at considerable expense but a few years convinced me and most group members that screaming produced more hoarseness than healing.

Experience with marathon groups, on the other hand, was positive. A common practice was to obtain a suitable location, a roomy apartment, a farm or a country house and convene the group early on a Friday evening. Group therapy would then go on hour after hour with short breaks for food or, by common agreement, for a few hours of sleep following which the group would reconvene and continue the discussion and interaction until Sunday evening. The impact of fatigue and exhaustion eroded inhibitions; long-buried hurts and resentments would be aired and shared, often with sobs and tears of pain. Barriers to accepting the sympathy and caring of the group would disappear as healing and growth took over, indeed, became the expectancy.

Innovative suggestions led to interesting experiences and adventures. One group chartered a schooner and a week's marathon was conducted in the Caribbean against a sunny background of sea, sand and sky. A member of another group offered his house in Bermuda for weekends—airfares were nominal in the sixties—and a lovely harbor-side home became the site for monthly marathon therapy sessions. Periodic marathons continued for years. I finally reached that age when missing a night's sleep—or two or three—began to take its toll; marathons were turned over to younger colleagues. Meanwhile, weekly meetings continued as the basic group approach bringing healing to the hurt and growth to the hesitant—and, occasionally, demonstrating the power of the group to work miracles.

The case of Chuck B., a patient of a colleague, illustrated just how remarkable this healing power of the peer group alone could be. Psychiatrists, like other kinds of doctors, are given to swapping stories about interesting cases and at a group therapy convention several of us were discussing the value of the alternate group, a weekly meeting held without the inhibiting if not restraining presence of the therapist. In illustration, my colleague presented one of his own cases. He practiced in Westchester County, in one of the wealthier New York suburbs, and his practice was devoted entirely to group therapy. He, too, had always provided his groups with the option of the alternate meeting, that is, a meeting without a formal leader or authority figure.

A member of one of his groups had come with a strange request. He had a friend, he said, who wanted to meet only with the alternate group and not ever meet the therapist. Although the psychiatrist's first impulse was to give a flat out, "no," he suggested that the member discuss the matter with the group. His thought, he said, was that the group would see how absurd it was and would veto the idea. The group, however, agreed with their fellow member on admitting the newcomer.

With some head scratching, the psychiatrist went along, hesitantly and with trepidation. He wondered about his professional responsibility and a funny thought crossed his mind that if things went badly he could be sued for malpractice by a patient he had never seen and who had never even paid him a fee. As the weeks went by, he pushed the matter out of his mind and refrained from asking questions. And so it went. Months passed. One evening as he met with the group he was introduced to a young man in his early twenties, well dressed and soft spoken.

Chuck B. had now been a member of the alternate group for more than two years. Over the next months the psychiatrist congratulated himself on having permitted this strange arrangement, and Chuck became a sensitive, actively participating member of the group. Gradually, his full story unfolded.

When Chuck was three years old, both his mother and father were killed in a crash of their private plane. The only living relative was an aged eccentric aunt, a great-aunt of his mother, who possessed unlimited wealth and lived in a vast and rambling estate, high above the Hudson River, surrounded by walls and a wrought iron fence seven feet high. She behaved like a semi-invalid, spent most of her time in bed, feared the environment was poisoned and carried her health concerns to freakish lengths. She was a vegetarian, had a special brush for washing each variety of vegetable, and was known to fly into a rage if the carrot brush was used on a potato. She lived in one wing of the vast mansion, and another wing was turned over to Chuck and whatever nurse or tutor had been assigned to care for him.

He saw his aunt only once a week, but a notebook was kept of every detail related to Chuck's health. What he ate was recorded. His daily urine volume was recorded and his bowel movements were weighed and measured. He didn't know what kind of doctors took care of him in the early years but later he learned that his aunt never saw anyone but strange assortments of self-styled nutritionists, crystallographers, and psychic healers.

For years there was a constant turnover of nurses and tutors for Chuck; every time one of them made a mistake of any kind he, or she, was fired. The butler was an alcoholic, the chauffeur was usually having an affair with a current maid or the tutor. In the afternoons, Chuck was free to wander about the place but with nobody to play with.

One day, in a far corner of the estate, he found a loose bar in the fence, squeezed through and wandered about outside for a short time before he hurried back, undiscovered. Carefully hiding his escape route he would, each day, return and would wander a little further. He discovered a playground with kids at play, and, for days, he stood on the outside, gazing in. Then, one day, a few of the boys and girls urged him to come in and join in the fun. He would play for a short while, and then hurry away, afraid that he would be caught either by the tutor or the chauffeur. He was always certain to finish his tutoring lessons in the morning so his tutor wouldn't take away his afternoon freedom.

In his wing of the house was a vast domed and walnut paneled library with books that stretched to the ceiling. Nobody went there and he discovered that if he told the tutor he was going there she would never check on him. Eventually it dawned on Chuck that neither chauffeur nor tutor would report him to the aunt, anyway. She would fire them, and, besides, she had taken to her bed permanently and seemed to have no interest in seeing Chuck more than once a month. One thing the tutors had done well was to teach him to read. He read fast and remembered what he had read. Alone in the vast library, books and reading became the main pastime, neither radio nor television being permitted. He developed great skill in maintaining his double-life; if any of the servants knew about it they gave no sign. He recalled thinking, on reading Oliver Twist, that if Oliver had been a little smarter he wouldn't have gotten beaten all the time.

This pattern of living continued until his teen years when he was sent to prep school. Most of the arrangements for this were handled by the aunt's lawyer, even older than the aunt, who had little personal interest in Chuck whom he duly escorted to school and duly brought back to the estate every vacation and holiday. Chuck made a few friends at school, but there was no way he could invite them to his home and he would never ask the aunt for permission to visit them. He continued to visit his old playground whenever he had time off from prep school and his only close friends were two or three of the boys he had played with through the years who knew of his background. He was finishing his third year of college when one of the friends from the playground days coaxed him to come into the alternate group.

After two years, they also convinced him that he should consider revising his views of the adult world. Heretofore, Chuck had tended to divide the adult world into two main groups; servants and weirdos. Sometimes, as with professors at college, he would have to decide which category to put them in. He was never troubled for long and they were neatly placed in one or the other. He did make progress; he began to relax, to change his views and, gradually, began to accept the therapist. The peer group was, however, his life. It had served Chuck, an orphan, for all practical purposes as both a mother and a father.

Over the course of months, Chuck kept remarking that the therapist was beginning to look younger. It dawned on the group and, finally, on Chuck that he was changing the therapist from a part weirdo, part servant into a peer and friend. Eventually, he began to do that with a few other adults and, finally, he himself, entered the adult world. After the aunt died, at the age of 102, Chuck married one of the girls in the group and, according to my colleague, they, as in the fairy tale, lived happily ever after. Such is the miracle of the playground, the healing power of the group, the healing power of friendship.

Utilizing the group approach for social problems—wider in scope than individual therapy—does not always lead to rewarding endings, even those launched with enthusiasm and promise. One thinks of the difficult beginnings of Alcoholics

Anonymous. An interesting example was the unhappy fate in New York City of The GROW School. Born out of the desperate social convulsions GROW, founded in the late 60s, was an acronym for Group Relations On-going Workshops, an experiment in education to train people for active involvement in confronting current social ills. Founded by a number of socially conscious young people, the school sought to develop leadership and group skills for solving the mounting number of serious social problems. It chose an alternative to the conventional teaching methods of schools and colleges that explain rather than challenge the status quo. Group workshops of ten to twenty persons replaced classes, group leaders replaced professors and dialogue replaced lectures.

Rather than courses in liberal arts or in science and technology, the workshops offered courses such as Basic Communication Skills, Techniques of Leadership, How to Organize Groups, Family Structure and Dynamics, Community and Neighborhood Activism, The Roots of Racism, Eradicating Racial Prejudice, The Social Aspects of Drug Abuse, An Overview of Crime and the Criminal Justice System and many others. Giving examinations and grading students was done away with; instead each student chose and developed his or her own social project with the help of the faculty who advised and evaluated.

GROW thrived from its inception; within six months it became a magnet attracting students from every walk and level of life. It also attracted teaching talent, therapists, psychologists, psychiatrists, pastoral counselors and a number of professors from nearby universities, chafing under Academia and anxious to lead groups and teach courses of their own design. Within a few years the student body had grown to over seven hundred, the school catalogue listed over two hundred workshop leaders and two hundred and fifty different workshops. The number of student projects filled a directory. Grass roots organizations dealing with high priority community problems—child care nurseries for working mothers, training for the single mother, block organizations to fight drugs, pocket parks from vacant lots—began to spring up in many New York City neighborhoods.

Most GROW students had jobs or were enrolled in degree programs at universities and news of GROW activities was widely circulated. GROW students often stood out as good workers or students and became known wherever they were. Many worked for the city government and a number of departments of the city began to offer free tuition for workers enrolled at GROW. The state education department authorized granting certificates for different levels of leadership skills and several colleges offered advanced standing for students taking GROW workshops. A combined degree program with a theological seminary attracted students of the ministry dedicated to social reform.

One of GROW's many endeavors, the result of the combined effort of GROW students and faculty along with New York City government officials, was the LIFT project. Sparked by the urgent need to do something constructive about the prison and criminal justice systems, the initials L.I.F.T. stood for Lift Inmates Forward with Training. The Riker's Island jails and prisons were overflowing and the log-jam of court cases was worsening. GROW was convinced that screening Riker's Island prisoners might reveal persons of basically sound character and leadership potential worthy and likely to profit from rehabilitation and education by GROW methods.

The suggestion was met at first with resistance from the directors of city bureaus but the desperation of the situation finally convinced city officials to endorse a pilot project. GROW faculty interviewed many inmates from Riker's Island and finally selected fifty young men and women on the basis of intelligence, character and motivation to receive GROW training. Preliminary to attending GROW, the fifty candidates were sent for evaluation and intelligence testing to a local university. Inmates were school drop-outs and most were simply—in conventional labeling—"street" kids. The test results were unsatisfactory, many of the inmates were listed as "untestable".

The GROW School occupied a large brownstone on the west side, a considerable distance from Riker's Island and prison officials were aghast at the thought of letting fifty prisoners out to run free on New York streets. To circumvent existing laws it was necessary to designate the school as an annex to the Riker's Island prison facility and uniformed officers were always on hand as a reminder. Inmates were brought by prison bus daily and duly returned by prison bus at the end of the day. After a few months, when not one individual had gone AWOL, the atmosphere of tension relaxed, inmates were no longer identified or identifiable and they blended in with the rest of the student body.

Having heard about GROW from the beginning and being interested in GROW's potential for promoting individual growth, I had agreed to serve as an advisor and, occasionally, when my schedule permitted had led workshops. Leading a group at GROW was a stimulating and often surprising experience, particularly if the group included participants from the Riker's Island LIFT project. The make-up of a GROW workshop often varied to the point of appearing chaotic, the only admission requirement being the participant's dedication and hopes for social betterment. Age, color, size, gender, religion, profession of group members all varied from one group to another. To a group which could include a nun, a rabbi, a nurse, teachers, social workers, therapists and students was now added drug dealers, pimps, prostitutes, shoplifters, thieves, and armed robbers—or so read their indictments.

When the groups met during the first weeks of the LIFT project, the Riker's Island inmates sat virtually pressed against the wall—most meeting rooms were furnished with cushions rather than chairs—and remained silent, responding to questions or encouragement with little more than a sound or a word. Although discussions ranged widely, covering topics as diverse as experiences in childhood and contemporary Washington's political scandals, LIFT students resisted any suggestions to express their views. Faculty advisers to the GROW project suffered through doubt and discouragement and fears that the project would fail spread. What to write in reports to prison authorities posed a difficult question. Hope faded and optimism continued to flow from fewer and fewer of the faculty, mostly those with a religious orientation.

About the time that things began to seem totally bleak the first breakthroughs were reported. One inmate confided to a group leader that it was not distrust of the group or the leaders that was responsible for the silence. GROW was a possible path to freedom and the inmates didn't want to jeopardize it. Further, coming to GROW was a lot better than the cement floors and crowded cages of Riker's Island so it was best not to rock the boat. Slowly, group leaders emphasized that confidentiality of group discussions was a GROW rule that should not be violated. Slowly, it was emphasized that growth was based on two things, a willingness to learn and spontaneity—including the ability to express an unpopular view.

The impasse' was broken seemingly all at once. In one group where the inmates had begun to share some of the circumstances that had led to their arrest, a young nun suggested that it might have been avoided if they had just gotten a job and gone to school. This met with a stony silence until one of the inmates let out a restrained chuckle that triggered a giggle from the others that released an unrestrained convulsion of laughing that spread to the entire group.

When the laughter had subsided one of the inmates said, "Yeah, Harvard maybe—or Yale? Sister, it's not like I wanna tell ya what t'do but you oughta be out there on the street—maybe once."

Thus ended the session but not the dialogue that had been opened up. The same nun continued in the following meetings to suggest that there must be some way they could get further schooling. One of them replied that he'd learn if he had the chance.

"I'll read da books; where'd ya get'm."

"I'll get them," said the nun, quietly.

The LIFT project underwent an unexpected revision. LIFT participants were asked if they wished to study for a high school certificate and all but a few of the fifty subscribed to the idea with enthusiasm. For the next two years the remedial program became part of the LIFT project with students and faculty volunteering to help in one capacity or another. Second-hand school books were obtained and special kinds of help or tutoring were readily available from among the student body. At the end of two years LIFT students were tested once more. Forty-two of the fifty "untestables" passed their high school equivalency examinations. A few years after the project was completed, thirty-eight of the original fifty had jobs and those with children were supporting their families. The potential savings to the city and state of such projects could be thought of only in millions of dollars.

As an institution GROW was a young and sturdy organism, secure and thriving, just beginning to build a track record in tackling social problems. What then could possibly go wrong?

For years doctors of psychology had been having a difficult time. Not having a license to practice medicine, their right to treat mental diseases was questioned and they were restricted in hospitals to doing psychological tests rather than treating patients. Their training was long and arduous and their resentment was understandable. They were arguing in the state legislature for a psychologist's licensing law and lacking the lobbying power of the medical profession, were making little headway. Searching for a strategy they launched a campaign in the media calling the public's attention to the dangers of unqualified counselors and therapists.

No license is required for any individual to counsel another or to give advice or to call themselves anything as long as he or she makes no false claims of training or expertise. Anyone could put a sign on the door reading, Therapist, Marriage Counselor, Guidance Counselor or other euphonious label. The psychologists, therefore, targeted questionable credentials, raising alarms about marriage counselors and sex therapists who exaggerated or falsified their training.

GROW, of course, made no false claims and would seem to have been safe from attack. The media, however, knows a good story when it hears one and the attack of the psychologists and their well-financed official associations upon GROW quickly found its way to the front pages of the newspapers. The charges, while false, were examples of inflammatory journalism at its worst. GROW was accused of being a diploma mill, certifying group leaders and counselors without adequate training. Endeavoring to respond to the charges, GROW answered with documented facts only to be faced with new charges more outrageous with each passing day. Sources of information—or misinformation—were said to be confidential, some hinting that informers from the student body were providing facts.

The media stories—devoid of truth but graphic and provocative—continued. *GROW was a little red school house, espousing communist ideologies, agitating for revolution and laughing at religion. GROW conducted nude encounter groups in a pool in the basement of the school kept at womb temperature. Pot smoking was permitted in the corridors, the use of LSD and other psychedelics was encouraged and drug sales took place in classrooms.*

I did what little I could to help, personally calling the editors of newspapers urging them to tell the GROW story in full. I said that since they constantly printed stories of the war on crime, the war on drugs and the war on poverty, what GROW was doing, namely training the foot soldiers and leaders for those wars was a praiseworthy endeavor. When the controversy spread to radio and TV, faculty members tried to tell the GROW story but the talk shows routinely became adversarial, lurid and pointless.

It was an exercise in futility. News stories, the editors with obvious pleasure and amusement, said, run their course and the truth will surface. In fact, the media had turned the event into a circus. I was reminded of William Randolph Hearst's remark to the effect that if there were no news one had to manufacture it. GROW had been irreversibly damaged. Many in the faculty resigned, fearful that their other appointments might be endangered. The city withdrew its support of tuition for city workers. A number of board members, substantial citizens, resigned pleading the necessity of not being involved with controversial institutions. Students, too, constantly confronted with the charges were afraid to continue their association even though they knew of the falsity and fabrications. Reserve funds were exhausted. GROW had neither the financial nor the human resources to continue the fight.

I was convinced of the rightness of the GROW aims, goals and methods. The faculty had been composed of dedicated and intelligent people. The student body, too, creative, constructive and energetic—had won my respect. Most of all, having studied and been involved in the dynamics of groups and having experienced the power of the group for constructive cooperation I was interested in any experiment using such energy for social betterment. The crushing of GROW was a sobering experience in social and political dynamics. GROW had run afoul of the power of vested interests and was the target and victim of two behavioral patterns I had studied for years, dominance and territoriality, vehement and ruthless—and, sadly, male.

Time healed. The young people of the country continued their struggles. The Vietnam war was brought to a close ushering in the ensuing decades of struggle centered on the murky dynamics of power politics—seen through the piercing eye of television as it focussed on both the national and the international stage.

Group therapy is not, of course, an unrelieved struggle involving pain, resentment and suffering. Composed of human beings much like all of us it is often a micro-model of society, replete with banter, teasing and humor. Amusing mannerisms and idiosyncrasies of self and others are revealed along with memories of the problems and pain of growing up. When members of groups—as when members of families—feel good, their playfulness comes out. They also become skilled at detecting foibles and flaws in the leader—or parent. I recall an amusing incident with one therapy group. They had decided that I was a bit obsessed with the mystery surrounding the origins of caring and, specifically, that I held some firm convictions concerning the significance of mothering behavior. On Christmas I received a life-size, sterling silver hen's egg from Tiffany's. On it was engraved "To Mother Rule," along with the signatures of all the group members. After decades, it still evokes a smile and it still occupies a place of honor on my desk.

Chapter Eighteen
NEW WAYS IN THERAPY

During the sixties and on into the seventies the human potential movement whose Mecca had been Esalon in California spread throughout the country. Rolfing, Feldenkrais, sensitivity training, EST, progressive muscular relaxation, autogenic training, Zen, and many other methods of consciousness raising, mind management and self-discovery became available, not just on the East and West coasts, but increasingly in most big cities.

The space age also brought, along with computers, other remarkable electronic devices. One evening a young engineering student came to a group with an assortment of electronic gadgets which he then—with enthusiasm—proceeded to demonstrate. Although I had read of research in a new field called biofeedback I had not seen the instruments. Compared with the crude laboratory apparatus of an earlier day these were marvels of miniaturized instrumentation. Originally designed for recording the reactions of astronauts in space, the devices— when attached to the body with simple electrodes—measured various physiological functions such as pulse, respiration, skin temperature, muscle tension and brain waves.

As most everybody knows, when we are emotionally upset our physiology gets upset, too. Breathing is rapid, pulse is faster, heart beats forcibly and muscle tone increases—the physical manifestations of ancient emergency reactions. Some people feel stress much of the time—completely unaware that it stems from repressed emotions, hidden fear and anger mostly—and psychiatrists endeavor to relieve tensions by helping patients resolve old resentments and hidden conflicts which produce such feelings.

Biofeedback training, the research indicated, teaches patients to relieve tensions in an entirely different way. The instruments measure minuscule changes in muscle tension, skin temperature and other functions, changes we are insensitive to or ignore. A dial or buzzing sound informs the patient of variations in these body functions. The twitch of a muscle can send the indicator on a wide swing of the dial, and changing from one thought to another can produce a loud roar from an instrument that measures skin resistance. With time—just sitting quietly attending to the signals—the patient discovers through trial and error new ways of relaxing that succeed in lowering the readings on the instruments. Continuing practice gives the patient more and more control over these involuntary body reactions and the ability to remain relaxed under stress improves steadily.

Intrigued, I practiced on the instruments and was gratified to discover that by relaxing I could slow my pulse, reduce muscle tension and increase—or decrease—the temperature of my finger tips. I felt calm. Even more rewarding was the fact that headaches which for years had occurred every few weeks eased off. I was impressed.

Biofeedback—like so many new treatments—offered extravagant promise. The flight or fight reactions, survival mechanisms built into the body millions of years ago and operating unconsciously could be brought under control. By reducing stress biofeedback training would make possible a relaxed approach and a reasoned solution to psychological problems. Psychoanalysis and other expensive treatments might be eliminated—or drastically shortened. Patients were more than willing to volunteer to try the instruments and the results were encouraging. Relaxation training not only led to their feeling better but therapy, too, seemed to progress more rapidly.

The promise offered by biofeedback created considerable excitement among the healing professions. Here might be an answer not only to ailments like headaches, spastic colitis and anxiety attacks but to such killers as high blood pressure, heart attacks and strokes. It was important to find out. Once again, clinical meetings, conventions, new journals and a flood of reports with publications of case studies became the order of the day. Local biofeedback societies sprang up and buzzed with activity and argument.

Reports continued to be enthusiastic. Research papers stated that the amount of insulin required to control diabetes could be reduced. Lower doses of medication to control high blood pressure or to control seizures in epilepsy were reported. Furthermore, biofeedback training, unlike dangerous new medicines or techniques such as the recently developed open heart surgery and coronary by-pass operations, was painless and harmless.

Many patients wanted the biofeedback relaxation training, groups as well as individuals. Eight to ten individuals would sit around a table, each attached to a biofeedback instrument for twenty to thirty minutes before a therapy session. Practice became busy, even hectic, as one group followed another throughout the day. As the months went by patients reported many changes, most of them positive and some remarkable. A patient would quit smoking, for instance, and not think to mention it. The same was true of sleeping pills and tranquilizers; patients would report that they had stopped taking them, they had just "forgotten" or "hadn't bothered". These unexpected reports of improvement were difficult to evaluate. They may have been the results of biofeedback training but, on the other hand, they could be due to suggestion or the placebo effect or to group support. Whatever the reason some improvement in well-being in patients seemed to be occurring.

Individuals varied greatly in their aptitude for relaxing with the help of biofeedback instruments. For some it seemed routine and easy, within a few weeks the instruments measuring skin resistance, muscle tension or skin temperature began to register the barely audible clicks or buzzes of a sustained low reading indicative of the body's physiological resting state and with time patients would say that a relaxed feeling was becoming a regular part of their day-to-day experience. For other patients, weeks would go by without progress, they seemed unable to relax or to calm the inward turbulence and tension. The early claims made for cure of high blood pressure, colitis and other ailments failed to materialize.

One result of the practice of biofeedback relaxation training—human curiosity being what it is—was thinking about the relationship of mind and body. Questions and curiosity arose with the daily watching of biofeedback instruments as relaxation training progressed. What did go on inside one's head? How did the brain think? How did a thought have its effect on the body? Could the right thoughts heal an illness? Biofeedback training didn't seem to provide any new answers. The one conclusion most patients agreed upon was that relaxation training brought about some improvement in thinking and emotions but it was hard to explain.

Two or three times in those years a patient would appear who could—within one or two minutes—bring the readings of biofeedback instruments to low levels, an ability unusual and puzzling. I routinely asked patients about their methods of relaxing and had kept lists of answers and comments. Some patients had simple and direct responses.

I count sheep. I picture myself sitting on the porch of our summer cottage looking at the lake. Some comments had a touch of the comic or whimsy. I think of my clothes, freshly washed, drying on the line. I touch my eye-balls and then pretend they're becoming soft-boiled. Other responses were more complex such as thinking about each toe, finger, foot, hand, leg and arm and alternately tightening and relaxing muscles one by one—a technique known as progressive muscular relaxation.

The two or three patients who had shown the remarkable ability quickly to lower the readings of the instruments had one thing in common, all had done TM or Transcendental Meditation. I had, of course, read about the Beatles and their Maharishi yogi but this was solid evidence, more tangible than a verbal testimonial to the potential benefits of a meditative exercise. The evidence provided by those practicing TM could not be dismissed simply because activities associated with rock groups—psychedelics, drug abuse, noisy music, and the sexual revolution—had reached levels shocking to the stodgy and alarming to conservatives.

The meditators with their beards, long hair and distant manner seemed strange—in those days—and they made no converts to TM from group members. Their ability to relax, however, left a strong impression. The demonstration of the clear superiority of a meditative exercise to induce relaxation when compared to psychotherapy, biofeedback training, or even a new tranquilizer called Miltown was something that could not be ignored. Facts are facts. Not one to embrace fads I nevertheless took myself to a midtown suite of rooms leased by the TM Foundation, paid the then nominal fee, attended the introductory lectures, brought my offering of fruit and kerchief, took the indoctrination, received my mantra and began to practice.

The few patients who tried meditating were basically skeptical, an attitude typical of those steeped and conditioned in the cultural traditions of the Western world; the daily attempt was an encounter with restlessness and impatience, often ending in frustration after a few minutes. With time the struggle lessened and the exercise ceased to be a pointless bore but for most it took months before the state of stillness became tolerable, much less sought out as an opportunity—an adventure— to explore the unknown.

Although meditative practices of Eastern holy men had long since been known, the practice was viewed in the United States, except by a few Buddhist scholars, as quaint and curious. After World War II and into the 1950s, with the talks of Shunryu Suzuki, Zen exercises were offered in San Francisco, at Esalon, and a few other places. Although an increasing number had pointed to its benefits, the practice of meditation met with indifference and resistance.

Basically meditation was alien to the Western way of thinking. Western philosophy, methods of raising children and general cultural indoctrination ran counter to concepts calling for stillness—even brief periods of stillness. Western values with roots in the Protestant work ethic emphasized action and achievement. Even prayer, like Puritan sermons, was active and vigorous. To further these ends anything that appeared different was ignored or rejected. Stillness—consciously and unconsciously—was associated with laziness, illness, stealth, sinfulness, punishment, banishment and death. The devil had work for idle hands to do, the dreamer caught nothing but moonbeams and cobwebs, the children who sat still, woolgathered or let the grass grow under their feet were candidates for sassafras tea and blackstrap molasses.

Meditation had once been an important component of ancient Christian practice but with the passing centuries had received less attention and emphasis than prayer, rituals and indoctrination. In a church becoming more and more rigidly hierarchical the freedom proffered by meditation was dangerous. It took on more and more of a negative cast. Meditation became suspect. Meditators, it was believed, practiced strange religions, associated with the abnormal and the mystical—and possibly with Satan.

Christianity was active, dynamic, proselytizing. Christianity became the hand maiden of expansion and the Western course of empire, the conquest of the material world employing the latest tools and weapons. The inward, non-material world became a secondary matter—largely employed for prayer, entreaties for help in triumphing over the pagan, the infidel and enemies in general when not neglected altogether.

NASA scientists in the sixties and seventies, studying problems of space travel, had placed subjects in isolation chambers in complete silence and darkness, in some cases suspending the subjects in water to provide weightlessness. Within hours subjects became disturbed, began to have visions, hallucinations and delusions with loss of orientation for time and place. Many such experiments, known as sensory deprivation studies, were conducted and the initial fears that they might induce psychotic conditions in healthy people proved to be unfounded. Healthy people, in fact, who take the trouble to notice experience strange blips and bits of mental phenomena once classified as abnormal, such as a vision, a delusion or hearing a voice. Dreams, which all of us experience, can be pretty weird creations. Meditators recognize and acknowledge these and proceed undisturbed. Years passed and the experience of sensory deprivation was sought out for its claims of providing deep relaxation and evoking insights. Commercial enterprises featuring Samadhi tanks, dark, quiet, filled with tepid seawater and rentable by the hour, sprang up in California and New York—some had room for two.

The interest of the scientists in isolation experiments, relaxation and meditative exercises had not, of course, escaped the medical community at large and by the seventies research projects had been set up at Harvard, the Menninger Clinic, The Hartford Retreat and other institutions. Most of the volunteers for the experiments were enlisted from among the followers of the Maharishi; by then the TM movement had begun to spread. Articles on the positive effects of biofeedback, meditation, and comparisons of various relaxation techniques were published in a variety of scientific journals and, a few years later, *The*

Relaxation Response, a book by Herbert Benson, a Harvard professor, reached the best-seller lists. Expeditions were dispatched to study the yogis of India and Tibet and of other branches of Eastern religions and sects. Despite the positive findings of many studies, however, interest in meditation grew slowly and information on trends was sparse and scattered.

One learned whenever and however one could. I talked with meditators or anyone knowledgeable in Eastern philosophies whenever possible.

A student majoring in Tibetan studies at Columbia University had become acquainted with several visiting rinpoches. From the same order as the Dalai Lama then in exile in Darmshala, India, three lamas in their priestly robes, heads shaved, visited the office and joined a biofeedback group. Responding as graciously as we could to their deep bow we served them strong tea mixed with regular butter—not having yak butter—which they drank with appropriate ceremony.

With all of them the instruments revealed immediate low readings, remaining in a steady state which continued throughout the better part of an hour as the lamas' posture, deportment, and facial expressions conveyed—what we could only interpret as—tranquillity, equanimity, and inward peace. The graduate student's Tibetan was halting as was the English of the lamas but the gist of the lamas' answers to our questions as to how they achieved this state was something about years and years of training. They were intrigued by the instruments and asked a number of questions about the "music" the machines made. One of the lamas said that the machines seemed to tell about the "strength of the winds that blew through the mind" but did not tell anything about either the wind or the mind.

Although biofeedback became a useful healing aid in a number of medical conditions, especially in rehabilitation after chronic illness and injury, meditation eventually proved to be generally superior to biofeedback for teaching relaxation. Being wired up to the biofeedback instruments was a distraction instead of an aid—like training wheels on a bicycle which a child discards as soon as he catches on to the trick of balancing.

In the early years, when meditation was associated with the exotic, the flaky, or the off-beat, fears that it—like the sensory deprivation experiments—might be harmful were common and held by psychiatrists and laymen alike. One of my colleagues who was the professor of psychiatry at a leading medical school had evinced considerable interest in meditation and I had given him simple instructions in how to begin. A few weeks later he took me aside to report that while meditating he had experienced an impulse to jump out the window—his office was on the twenty-fifth floor—which had precipitated a severe anxiety attack. He would have nothing further to do with meditation and rationalized—with a sidelong glance at me, I thought—that such exercises were probably not indicated for those with the finely honed mind characteristic of academic psychiatrists.

Through a friend I had met Alan Watts, preacher, poet, philosopher who visited periodically in New York and was a gifted and convincing salesman for Zen and the wisdom of the East. I enjoyed a number of evenings in his company at small social gatherings following his popular lectures. His zeal and enthusiasm was infectious. Hoping that I could gain some important, first hand revelations and tips on meditative techniques I was somewhat puzzled when he told me that his main difficulty seemed to be just finding the time. I was further puzzled by the fact that he was a chain smoker. Another guest reassured me.

"Alan has seven children," she explained.

I had only three but I understood.

At the suggestion of Eric Fromm, a psychiatrist and philosopher who was one of several leading thinkers challenging the prevailing psychiatric theories, I undertook to study with

Charlotte Selber, a pioneer in the field of sensitivity training. I attended her studio classes once or twice a week for several years to stretch out on a little mat and go through her remarkable exercises in awareness practice which led to increasing one's sensitivity to body sensations previously unobserved and unnoted. An exceptionally intuitive human being and teacher, Charlotte had rightfully been referred to as the "living Zen". Under her tutelage I learned to recognize the infinite and on-going symphony of body sensations occurring in all of us to which we ordinarily pay no attention—indeed, are often taught, in the conditioning process called growing up, to ignore. I began to realize how much more vast was the Unconscious than what I had understood it to be during the years of psychoanalytic training—which mainly focussed on recovering forgotten memories and motivations.

I was getting hints of ancient meanings that humans are asleep, hints of why Enlightment is referred to as awakening. Skeptical whenever evangelical or organizational zeal reached high levels, I resisted joining any of the movements I encountered while attending various lectures, work-shops and demonstrations. One would naturally be warmly disposed toward the general philosophies expounded, since all held strongly affirmative beliefs in the brotherhood of man—some had begun to include sisterhood.

When, however, there were hints that by becoming a convert one could develop miraculous, magical powers—beyond one's capacity to imagine—my interest tended to wane. The TM practitioners, for instance, spoke of the ability to levitate—to defy the laws of gravity and float up in the air—and striving for such was taken seriously by many of them. The claims triggered heated controversy with scientists; a research mission—whimsical in my view—dispatched to India and Tibet failed to uncover a single yoga with the power to levitate.

Discussions of reincarnation, too, became elaborate and

fantastical beyond my ability to remain within the frame of the discourse. I was willing to accept—the First Law of Thermodynamics says so—that not a single atom making up the corpus of my material self would be destroyed at my death. Further, re-arrangements of the atoms making up my body were already so extensive that photographs of me taken as a young man bore little resemblance to my present appearance, a reincarnation of sorts. What the re-arrangement would be after death was a very interesting question but a question for which, I felt, I could not demand an answer.

In my years of residency in mental hospitals a considerable number of patients claimed to possess a variety of magical powers, transcending time and space, life and death, although they were not able to demonstrate them to others and derived no particular benefit that I could discern. Exploring and understanding, not defiance of physical laws, seemed more reasonable.

Several years later the Dalai Lama, on his first visit to the United States, greeted a small gathering of us on the second floor of a small Tibetan center somewhere in the East Thirties and, afterward, a few of us were invited to spend the evening with the Dalai Lama's physician who—through a translator—talked about and answered questions about Tibetan medical practices. One could only be impressed by the air of composure and equanimity which the Tibetans—one and all—exhibited along with what was so clearly spontaneity and joy. What we were experiencing certainly had an important message for Western medicine. We didn't have all the answers.

Reading in Eastern philosophies became not just a passing interest but part of growing and learning. At first confusing, almost bewildering, it became clear that—unlike Western thought—Eastern religion, philosophy and science were not separate categories taught in different departments by different professors but were all one; blended, not classified, integrated, not subject to reductionism. Starting late, one could never hope to acquire more than an overview or, perhaps, a reasonable appreciation of fundamentals but it was intriguing and challenging. The origins went back centuries before Christianity, the varieties and numbers of sects, rituals, writings, symbols and artifacts extensive and complex. Translations varied greatly in quality, the Pali and Sanskrit terms endless and difficult, yielding rewards begrudgingly.

Slowly, the studies led me—as it had others—to new ways of thinking about Western medicine with its Science, Objectivity, Experiment and its emphasis on quantifiable data, classification of facts, followed by logical deductions and descriptions, and, finally, laws and theories. The scientific West had long ago dismissed the Eastern practices as religions, not subject to logical evaluation, even though the Buddha repeatedly declined to be considered divine and asserted that his teachings were simply part of a philosophy and methodology leading toward inward peace and uncluttered truth which came to be known as Enlightment. The wordless Eastern practices—perhaps describable as Detachment, Attention, Intuition—began slowly to offer a welcome antidote to the deeply ingrained drives to think, to do, to act, to get, to achieve—update of Julius Caesar's Gaulic Wars learned by every first year Latin student, *veni, vedi, vici*. The alternative offered was the opportunity to practice and acknowledge *being, awareness, experiencing*.

Having done my best as a late comer to grasp the contributions of Eastern philosophies I was sufficiently impressed to follow some basic disciplines. I now begin every day with a simple meditative routine and have done so for the past twenty-five years, the time commitment being less than that spent at the breakfast table with the morning newspaper.

Chapter Nineteen
TURBULENT TIMES: EAST MEETS WEST

The various disciplines and exercises in the practice of
relaxation and meditation led over the years to modifications
in the practice of psychotherapy. When we humans stumble
across a new and helpful way of feeling better we often want
to share it with others, psychiatrists perhaps especially so.
Meditation had enabled me to feel much more patient, much
less demanding of self and others, relaxed mentally and physically. Others could surely benefit. It was one thing, however, to
undertake the discipline of silent sitting and quite another to
convince patients that the solution to problems would be fur-
thered by their doing the same.

Efforts to do so were disappointing. I found a tone of
insistence creeping into my suggestions which made me wonder about my own newfound equanimity. Patients would readily agree that Santyana was right—*A life unexamined is a life
unlived*—or with Socrates that such a life is not worth living.
They would agree that in stressful times some practice of
relaxation is necessary but still they resisted—even bristled—
at the suggestion that they try meditation. Do something, take
action was the prevailing attitude; no problem could be solved
by "staring at one's navel". Slowly, I realized what I was up
against, how rarely most people search for inward peace or
even concern themselves with a genuinely contemplative approach to living. Other than prayer, our culture has no established disciplines or methods of working toward such goals.

In our striving for material things, most of us, Thoreau
pointed out, lead lives of quiet desperation. Meditation often
makes this apparent. The few patients who—reluctantly—
followed my suggestion to learn meditation encountered un-

comfortable feelings and then blamed the meditation or me. I tried to assure them that this was quite normal and to point out that they were focussing—paying close attention to how they felt—for the first time in their lives. They were not persuaded. Some said that they felt humiliated, that their friends had howled with laughter. During those years, convincing a patient of the benefits of meditation was a thankless endeavor. Few patients opted to try meditation, none with enthusiasm.

Even those who agreed that it might be a good thing insisted that they had their own ways of relaxing which they felt were just as good. They preferred to stick with these rather than undertake a new method. Questioned about their method of relaxing the answers ranged from the sensible to the absurd. A few did say that they liked to go into the church and sit quietly off in a corner, some said that they liked to take a walk, such as going to the park, finding a comfortable bench and watching the children, the squirrels and the birds. Some mentioned reading, knitting or crocheting. Alcoholics pointed out that AA called for meditation in addition to prayer in the eleventh step. Some said music was the answer—including rock music—and others said that tennis or their weekly game of golf provided sufficient relaxation. Many felt that any change from the daily grind was relaxing. A double Martini at the end of their work-day was all one needed.

Having struggled to master meditative skills I could understand; however difficult the Western struggle may be, it had to be less frustrating than confronting the confusion of the Eastern path. The Western mind, in fact, reacts strongly to confusion; the Eastern accepts it along with ignorance as just another truth, like one of the five senses or "the obscuring passions." I stopped trying actively to persuade patients to meditate but continued to suggest that some form of relaxation would improve therapy. Every so often I would gently introduce the subject of meditation and occasionally a patient would agree to try. A tug of war ensued, subtle in nature, not unlike what the parent encounters with a plaguy child.

Frustration and resistance typically characterize the beginner; a patient who did not complain about the practice was simply not meditating. Conducting this tug of war artfully and playfully became a part of therapy. Coaxing was helpful; I would urge the patient to sit quietly and repeatedly count ten breaths for one or two minutes, stopping at the first sign of frustration. Then, at the next session, I would ask how many minutes had gone by before frustration set in and congratulate them on how skilled they had become at precise monitoring of what went on. Patients would begin to report extensions of time spent meditating to five minutes, eight minutes, twelve minutes until they reached a stage after some months where they no longer had constantly to count breaths to maintain concentration. Sometimes to help patients I would suggest that they come early so we could experience a few minutes of breathing and stillness together. We would share feelings of frustration and the seemingly unrewarding nature of meditation. In a few weeks or months I would often hear from the patient that something good was taking place which was difficult to put in words. After a smile or a shrug we would proceed with therapy.

Things were changing, however slowly. From isolated beginnings a general interest in meditation grew steadily over several decades. The "me" generation of the sixties, identified with sexual license, drug abuse, and war protests became the YUPPIES of the seventies who in the eighties inspired the slogans reading "you've come a long way, baby" and "get it all, you only go around once." While unrestrained hucksterism, selfishness and materialism were manifestations of uninhibited and noisy individualism, a quiet development had also been taking place. The signs of a widespread cultural revolution, a revolution in ways of relating to others and to the planet, a revolution in the search for the Self became obvious to the attentive.

Not the least of these signs was an acceptance of meditation and the inward search for meaning. Other changes followed. The practice of meditation attracted the interest of psychologists, self-help groups, the alternate health movement and many others. Visitors from the Far East, both secular and religious, the yogis and the priests—Buddhists, Hindu, Sufi and others—gave talks and work-shops in various cities throughout the United States. Several denominations of Christian churches explored long abandoned roots of mysticism and soon the meditative traditions of Western religions experienced a renaissance. Various denominations offered retreats for week-ends of silence, meditative practice and spiritual growth.

The change in social attitudes continued. Within ten or fifteen years the skepticism and fears had withered away. A flood tide of interest in all things Eastern, spiritual, mystical, and magical spread widely. Heralded as the new age, the Age of Aquarius, it took on an American flavor. Driven by commercial energies, a rash of goods and services were offered by direct mail and magazine advertising with promises of attaining miraculous powers, cure of disease, success in sex, love, business or any chosen enterprise. Exotic herbs and other health giving substances, amulets, crystals and gems, audiovisual aids, books and courses leading to careers in healing arts were offered in catalogues, at conventions and health bazaars, all available to individuals restless and dissatisfied with the experience of life in the eighties and nineties. Classes in yoga were featured on TV and meditative exercises of various kinds became part of health and fitness programs along with diet and exercise. Some athletes became, like the Samurai of old, disciplined meditators.

Although fringe movements, cults and colorful gurus captured media attention, genuine Eastern views and traditions,

Buddhist—Tibetan, Southeast Asian, Zen—as well as Hindu, Sufi and others spread widely. As more and more students returned from years of training under the guidance of masters in India, Japan and Southeast Asia, centers for study sprang up throughout Europe and the United States. Now, in the nineties, centers are within easy reach of most anyone interested in learning meditation. A Zen center in New York conducts an indoctrination session once a week for beginning meditators. Instruction is supplied at no charge although small contributions are welcomed. A number of centers offer week-end retreats or more extended periods of meditation practice along with instructive talks. Over the years books and pamphlets, audio and video tapes by scholars and teachers became available in increasing numbers. Newsletters, magazines, newspapers kept followers informed.

More than half a century after a few had pointed the way, a bridge between the wisdom of the East and West, stable and thriving, largely free of cult and sect mentality, had been established. Science and religion after centuries of friction now shared an area of interest. Meditation, an exercise that called for silence and stillness without stimuli, was for religion a pathway to spiritual growth. For science it was a method of inducing physiological relaxation, of studying unconscious psychological processes and for exploring the nature of awareness. Eastern wisdom states that inward peace is the foundation of hope, happiness and love. Western science states that deep relaxation contributes measurably to health—with a hint toward happiness and a long life.

Meditation, nevertheless, continued to be ignored by mainstream psychiatry, less from professional ignorance than from the workings of the market place. Psychiatry itself had undergone changes. Insurance companies became reluctant to cover the cost of extended psychotherapy which meant that only the wealthy could afford such therapies as psychoanalysis. A psycho-pharmacologist, the psychiatrist who treats emotional illness with chemicals—new kinds of anti-depressive and other drugs were announced every month or so—could earn three times what he or she could earn by practicing psychotherapy. Fewer psychiatrists chose a career in psychotherapy or took more than rudimentary training to do so. The field was left to the psychologists, psychiatric social workers, pastoral counselors and lay therapists. Like fresh air and sunshine, meditation might lead to health but it did not lend itself to marketing. One cannot expect sizeable financial returns for advising people to sit still.

With the widespread change in attitudes, convincing patients of the value of meditation got easier. This had little to do with improved powers of persuasion on my part but rather with a rising tide of awareness that relaxation exercises were important to health and fitness. By the nineties these beliefs were backed by research which demonstrated that strengthening the immune system through meditation and psychotherapy increased the body's power to resist disease including—according to some researchers—resistance to cancer. A new multidisciplinary research field called psychoneuroimmunology reflected a hope that the connections between the workings of the mind and the body—long outside the realm of science—might be revealed. As these advances became known, patients were willing to practice meditation as legitimate homework on the way to healthy growth and self discovery. What was the best way to go about it?

The varieties of meditative exercises fill volumes and the practices and routines of the individual meditation masters multiply these ten-fold. All types of sitting exercises— as distinct from the walking or rhythmic exercises—have two basics in common, a proper sitting position and something on which to concentrate. The TM followers, for instance, sit in a relaxed upright position and are given a mantra, a secret word or sound which is repeated—silently or mentally—whenever the mind wanders. Other types of yoga exercises call for the cross-legged lotus or semi-lotus position—easy for the young and limber—and frequently employ a visual object or mandala as the object of concentration.

The most practical meditative practice, concentrating on breathing, is described at length for every branch of Buddhism—Tibetan, Zen, Indian, Burmese, Thai and others. The standard instruction is brief and simple. The student is told to sit quietly with spine, neck and head in erect and effortless balance, then concentrate on the experience of breathing disregarding outside noises or other distractions. That is the extent of the directive. A few helpful hints are offered from time to time, suggestions about position of arms and hands, where to direct the gaze, but all emphasize returning to awareness of breathing, counting breaths whenever the mind wanders.

For some time beginning meditators may notice nothing or may have some sense of confusion, or may wonder why they're doing it. Trying to make sense of it persists but eventually the student learns not to bother. After a few weeks the jerky, uncontrolled action of the untrained mind as it bounces from subject to subject becomes obvious. The human mind, goes the Eastern wisdom, is like a drunken monkey—jumping from branch to branch, grabbing at this and that, its attention captured by every fluttering leaf—an image that aptly describes the experience of the beginning meditator. As a psychiatrist, I had originally become a meditator to find ways of helping patients relax. It didn't take long, however, to realize that my own monkey mind was—even after years of psychoanalysis— as jumpy as the next. Sympathizing with the beginner I would urge that he or she continue to focus awareness on breathing, counting breaths if necessary to help concentration.

Does your breathing know it?—is an example of one of those strange Eastern questions or koans used for centuries to get students to stop thinking and get back to experiencing. The

experience is not of I am breathing, a declarative Western assertion but rather the experience of *It breathes me*, the Eastern
acknowledgement of mystery. With sharpened awareness the
student begins to note mental events as they stream through the
mind in a kind of endless parade. At first, more a jumble than a
parade, what the meditator encounters is a blur or barrage of
sensations, emotions, imaginings, thoughts, and cravings. As
my patients began to master the discipline, as they experienced the effortlessness of stillness and breathing, they would
report increased awareness of muscle tensions and other body
sensations as well as awareness of the coming and going of
emotions, of fantasies, of thoughts and impulses. With awareness came a feeling of relaxation and the privilege of options,
the choice of reacting or not reacting.

As patients continued their practice they found the Eastern
literature to be a rich source of help. In the West we have
slogans, aphorisms, and mottoes that offer guidelines for behavior. *One day at a time. Easy does it. Haste makes waste.* are
examples we find helpful. The Eastern world has been equally
generous. Over the centuries many teachings have been handed
down to stabilize and strengthen the discipline of the struggling meditator.

As with the koans, understanding some of the Eastern
writings could be slow in coming but when meaning finally
dawned it would become richer with repetition.Helpful to
beginners was the question *Thinking neither of good or bad, at this
very moment, what is my own true nature?* Repeated in rhythm
with breathing it would at first seem futile or meaningless but,
since it was a time-worn and time-proven device, patients
would continue and they were rewarded for doing so. They
came to realize how much of their time and their intellectual
energy was wasted in making endless evaluations and judgments. *Thinking neither of good or bad . . . .* hour after hour,
unconsciously, the process went on. This is good, no, that

would be bad. I should have done it. It was a mistake. Much of this was obsessive or habitual rather than practical or necessary.

The same was true of the next phrase . . . *at this very moment*. How seldom one lived in the moment. Patients began to note how much time was spent, lost in mindlessly reviewing the past or regretting something that occurred years ago. Unpredictably the mind would jump from preoccupation with the past to worrying about the future, vaguely apprehensive about tomorrow or next week, often dreading the future while clinging to fantasies of a happy outcome. Repeating the phrase as part of their daily meditation helped patients notice how much time was dissipated in rumination over past or future, how little time was spent in the here and now. Even the taste of food, the pleasure of music, the joyful hug of a loved one was lost or muted by the mind's jumping to something or somewhere else, long since gone or not yet here. Little wonder one never paused to ask oneself about one's own true nature; few had sufficient composure to wait for an answer. The Western world, indeed, seemed reluctant to ask such questions. Concern with the mystery of the self was pointless, self centered, adolescent—like the soldiers in the poem "ours not to reason why, ours but to do or die."

As more and more of my patients took up the daily relaxation exercise the nature of practice changed. Patients felt less dependent on me—a change in what psychiatrists call the transference. The attitude of the patient toward the psychiatrist, which can range across the extremes from love to hate, is a re-run—transference—of attitudes from the patient's childhood. Patients view the analyst through the same lenses that they viewed the loved or hated caretakers of their early life. These convictions can be stubborn; clearing up the confusion takes up much of the work of therapy. When patients followed their meditative routine the time consuming exploration of the transference was no longer the central issue, a revolutionary change from conventional therapy. As self-discovery through meditation came to the fore, the patients' views of me and my role in the process became much less important.

I was no longer seen as the central power, an all-knowing parent, caring or not caring. Something more important, a journey into the unfamiliar regions of the psyche had taken over and I was simply an older and more experienced guide. Together we were taking that journey, a necessary journey, a sometimes difficult sometimes rewarding journey, but one increasingly seen as hopeful, hopeful perhaps beyond our ability to grasp. I was no longer a final authority but rather a dedicated explorer—perhaps more experienced—and fellow pilgrim. Together we were discovering that Buddhism and other ancient Eastern writings were a rich source of meditative practices, insights, complementary, supplementary or alternative to the truths of Western psychology.

My patients and I were discovering—through the experience of stillness in solitude and together—that there was within each of us a mysterious and unknown creature, first exhibited on the day we were born, that had taken Nature millions upon millions of years to create. From the moment of birth that creature encountered a chancy and variable conditioning process which was from then on imposed upon it. Eventually, unless it was lulled into numbness or the oblivion of material comfort, that creature was left, bewildered and lost, to figure out what had happened, to puzzle over the forces that had shaped it—having no memory of the kind of creature that began the journey and only fragmented awareness of what happened afterward. With no answers it then discovered that there was no source of knowledge or wisdom remotely capable of supplying answers free of bias or advocacy.

Today, the combined lore of East and West agree that such answers are to be found. Brain research of the Western world suggests that every experience of the human being is recorded and stored, a simple fact of cellular and neuronal functioning. The Eastern world can best speak to the question of retrieval. Relying on the process of meditative practice and the strengthening of intuitive powers, retrieval is possible; the creature that began the journey is knowable. Shedding the smothering layers of conditioning is awakening, Enlightment. To further those powers the East goes to great lengths to negate restlessness, doubt and clinging to rationalizing and logic. To the struggling neophyte, who cannot suspend the habit of using logic, assigning a koan such as the classic *What is the sound of one hand clapping?* can help him or her abandon the habit. Eastern wisdom reassuringly asserts that what the knower seeks is beyond mental concepts and verbal definitions to which the Western world has been inordinately attached.

Patients who regularly followed their meditative routines discovered that Buddhism and other ancient Eastern writings were a rich source of psychological insights that provided refreshing alternatives to the excesses of the Western world. In the early years of practice I rarely encountered patients who questioned the materialist values. Most patient's complaints were of not getting enough of material rewards; unhappiness was the result of injustice and unkindness, of not having been given one's fair share. From its beginnings in the sixties the opposition to greed, materialist frenzy, power and individualism had spread slowly but steadily. Hope for illumination—spotty and uneven—began to appear. Buddhist philosophy was no longer dismissed as flaky, spiritual, mystical but was accepted as a legitimate field for psychological inquiry.

Patients varied in their aptitude for Eastern disciplines; natural talent, obvious in learning a language or a musical instrument, applies equally to the discipline of stillness. To help, particularly those who felt discouraged, I set aside two hours on Sundays, late in the afternoon, to meet and meditate with whomever chose to come. There was no charge; it was for my benefit as well as theirs. We would finish these sessions with a few minutes devoted to exchanging helpful suggestions or sharing newly acquired lore and learning.

With no pretense of becoming religious scholars in general or Buddhist scholars in particular, we did in the course of the years take up most of the central themes of Buddhist philosophy. The truths of suffering, craving, impermanence, the non-existence of an "I" or a "self" or an external caring agency and the steps to be taken toward awakening or Enlightment were subjects of informal Sunday afternoon discussions.

We sometimes sounded more like classes in ethics than psychotherapy groups but Buddhist philosophy provides easy adjustment to paradox. Proper human behavior is not so much a question of right or wrong, taking place under a canopy of guilt, shame and punishment, but is simply a practical way of reaching harmony and inward peace. Another pleasant discovery was the fact that small gains were rewarding; one didn't have to reach ecstacy, bliss or transcendence to have lasting good feelings. One didn't have to live exclusively on fruits, grains, broccoli and spinach with nary a glass of wine or beer to experience the rewards of Buddhist philosophy. One didn't have to love every little nasty bug or germ. Even the Dalai Lama, a patient pointed out, will swat the overly persistent mosquito.

I continued to be a psychiatrist, an advocate of meditation without pretensions of being a guru, and patients pursued their own inward adventure in any ways that their creativity and energies led them. Some patients did, in fact, journey to the Far East to seek out a Master for advanced guidance. Others spent week-ends or longer at one or another meditation center in the United States. Most, however, pretty much continued to follow what would appear to be conventional lives but with an inner awareness and richness which brought new rewards in relating to—and caring for—others. I was one of them.

Chapter Twenty
SUMMING UP

Slowing down, seeing only a few patients a day left time for reflection—for summing up. Nearly fifty years had gone by since Debbie, an attractive young woman, had come to my office suffering from a painful and difficult emotional problem. The outcome had been heartening. Debbie got well. Working together we had enabled her to get over a long forgotten hurt which had made her life miserable and unmanageable.

The key to helping Debbie had not come from my years of training to become a psychiatrist, nor from advice from colleagues; neither had provided it. The key had come from research scientists, specifically their observations of the great harm done to infants by separation from their mothers. The observations, however, were not of human babies but of animals, in this case, monkey babies; years ago, documented observations of human babies suffering from severe deprivation of mothering were not to be had.

If observing a monkey mother and her baby could provide valuable clues about humans, clues leading to improved therapy and recovery from severe psychological injury, how much more could be learned by studying the full range of animal behavior? The question persisted and, in time, turned into a project—midway between a hobby and an obsession. For years the daily practice of psychiatry was—as it is for most psychiatrists—a career dedicated to finding better ways of helping humans. The search during free time—off-hours, nights, weekends, and holidays—was in the field of animal behavior, the behavior of the living creatures of the natural world, a vast and multidisciplinary endeavor lacking boundaries or guidelines. It was a pursuit rewarding not only for itself but as change from years of medical training that had emphasized experimentation and vivisection—not a good way to learn about animal behavior. The naturalist's way, by gaining entrance into the world of each animal can be a revelation.

The intricate strategies of survival of even the simplest creature strains the comprehension. The wood tick clings to a twig or a blade of grass and waits in suspended animation for months or years for the whiff of butyric acid given off by the sweat of a passing mammal. That chance event triggers the release of the tick's grip enabling it to obtain temporary residence and a blood banquet on its innocent host. Bloated, it falls off and, with luck, starts the cycle again. Creatures share such secrets only with gifted naturalists, in this case a clever researcher strolling through the woods, hands extended holding a pan coated with rancid butter, being rewarded with a generous supply—a full pan—of ticks tricked by the procedure. He or she might have been interested in ticks or, on the other hand, in finding out about Lyme disease for which such creatures are agents.

Baby birds gape in response to the vibration of the mother's alighting on the edge of the nest and she, in turn, will stuff food into the baby's mouth as long as it gapes. Naturalists, needing to determine the full range of the hatchling's diet, can place in the nest a mechanical imitation bird that gapes and the mother will stuff a full sampling of the diet into this novel receptacle. Naturalists' notes abound with many such methods of getting facts without vivisection and without unduly disturbing creatures in their natural environments. Poets tell us that for those with imagination there are millions of worlds; for the naturalist, too, there is a specific world for each of the millions of species.

Discovering the details of these worlds is not easy; difficult questions beset those who would plumb Nature's secrets. How does this creature explore its environment? What does it eat and how does it get its food? How does it defend itself? How does it find a safe shelter? How does it find a mate? How does it dispense with rivals? How does it conduct courtship and produce offspring? How many offspring and how does it raise them to insure survival? Learning about the worlds of these creatures is to experience—however much or little—both awe and reverence.

Among classic studies the world of the honey bee has been described by vonFrisch, and the world of the herring gull or of greylag geese by Konrad Lorenz, and the world of the baboon by Maras. It took a long time, years, to acquire a general understanding of animal behavior. The field was vast, time limited, the opportunities to learn random and I often regretted the superficiality and unevenness of my knowledge. Eventually, limiting the scope of study was necessary.

Fortunately, the evolving standards and new methods of animal observation had led to the remarkable studies of gorillas and chimpanzees by Schaller, Goodall, and other pioneers of primatology. I went on reading about animals in general—a consuming curiosity about living things—including the lesser primates of which there are over two hundred species, but my main interest was with the primates whose brain most resembled ours, the greater apes.

Chimpanzees, having stopped short of humans on the evolutionary pathway, did not acquire the cerebral cortex capable of the refined judgments, moral and otherwise, that humans have developed over the last five million years. Dr. Goodall's studies of chimpanzees, however, demonstrated a capability for abstract thought. Her observations bear out their ability to make and use tools. Every chimp group studied has not only shown tool use but patterns of tool use which vary from group to group. Complex social behaviors involving teaching and learning demonstrated that the culture, not the genes, transmitted information. During the same years paleontologists were uncovering more and more fossils of ancient creatures who no longer used their knuckles in walking—being truly bipedal—but whose brains were not much larger than chimpanzees. A new look at our relationship to the animal world was necessary.

For psychiatry it was a challenging opportunity. Thirty years ago the various theories to explain human behavior were in a sorry state of confusion. Turmoil, seething rivalries, petty bitterness tainted relationships between professionals. A colleague—echoing the general frustration—wrote that the field of psychiatry had become a gaggle of cults exhibiting rituals and dialects, isolated from one another, none possessing a broad, integrated, and scientific view of Man. Through the studies of primates I hoped for a new perspective and a hint of getting at the roots of human behavior. The step by step study of the qualities and behaviors we shared with primates, particularly the chimpanzee, eventually provided new views of why humans do what they do. A new theory of human behavior became a possibility.

All knowledgeable people agreed that in their anatomy, physiology and chemistry, humans were much like other primates. Further, all primates, humans included, evolve behavior in response to basic needs and drives—food, shelter, mates, getting and giving care, defense and the like. Next, for a human growing up, just as for the highly social chimpanzee, in-born behavioral patterns sufficient for independent living are not yet developed and necessitate, not only care, but extended learning. Beyond mastering certain fundamentals about the physical surroundings, growing up requires experiencing and practicing three basic social behaviors; being mothered, peer-play and courtship-sexual.

Finally, living in a social group requires the individual to master three additional socializing behaviors, namely territoriality, spacing and dominance. For day to day living humans—and chimpanzees, too—must learn their "turf," must learn who they can trust or "to get close to," and, finally, must learn who bosses whom, "who calls the tune."

Individual modifications of these behaviors occur for humans—and chimps, too; tricks and variations abound. Humans, however, over the centuries have modified basic behaviors to such an extent that recognizing them is difficult and confusing. The chimpanzee carries out behavior with a remarkable and artful complexity but nothing comparable to the extent—and often diabolical complexity—characteristic of humans possessed of their larger cerebral cortex. A few moments reflection on the tricks and scams humans use to acquire money or power should illustrate this.

Except for the outer layer or cortex, other parts of the brain of chimpanzee and human require an expert to tell the difference; below the cortex in the regions of basic drives, emotions and physiology, chimp and human are much the same. The question was not whether we shared behaviors, but rather how the behaviors changed in five million years of human evolution.

That, too, had straightforward answers and illustrations. Along with the growth of the brain, every behavior—individual or social—underwent progressive modification through the processes of refinement, elaboration and accumulation. The saying, "Live and learn", had been operating for five million years. Tool-making is a good example. The chimpanzee tool-maker fashions a few simple tools, a stick or twig to probe a termite's nest, a sponge from chewed leaves to soak up water from a cleft in a tree, a choice selection of rocks or wood to serve as hammer and anvil in cracking otherwise inedible nuts. Chimpanzees also choose a wide variety of medicinal herbs, the selection differing from one chimpanzee group to another. A chimpanzee exhibiting exhaustion and bowel upset is observed chewing shoots of *Vernoni amygdalina* and swallowing the bitter juice. Local natives do the same. One may have learned from the other but it is doubtful if the natives taught the chimpanzees. Two other medicinal plants, *Aspilia* which kills bacteria, fungi and parasites and *Rubia cordifolia* have been identified in similar contexts.

Another important modification and elaboration of basic behavior is team forming. Chimpanzees, as do humans, form teams; periodically they form teams for hunting, for patrolling borders of their territories, and for raids on enemy groups possibly obtaining females. Evolving humans, however, became the premier team formers. The chimpanzee invents a probe to explore a termite's nest, may share it with an offspring or companion and the skill spreads through the group. Humans add team forming to their tool making skills. Ancient man formed teams to build ziggurats or pyramids to probe the heavens; modern man forms a team to probe outer space. Both exemplify primate creativity.

Human tool-making, which began with tools as simple as the chimpanzee's, is a fascinating story of cultural and material accumulation over millions of years but the underlying behaviors of chimp and human tool-maker are the same. Both reflect abstract reasoning, both involve trial and error over time, both involve foresight—the chimpanzee often has a spare twig tucked under an arm as he hunts termites. The difference is simply the human superiority in storing, processing and transmitting information.

The modifications of basic social behaviors are not always easy to trace. Mothering in chimpanzees is straight-forward and on a one to one basis. This continues in humans but mothering became parenting when the female obtained male help. The advent of fathering produced the family, a mothering team which—as teams do—became more and more elaborate. The forms the team or family has taken—patriarchy, matriarchy, kin networks, etc.—are many and provide standard puzzles for social anthropologists. We are familiar with a form of extended families assisted by nursemaids and nurses, teachers and tutors, coaches and counselors, pediatricians, etc. No one doubts, however, that the team's function has remained the same, caring for and raising children.

Virtually every basic human cultural phenomenon has its beginnings in chimpanzee society. Social and political maneuvering of remarkably subtle nature is well documented. One particularly amusing story of Dr. Goodall's was the case of Mike, a low ranking male chimp, who developed an impressive display in kicking and hitting two empty five-gallon oil tins in a soccer-like performance which was extremely noisy and intimidating—chimpanzee ears may be even more sensitive than human's to disturbing sounds. He rose to the top of dominance hierarchy in a manner reminiscent of many a meteoric political career, replacing a bigger and more aggressive leader, and maintained the dominant position for a number of years— powerful males showing submission to his polished and practiced performance.

Over the past few decades, the studies and books of Dr. Goodall and others have circulated widely and excellent wildlife TV documentaries are familiar to millions of people. Complex and sophisticated chimpanzee behavior in the areas of friendship, courtship, alliance formation and various other social behaviors are common knowledge. Even primitive forms of the darker human behaviors, warfare, cannibalism, infanticide with subtle variations from group to group are now well known.

The primate brain evolving over the millions of years is a complex structure made up of three brains set one on top of the next. The bottom story of the three-storied brain is the most primitive—variously referred to as the reflex brain, the instinctual brain or the nose brain—a brain found in cold blooded creatures like snakes and lizards which functions largely with reflex responses to physical and chemical stimuli. The next modification led to the more complex brain found in mammals. This brain has been referred to as the emotional brain in contrast to the instinctual brain it superseded. More complex reactions such as curiosity or fear supplement physico-chemical reactions in guiding behavior. The final and top-most story, the cerebral cortex, became prominent in the brains of primates, reaching its present size in humans, the faculties of reason and logic assuming priority over both emotions and reflexes.

The step by step evolution of this triune or three-storied brain has been traced in great detail in fossils and in the comparative anatomical studies of creatures living today. Embryologists who study the fetus in the mother's womb also confirm that the developing brain goes through these three stages of growth, repeating evolutionary history. In the scientific jargon of the biology professor to his first-year students, ontogeny recapitulates phylogeny—the technical description of the process that the development of each one of us, beginning with the fertilized egg, retraces the history of our evolution from ancient forms.

The human infant is born with this three-storied, complex human brain—fully formed but not developed. The brain of reasonableness and logic, of judgment and creativity is a hope, a promise, a gift which blossoms only after years of enfoldment by or within reach of mothering arms, then carried on by family, society and culture. Scientists tend to use less flowery similes; they compare the cortex of the newborn to a preprogrammed computer to be further programmed by experience.

The lower, primitive brains control operations at first. The infant cries when cold or hungry, coos when fed. Later, the emotional brain manifests itself; it calls for mummy to fulfill its needs and gets upset if she doesn't comply. As adults these primitive brains continue to function. When we accidentally touch something hot we jerk our finger away without deferring to reason and judgment. The reflex brain manages important functions like breathing and heart beat without consulting the front office and the emotional brain regulates the ups and downs of our feelings, selecting, guiding and coloring our activities and taking over only when we are hit hard with misfortune or tragedy—or joy.

Under the best of conditions things work out well. The youngster develops its skills and talents, it learns and it learns to learn, it embarks on a life-long process to discover who it is, a Self—in relationship to others and to society. Trusting others leads to increased awareness of self, to confidence, competence and capacity for satisfaction, to fairness in one's dealings, to caring for others and to a sincere interest in understanding right and wrong, the moral and ethical imperatives for full and functioning membership in society.

But things go wrong. The infant can begin with a grave genetic or other health burden or can be the offspring of a mother lacking in mothering skills. The ready finger of blame often points to the mother, particularly if her confusion, immaturity and distress is reflected in abusive, addictive or other negative behaviors. Little attention is given to the handicaps of poverty, overwork, ill-health, a poorly functioning, absent or abusive father and the indifference of a society that ignores its children's health and education.

As the wrong things accumulate and such circumstances prevail, increasing numbers of society's young are governed, not by the maturing cerebral cortex but by impulses from the more primitive centers, triggering fear, anger and violence. Deficient parenting leads to isolation from or deprivation of the socializing process, produces wanton behavior, sexual promiscuity, drug and alcohol abuse, delinquent and criminal behavior and, occasionally, the cold-blooded killer: impulsive, reactive, ruthless, guiltless. Under sufficient provocation antisocial behavior, bizarre and cruel, can surface in the seemingly normal among us.

A young woman patient who worked as a guidance counselor at an inner-city center for adolescents shared an experience that had left her shaken and bewildered. The police stopped by her office with a teen-age boy in custody, bandages covering several wounds, who had stabbed another in a street fight. The boy had asked if the counselor—of whom he was fond and whom he trusted—could accompany him with the police and they had agreed to his request. She had assumed that they were going to the local precinct for booking. Sitting in the back of the squad car the boy whispered to her that he hoped the other boy hadn't been hurt too much in the fight. The counselor was shocked and sickened to discover that the police were taking the boy to the morgue to identify the body of the victim who had been stabbed more than twenty-five times. The teenager, whom the counselor knew to be an honest lad, vaguely remembered being in a fight but could recall little else. Such is the primitive reflex brain driven by survival instincts as it functions independently of the cerebral cortex.

The objection most often encountered in comparing humans and chimpanzees is, surprisingly, not superior intelligence but the possession of language. We humans can talk. Our capacity for speech—so the argument goes—is the unbridgeable gap that separates us from the chimpanzee. The generally accepted view is that the ability to talk is a gift, wondrous and special, and—the primitive, magical explanation—like other gifts of Nature, put on earth for the exclusive benefit of Mankind. The Noam Chomsky school of linguists agree—at least in stating that only humans have it. We are born with it. Children don't learn language, they don't have to, they inherit the "know-how", a "hardware," wired-in structure or "grammar" of thought which blossoms into spoken language as the infant grows into childhood. Whatever the culture into which they are born, humans are prepared by instinct to speak any of thousands of languages. Not so the chimpanzee.

Those who have studied chimpanzee communication, however, will assure you that if chimpanzees can't "talk" like we can—if being exactly like us is so important—they make up for it by posture, gesture, facial expression and vocalization. Under natural conditions where the subject of concern is obvious, the chimpanzee's meaning is clear—a single gesture may suffice. Words would be redundant—as they so often are with humans. While chimpanzee grimaces, grunts, whoops, pants, barks, bellows, and calls of various kinds are not as specific as words, they bring about appropriate responses. Even with monkeys—vervets, baboons—a warning call, recorded when a group has spotted a leopard and played back by loudspeaker will send the group into appropriate patterns of defense and dispersion. A different but appropriate response occurs in response to a warning call recorded when a group has spotted a snake. Warning calls, food calls, social joy calls—extensive classifications of calls are constantly being updated by observers.

Dr. Chomsky's theories may help brain researchers and they may lead to new ways to teach (or not teach) children and languages but they are of only peripheral interest in comparing chimpanzee and human. Whatever the chimpanzee's ability to deal with symbols or abstractions—and each new study adds evidence of chimpanzee cognitive abilities—the chimp is, admittedly, no great shakes as a grammarian.

More to the point is that our glorification of the spoken word makes it difficult for us to understand that verbal communication isn't all that important. Verbal capability is one thing; communication is something else. Communication is not only the *word* (or our *grammar*); it's what happens "afterword." It's the response you get, whether you intended it or not.

Speech, a verbal communication system, is a natural and not surprising outcome, evolved from the extensive primate communication system of posture, gesture, facial expression and vocalization which is millions of years old. When humans, much later in evolution, developed a verbal language the more basic, emotional, non-verbal components of communication—posture, gesture, facial expression and vocalization—tended to drop out, to become covert. Humans discovered the rewards of keeping things hidden. Speech acquired a new function, namely, to cover up the truth—to confuse the other. Speech may or may not convey something but it always hides something; harshly, it could be said that every statement contains a lie. To understand fully what a human is talking about we would have to know what he or she has decided not to talk about. The non-verbal components of communication can give one away; humans restrain or hide them—e.g., the poker face. However, when humans get to crucial, emotionally meaningful issues, they see-saw between the verbal and non-verbal, and the basics readily return: posture, gesture, facial expression and various vocalizations such as sighs, cries, gasps, and so forth. Words may be eliminated entirely. In the grip of fear, anger—or love—we are speechless.

Talk, a purely verbal communication system, is a comparatively recent development—appearing somewhere in the two million years between H.habilis and Neanderthal—occurring after evolution had led to bipedalism, increased brain size and a larynx located further down the throat which, along with better control of the diaphragm, made word formation possible. A project devoted to teaching a chimp to talk by a determined husband and wife team—in spite of the chimpanzees' lack of phonation equipment—resulted after years of tutelage in a vocabulary limited to two words, cup and papa. After learning sign language the chimpanzees' vocabulary increases to hundreds of signs which they combine in meaningful—and grammatical—ways. The understanding of the spoken word—in the chimps I have talked to—compares nicely to that of a three year old child.

Instead of understanding speech as the outcome of evolution we tend to focus on its role—remarkable certainly—in enabling humans to communicate about an object that can't be pointed at or an event that took place in the past or would take place in the future. Time awareness, the capacity to transmit abstract formulations and the accumulations of culture—material, religious, artistic, scientific and otherwise—became possible and, with writing a few million years further on, infinite. These accumulations are vast, awesome—and increasingly confusing. Hence, our mixed feelings about speech or, more specifically, doubts about where the so-called miracle of speech and writing have taken us.

To summarize, study of the spoken word can be accepted in the research scientist, enjoyed in the poet, endured in the lawyer and tolerated in the politician but for a psychiatrist—or anybody—trying to help others it is merely a communications tool and a means to an end. A shrug of the shoulders or a smile, if it accomplished the same thing, would be just as good. Mothers have known this for years. Grammar. What is grammar? Is there a grammar of male and female? Is there a grammar of mothering? Is there a grammar of play? Is there a grammar of power? Is there freedom of speech? Children are taught to speak only when they are spoken to—and so are lots of others at lower levels of the power hierarchy.

Most thought that goes on in the human brain is wordless and unconscious although few people seem to realize it. The brute fact, leading theorists agree, is that most of living goes on that way. The reality of the mind is wordless. When we change it into words we leave the world of the wordless for the world of words which we then begin to believe—and worse, to insist—is the real world. We create worlds with words. Peoples of different cultures and languages do not live in the same world with different labels attached to things and events. They live in different worlds. This is what chimps and Chomskys argue about.

The world of animals and the real world of humans (or one might say, the world of real humans) is a wordless world. It isn't so much that people won't believe it; they don't know how to believe it.

Much of what has been said about speech should also be true for consciousness, basically, that it isn't all that special. The chimpanzee, for instance, shows early but definite signs of self-consciousness. Paint a red spot on the forehead of chimpanzees, sit them in front of a mirror and they indicate their concern with the human's most fundamental question of consciousness, namely, Who am I? Staring at their image, chimps soon start a somewhat puzzled exploration of their own forehead with a finger. Creatures a step down on the evolutionary scale do not; they keep peeking behind the mirror.

Animals below primates on the evolutionary scale live constantly in a state which we humans would define as *out of sight; out of mind*. The animal reacts to—can only "think about" what's going on in the here and now. As scientists put it, the animal is sense dependent; it spends its waking hours imbedded in—and reacting to—the evidence presented to its senses. Studies of chimpanzees reveal that in areas like planning to hunt termites or small game, or in mourning for a lost loved one they, like humans, are not embedded in immediacy but in memory.

Animal behavior which clearly involves response to stimuli is intriguing in its complexity; e.g., the seasonal migration of birds with navigation on the basis of the stars or the Earth's magnetic fields. So intricate are some behaviors, nest building, infant tending skills, for instance, as to create the illusion of foresight and other human-like capabilities.

Human acts can appear to be mechanical, automatic, robot-like. Much behavior, variable, complex and intricate, takes place outside of awareness. A boxer having suffered a blow to the head may fight for many rounds—and win—with no memory of what took place. Subjects under hypnosis can undertake all kinds of complex behaviors requiring speech and other manifestations of intelligence or cleverness without recollection of what they did or how they did it. Alcoholics report the same thing, calling them black-outs; the episodes are not necessarily related to the degree of intoxication, a few drinks or extreme fatigue can do the same thing. Defined simply as increased awareness, consciousness doesn't seem all that special.

Conscious awareness rises and falls independently of information processing and most information processing is unconscious; we don't even need consciousness—habit takes over—for most things we do. Most of us, absorbed in a task, lose track of time. When we are preoccupied, days and weeks may pass in a blur. Conscious awareness tends to brighten up when we relax and focus attention but usually it's a dim bulb, constantly flickering.

Pursuing theories of consciousness can get to be pretty involved. Theories are many, running on and on. Consciousness, says one theorist, is a property of all living things. No, says another, only those living things that have become capable of learning by experience. Or only when evolution reaches an advanced critical stage does consciousness, a special quality, appear; evolution is "emergent" and what emerges is not predictable. Another theory has it that all talk of consciousness is unnecessary; it's a non-essential, non-substantive phenomenon of life, like a shadow or a halo. Or it doesn't exist at all, humans are complex robots preparing for or involved in action, consciousness is at most the hum of a motor.

A recent view asserts that consciousness occurred comparatively recently—much later than speech—in human evolution, and postulates a time in pre-historic culture when humans, like other animals, were not conscious of their behaviors. Society functioned by a system of conditioning with directives embedded in each individual who remained quite unaware of them. A voice inside one's head, a hallucination, heard at times of indecision accompanied by stress and confusion, told the individual what to do and was attributed to a powerful leader, god or a god-king, and the individual obeyed it. When this system no longer made sense, consciousness or self-awareness took a forward step along with emerging glimmers of individuality and individual choice.

Neuroscientists have joined the academics and are busily exploring—along with the linguists—the neurochemistry, brain rhythms and neurocircuitry involved leading, hopefully, to understanding the mechanisms of consciousness—factors of alertness, arousal, and capacity for focussed-attention characteristic of all primates. The brain, they point out, doesn't store images like a photograph album. Sensations—visual, auditory, kinesthetic, etc.—exist as electrical blips or molecular configurations and are stored in different parts of the brain to be assembled in response to a master stimulus. Emotions are controlled by neuro-transmitters, chemicals such as dopamine, serotonin and others. Consciousness, a leading scientist states, is simply a manifestation and the outcome of complex neuronal activity—like parallel processing in computers. Consciousness is the highest—and the most efficient mode of integration—the final form of information in problem solving. The answer is stated, of course, in biological terms which have nothing to do with the experience of consciousness. It adds nothing much in the way of help in understanding the pervasive question underlying our interest in the mystery of consciousness: *who am I?*

Today, in the age of popular psychology most everybody, including clergymen, has become interested in exploring consciousness and searching for the true Self. Psychedelics, reports of near-death experiences, consciousness-raising programs are increasingly common. Consciousness has become something fascinating to be explored—the bliss of psychedelics, the aura of the epileptic, the quest for Enlightment, everybody's adventure—a miracle granted to humankind, their own wondrous, elusive private world full of demons and angels, ideas, plans, hopes, fears, fantasies, and ecstacies. Consciousness, say some, is everywhere. The cosmos and its galaxies are conscious. Energy and mass are interchangeable and so are Mind and Matter. Mind and Consciousness are a gift from God, granted only to Man. The inquiry is extensive, understanding consciousness has become the central thesis of today's preoccupation with subjectivity, with *Self* and—for the spiritually inclined—with *Soul*.

No one mentions mother.

Every event encountered by an individual is stored in memory, employing, incidentally, only a fraction of the vast storage potential of the human brain. The brain stores countless memories and, triggered by associations or deliberate recall, can bring many of them to consciousness, some easily, others—the unhappy ones as therapists will explain to you—only with patience and effort.

The brain processes memories, compresses, condenses and categorizes them so that recall brings forth versions which vary considerably from the original recorded experience, more and more so with the passage of time. Memories are also stored attitudes and guides to behavior without thought or image—moving away from a hot stove, for instance. The earlier the memory, the greater the emotional impact and the greater the frequency of the event the more influence it exerts.

There need be no doubt about what impressions in humans are the earliest, the most frequent and the most important. They are the brain's registered experiences, "candid snapshots"—thousands upon thousands of them—of *me and mother*. No human child but feels (in the deepest recesses of its being) that it once was—or should have been—the object of a constant, adoring, nurturing and endearingly interested gaze—

mother's. It's only a short mental click to sensing who she was looking at with such love—me, me, me. Me doing this, me doing that, me with others, me being good, me not being good, the seeds of self-awareness.

The process is validated by children themselves. Ask whose little girl or boy they are and you will find that "I'm mommy's" or "daddy's". Or listen to their soliloquies often carried on in a clear voice with proper intonation and directed toward self or doll or imaginary something. "Naughty, naughty. Now, be a good girl. If you're bad I'll have to spank you, etc.".

With the passage of time the mass—critical mass—of recorded memories of me and mother are processed, condensed, classified and modified. Mother's image fades slowly as it merges with images of all the others who have interacted with us. The "me" is emphasized and, in time, the me becomes "I", an ego, a conscious Self, a thinking, planning, dreaming, doing Self—as well as a Self that gets frightened, confused, defensive, or angry, and becomes highly conscious and aware.

Not only are we able in growing up to develop a sense of self, a fundamental element of consciousness, but based on our interactions with mother we gradually create our own epic, a story and a cast of characters which becomes a guiding scenario. Mother—and the mothering team—have been our source in setting up a program or process, an on-going *comedia del arte*, that enables us to live as social beings in complex societies. We have little or no recognition of this process. It becomes a scenario which fate has written for us and we learn to interpret and explain everything from the indoctrination inherent in that scenario. Not only is "the play's the thing," it's the only thing. With ourselves as the central character we—through observation and invention—determine the personalities and characters of all the other actors speculating on their motivation, speech and actions with, often enough, a remarkable degree of accuracy. We alter the script of Self, other and outcome as life unfolds as best we can, weaving and spinning multiple possible happenings. Hoping for the most favorable outcome—while keeping our mental fingers crossed against the least favorable—is the living, breathing, pulsing, the central, constant, conscious and unconscious, preoccupation of human beings.

Our deepest imperatives retain vestiges of the wishes of mother's little girl or boy attached often to remaining traces of fear or guilt. The Zen master is aware of this primitive bond. To help the neophyte get beyond it he assigns the koan, *What was your face before your parents met?* Enlightment, the ultimate expression of consciousness can be thought of as awareness increased to the point where concern for the self disappears.

As adults much of our mental processing becomes unconscious, our creations, calculations and conclusions become the on-going, rapid and routine functions of the brain. Our period of dependence drops away, we enter the adult world and base our decisions on values as set up and incorporated into the script with the passing years, a script that preserves bits and pieces of our previous dependency on mother.

A patient, Mrs. Herbert T. illustrates this. She was brought to my office by her husband who told of the accidental injury to his wife some months previously. The wife, a successful writer in her late fifties, had been working in the library of a local historical foundation when a section of a shelf of books gave way and she was hit on head and shoulders by several volumes which showered down on the table where she was working. She was stunned but denied losing consciousness, apologized for any disturbance she might have caused and hurried home. There were no fractures or lacerations and except for a few superficial bruises no evidence of damage.

Vague complaints of pain around her head and loss of power of concentration continued. Her husband assured me that she had never been overly concerned about health. At her husband's insistence, she was seen by a number of specialists but repeated neurologic evaluations, CAT scans, and electroencephalograms yielded no diagnosis nor any helpful answers. Seeing a psychiatrist was the last resort and she had agreed to see me only on the urging of a friend. The degree of fear and depression she exhibited was, according to her husband, totally out of keeping with her normal personality. She was doubly discouraged because of her feeling that something was wrong with her and the failure of all the tests to reveal any abnormality. For the first weeks, talking to her was slow and laborious.

I was frank to confess my own puzzlement. Knowing that she had written several successful detective mysteries I suggested that her skill as a detective might be our best resource, a remark that evoked the first smile I had seen. Piece by piece her life story—a moving story—unfolded. She was one of five children of Italian parents, and the first child born in the United States, the eldest two having been born in Italy. They were bitterly poor, the father abandoned the family, although some said that he left in desperate search for a job and money and met with tragedy. Huddled in a tiny apartment, they lived in a back alley in the slums of Baltimore and the mother opened a little grocery store in one of the rooms. It had survived because it was open all day long, seven days a week and handled items that people needed at off hours. Mother existed from month to month and year to year on the verge of exhaustion. Each and every child learned to cause no trouble, to help wherever needed, and to be an obedient and a good student at school. It was a story that might well have been added to those sagas we associate with Ellis Island and the Statue of Liberty. Every single one of the five children became achievers and unusually successful as adults.

As the patient was recounting the stresses of those early days she mentioned on several occasions that the one overwhelming dread of that struggling family and the one thing that threatened day to day survival was an illness in one or another of the children. So imbedded in the children's minds had this become that the children learned even when ill to keep it a secret from the mother. On more than one occasion an illness or injury in a child was kept from the mother by dint of a conspiracy in which all the children participated.

Several months had passed without signs of improvement in the patient and during one session Mrs. T. was sharing another recollection, an episode where her brother had fractured a wrist and the children devised elaborate stratagems to keep the mother from knowing. To encourage continuing flow of her thoughts I suggested that it was fortunate that her recent injury hadn't occurred during her childhood. Her face went suddenly white and she sat as though stunned. My first thought was that she had probably not been paying close attention to what I was saying and may have misheard. She left the office in somewhat of a daze but I had become so accustomed to her depressive feelings that I thought no further about it. The woman who appeared for the next session was a different woman, a new woman. She took the chair opposite with grace and composure, looked at me directly with the warmest of smiles and said something to the effect that she wouldn't have thought it possible. I was still puzzled as she explained to me that she had discovered what the trouble was, she now knew exactly what had happened. She was right, she said, in insisting at the library that she hadn't been hurt and that she didn't want her husband or anyone to bother. Since that time she had been in a trance of fear and confusion, barely able to mobilize the energies to get through the day. Whether or not my off-hand remark had triggered it, the reason had suddenly become clear. *What if her mother found out?* Her mother had, in fact, been dead for many years. The unconscious, said Freud, knows nothing of time, has no idea of past or future. The power of the hidden scenario governs all of us. Nature supplies the clay; mother is the sculptor and her work lives long after she is gone.

This process—as in the case of Mrs. H. T.—does not always work out smoothly. Where the interactions with the mothering one have been painful and unsatisfactory the resultant self-image and damage to self-esteem continues to produce pain and dissatisfaction, sometimes to extremes, with a severe disturbance in emotions and in one's ability to relate comfortably with others or to deal with the stresses of living. Of course, it is neither black or white. Few are the lives untouched by suffering. Few also are the hopeless.

Over the years of comparing chimpanzee and human behavior it was clear that we had moved far ahead of the chimpanzee in the areas of both speech and consciousness. We could feel grateful for the pleasure and satisfaction resulting but not overly proud of what we had accomplished as a result of it. Human behavior was still pitifully amiss in both communication and awareness. It was necessary to de-emphasize both speech and consciousness to further an understanding of behavior.

Over the years I periodically considered sharing my views of human behavior—somewhat novel and unorthodox certainly—with psychiatric colleagues. Eventually I wrote up the theory and, surprisingly— way back in the sixties— the paper was accepted for publication in The American Journal of Psychiatry. Not surprisingly, a theory that claimed we could learn about human behavior from animals evoked more indifference than endorsement. Two more articles published in university journals met the same fate. I put it all on the shelf where it remained for thirty years.

Thirty years later it was a new world. Technological growth produced a world linked by computers, information networks and instantaneous transfer. Politics closed a chapter in history. The threat of a world divided between two armed superpowers with weapons at the ready ceased with the ending of

Russian communism. The umbrella of terror of the H-bomb had been lifted. War as a basic policy of nations, now so closely interconnected, was being questioned as never before. Major powers cooperated in collective security and peace seeking efforts to halt the spread of and solve, regional, ethnic, and tribal conflicts.

With the fears and terrors of world-wide import lessened, important questions resurfaced, questions of human rights, of minority rights, of poverty and economic justice, of corporate greed, of the informal conspiracy between special interests and political incumbency which paralyzed reform. Economic dislocation aside, it was, nevertheless, a brave new world, dominated more by turmoil than by terror. Old stale political methods withered away. Old agendas were discarded, it was no longer business as usual, a general restlessness was evident.

Along with the world wide wave of movements for self rule there was another movement—it would have been called soul-searching in former times—to seek, to find meaning, to explore the nature of the Self. Freudian psychoanalysis had been pushed to the periphery in the field of psychiatry, new theories, new therapies, biological and psychological competed for recognition. Energized by the traditions of individualism and enterprise it took many forms and operated through many agencies, the human potential movement, self-improvement and fitness programs, new waves of religious awakening, group psychologies, The New Age, Eastern lore and mysticism.

My views of animal and human behavior once dismissed as far out were now mild and conservative. Jane Goodall, Diane Fossey had become household words. Some went further; animals had spiritual qualities we had never fathomed. Civilization had lost touch. Only unspoiled natives were in touch with such reality.

What were the underlying causes of such ferment? Had governments begun to recognize the collision course with disaster? Had the terror of the H-bomb truly ended? Could monitoring on an international level keep it so? Had the triumph of capitalism proved that the free market was the source of all economic wisdom? All of the above, said learned men and learned journals, but the explanations were less than satisfying. Hints that something was missing increased steadily and were—finally—heard.

The missing—and crucial—element was the voice of the female.

To the thoughtful there was, of course, nothing new about that voice: it was still the voice of caring, not of possessing; of peacefulness, not of violence; of affiliation, not of alliances; and of joy, not of triumph. At long last that voice, the voice of half the human race, might be listened to and—sometimes—understood. The male found himself listening, often without realizing it, perhaps from a quiet born out of perplexity.

Women, having discovered that woman's suffrage brought neither economic equality nor empowerment, began a new movement. The waving of banners to command attention, the assertion that on the primacy of women's rights hinged the hopes for all minorities, the demand for political and economic equality—sometimes noisy—reflected a ground swell of hope that women for the first time in history, participating fully in society, could bring justice for all. Males, often enough, bristled at noisy women who shouted down opposition. They belittled the advances of the new feminism, not realizing that it often made them more sensitive to quiet female voices— more and more in evidence—that they had hitherto ignored. A flood of new studies of infants and children explained the step by step development and the importance to society of the mother-infant bond as well as the vulnerability of mothering and the family.

In this new climate—political or cultural or whatever—the views expressed in the theory I had written so many years ago seemed less radical—even tame. The search for the roots of human behavior in the study of animals had become acceptable. That fathering could be defined as mothering learned and practiced by a male—the mothering male—that psychiatrists could be thought of as society's specialists in corrective foster mothering, that the male in dominating the female for millions of years had neglected to acknowledge what he had learned from her— these views now seemed respectable items for discussion.

The plight of children everywhere, of the world's children, could no longer be ignored. Women were the natural reservoir of important answers: one must listen to them. With the possibility of women in increasing numbers reaching policy making levels in many endeavors came a surge of what could be called "nurturance" concerns, the welfare of children, interest in nutrition, in ecology and the environment, in education, in civil rights, in prison reform, in health, in medical care, in drug and alcohol dependency. Along with all the other developments in human destiny, political, scientific and otherwise, the women's movement had finally reached a significant position in the parade of events.

Chapter Twenty-one
A HOPEFUL TOMORROW

As a new, multidisciplinary specialty primatology had come into existence in the '60s. Women had always played a crucial, even the leading role in its development. Courses I had taken had been led by women, many papers on the subject had been written by women. The field itself had had from the beginning a feminine imprimatur. When I began my study, it was customary in scientific papers to refer to monkeys or apes under observation as types: adult male, adult female, pregnant female, juvenile, nursing infant and so on. Abandoning the custom of labeling animals in this manner, Jane Goodall's research reports on the chimpanzees were punctuated with names like Flo, David Graybeard and Figan accompanied by comments on their temperament, personality and motivation that seemed dangerously close to by-passing scientific objectivity.

The attitude of the largely male scientific establishment seemed to be that this was perhaps excusable in a woman scientist. A remark of a professor at Berkeley at this time indicated the prevailing attitude toward Jane Goodall's first reports. Over lunch I asked him a question about Goodall's procedure in labeling subjects and he suggested, somewhat condescendingly, I thought, that research done by females usually had some gender bias inasmuch as females tend to minimize the violence and ferocity in the animals they observe.

The male establishment clearly found itself in an anomalous position with their material for vivisection being given names like Fifi, Freud and Mr. Worzle. Dr. Jane Goodall did not bother to provide scientific rationale for giving names to the subjects under observation. On the contrary she wrote, "I readily admit to a high level of emotional involvement with individual chimpanzees—without which, I suspect, the·research would have come to an end many years ago." This was the remark of a woman scientist who had sat month after month in the presence of wild chimpanzees, unarmed, undefended. The contrast with male attitudes was too stark to be ignored. It reminded me of a current joke describing the shortest known account of an animal behavior study—ostensibly conducted by males. *"The animals fled at our approach so we shot them."*

It was becoming clear. Resistance to a natural empathy for—or identification with—animals in general and the chimpanzee in particular stems largely from the male. Females—certainly female naturalists—seem less rigid. Anthropomorphic reasoning, projecting human traits on animals—or vice versa—doesn't seem to bother female naturalists all that much. A few seasoned women investigators have, in fact, told me that anthropomorphizing is a minor risk if one's emphasis is, first and foremost, on mastery of the facts.

Until a few hundred years ago the separation between humans and animals was tentative and uneven. Animals were brought into court to appear before the most august of judges; oxen, pigs, horses were tried for offenses against humans and, when guilty, hung or beheaded. Children—and primitives, too—remain uncontaminated by modern male belief systems. They talk to animals and accept the animal's response. I once heard my twelve year old nephew speak drowsily but clearly to his dog, Sugar, who was given to snuggling in bed with him at night, "for heaven' sakes, move over, Sugar." The explanation seems clear enough, females, children, natives—not being restricted by white male logic—accord more weight to fundamental behaviors such as care-giving, play, and friendly, non-aggressive responses than they do to the more superficial and recently acquired behaviors like talk, abstracting ability and formalized reasoning processes.

Females, having experienced the human male since childhood and having themselves suffered from classification by males, may be unimpressed by male preoccupations in general—male beliefs, male myths, male arguments, male displays and male definitions—since these are mostly for the benefit of other males. Male definitions of human personhood aren't all that impressive. Aristotle defined humans as symbol-using animals. John Locke, in denying Descartes' theory of innate ideas, made human language the basis of his logical system. Such definitions, in the light of our present knowledge, seem fuzzy.

As more and more evidence accumulated of the closeness of chimp and human, observers logically concluded that the chimpanzee—some insisted that gorilla and orangutan be included—should be re-classified as Hominids, the only other surviving members of the human family. Other members of the human family, the slightly stooped, hairy and beetle-browed Homo habilis, Homo erectus and big-muscled Neanderthal, are known to us only through their fossils and tools. All are long since extinct. To reclassify the higher apes as such close relatives, however startling, was scientifically arguable and not uncongenial to female primatologists who had so courageously spearheaded the defense of these endangered creatures. Diane Fosse, murdered as the result of her protection of gorillas, had, in fact, been deemed a martyr to the cause.

The suggestion to shift the classification of the chimpanzee to the broad human family strikes the average person unacquainted with the facts as ridiculous. Scientifically valid or not, it is more daring than absurd, involving as it does much more than a simple change of two Latin words. It means confronting another charge that humans have been guilty of—cruel and unusual punishment up to and including murder, torture, cannibalism and inflicting martyrdom. Even more, it means that we give up our unique and privileged position as somehow above nature. The resistance is a stone wall. Most of us, unthinkingly, dismiss the evidence and defy logic. The chimpanzee is a beast and that's that. Humans kill primates and eat them, hunt them as trophies, display them for amusement, imprison them for life and sacrifice them in experiments, just as they have done—and do—with other humans. And now they are on the brink of extinction. Again, the role of women—not only Goodall and Fosse but Galdikas and many others—in exposing this tragic situation and disseminating the truth is well established. Perhaps we should focus on even a broader truth: *A Sacred Kinship I will not forego binds me to all that breathe.*

Going back to the origins of human behavior millions of years ago, before evolution and culture combined to blur basic behaviors, what assertions have merit and substance?

FIRST: BEHAVIOR

Chimpanzee social behavior is human social behavior without the trimmings. The basics, the essentials, all are present in the chimpanzee social group: love, friendship, aggression, creativity, non-verbal language, humor, inventiveness, tool use plus trickery and cunning.

SECOND: MOTHERING

Mothering in its immediate pre-human form is mothering unadorned. It exists in all its dimensions and all its wonder, sensitively adapted to its purpose. Effective and consistent, the mother's dedication covers a period extending over years. She is vigilant and attentive, sensitive, tolerant, protective and nurturing. A wordless wisdom guides her behavior toward her little one. Her mothering is total, she is assisted by no one—although older daughters, observers note, may offer a helpful presence. Adult males in their comings and goings provide an umbrella of protection, but the real protector is the mother. She nurses the infant and after weaning she shares food and guides the little one in food finding and selection.

These descriptions of mothering may sound sentimental or romantic; they are, nevertheless, true. If not, chimpanzees—

with their limited population growth rates—could not have thrived for these millions of years; the chimpanzee infant with a poorly functioning mother does not survive.

More important, however, from the standpoint of group survival, is the mother's role in preparing the young for maturity, for full and effective group participation. She does so by helping the toddler enter the peer group and by continuing supervision of its progress during that extended period of juvenile learning, vigorous play, exploration of the environment, and daily practice of social skills leading toward adult status. By the time the maternal bonds are loosened, the juvenile at puberty is well equipped to function independently. The group's social life centers around the females, their infants, juveniles, and adolescent females until the onset of sexual receptivity. Pregnant females, too, remain close to their mothers. Adolescent males leave to tag along after the adult males to, over time, seek their level in the dominance hierarchy. Standard training for this endeavor, it should be noted, is through systematic domination of each and every female on the dominance hierarchy.

A paradox of the seemingly rugged and indomitable quality of chimpanzee mothering and its general effectiveness as recorded by naturalists is the fact that mothering is a fragile and easily destroyed behavior. Laboratory studies of lesser primates demonstrated that deprivation or abuse of the infant or young female effectively destroys the capacity for mothering behavior which normally unfolds in the years ahead. This general truth requires more extensive documentation for natural conditions but consensus seems to bear out that selective forces weed out the poorly functioning mother. The best of human mothering seems to spring from the mother's early experiences of nurturing, tenderness, compassion and joy. Battered by stress or illness, mothering skills are difficult to attain—for human females, battered by poverty or inadequate mates, they are difficult to maintain.

THIRD: MALES

While the female is central to the social group, the male is peripheral. Food gathering in chimpanzees demands considerable group dispersion—alternating fusion and fission. Few opportunities for feeding can supply the entire group. Foraging patterns may involve any number from one up to large components of group membership—when a fig tree ripens, for example. Feeding groups involve mixtures of the sexes though mothers with their young feed together.

The male has little interest in non-estrus females. Copulation is brief, random and promiscuous although occasional courtship with a single female coaxed away from the group may last a few days. In bonobus, the pygmy chimpanzee, courtship patterns are more involved. Copulation is no longer intermittent, it is frequent and occurs throughout the menstrual cycle. Ventral intercourse occurs. The implications of frequent, face to face intercourse for behavioral evolution are obvious; the pretty face and courtship behavior were forever joined. New forms of social bonding, peace-keeping and other social patterns evolved.

Male relationships with the young are superficial or incidental although males are protective, even tolerant and playful toward an infant or juvenile clinging or clambering over them. Between adult males relationship may continue over time but these relate more to alliances in group dominance interactions than to friendships. Male capacity to form teams for hunting, patrolling borders and possibly raiding neighboring groups for females has been mentioned. The organization of the chimpanzee group is crucial to survival; the peripheral male, ever vigilant, is a defense against leopards or other carnivores. Organizing leadership through dominance interactions is an important instrument in group survival where external threat is ever present. Millions of years of evolution and thousands of years of civilization have not yet obliterated this basic primate pattern of the central, affiliative female and the peripheral, exploratory, inventive, lonely, restless, vigilant—but promiscuous, ego-dominant and, often violent—male.

FOURTH: SOCIALIZATION

All social skills stem from the mother. This is true not only of the skills imparted to each child by the mothering one but also to the increase of social skills through succeeding generations. The long period of nurturing and dependence is a mutually reinforcing and learning experience for both mother and infant. The mother's skills steadily increase with each pregnancy and the young benefit successively; the juvenile social skills are a product of interactions with the mother, further developed through peer experience. As evolution progressed, this period of maternal dependency lengthened and social skills training was further extended. Mothering became the most important "school" in the educational curriculum.

The less obvious aspect of imparting social skills was the female role in bringing a more sociable, peripheral male closer to the center of the social group, finally leading to food sharing and pair-bonding which resulted in a radical alteration of the basic social structure, particularly of caring for and raising the young. The evidence points to feminine initiative. The female tended to mate—often, beyond the watchful eyes of the dominant male, employing ruses that strike observers as being close to feminine wiles—with males of a cooperative, attentive and friendly nature who also occupied a high position in the dominance hierarchy. Primate studies demonstrate that the status of the offspring reflects the status of the mother. Today, the mother is often credited or blamed for having produced dominant, successful sons. From the evolutionary standpoint, however, the qualities of friendliness, cooperation and affiliation predominate. Over generations the selective process led more and more to domestication, to a strong, intelligent, socially adept and friendly male. We have a long way to go.

Every positive male quality of tenderness, capacity for sharing, tolerance and teaching ability has its source in the female. She selected the male to provide the genetic material and then carried out the social conditioning of resultant offspring. With pair-bonding and the human invention of the mothering team these qualities are, of course, reinforced and passed on by fathers to sons or daughters. In its furthest reaches—as in humans—the male is quite capable of learning and taking over from an ill or absent mother the full range of mothering tasks. Not infrequently, in fact, males are doing this or fully sharing the mothering tasks in a forthright partnership.

Males often think of themselves as the architects of male-female courtship routines and relationships because they play the active role. In truth, it can be either way. Female chimpanzees, reversing the pattern of lesser primates, often leave the group when choosing a mate. Where there is a shortage of males in any primate society, the females actively initiate courtship; where males are plentiful females react to male assertiveness with seeming—almost coy—avoidance.

The sociality emanating from the mother is of an intimate and constant nature which lasts throughout the full life span. Both females and males as adults remain friendly and continue to gravitate toward their mothers. The bond of mother and child is the single permanent bond of the primate group. This bond created human society and the general sociability which makes such a society possible. It is this bond which serves as the foundation and training for all other social relationships, partnership, friendship, love, courtship, marriage—and culture in general. The on-going increase in these qualities will eventually dissolve the barriers, gender, racial, cultural, that divide and separate us from one another.

Sexual selection, operating largely through the female, predominated in the evolution of human society through the thousands of years of the hunter-gatherer societies and continued steadily until the beginnings of civilization.

FIFTH: MALE DOMINANCE

Male dominance, like mothering in the female, has undergone many modifications in the course of human evolution. In mammals below primates on the evolutionary scale, dominance is largely confined to winning access to females, and is often characterized by battles to the death during the breeding season. This occurs in some primate species as well. The male langur monkey extruded from a group when young may, when grown, displace or kill the leader of a group and then kill all the infants, too, whereupon the adult females immediately come into estrus. Male gorillas sometimes kill offspring of a rival male. Human males, too, commit and sponsor infanticide. More generally, however, they are indifferent to the fate of children other than their own and government policies reflect such indifference. Programs for the welfare of children are inadequate, spotty and uneven.

In chimpanzees, male dominance is rewarded with first choice in food selection, some advantage in choice of females, grooming, subservience and deference by other group members. Contests for group leadership do not—except rarely—end in death of the loser. In interactions between groups it is a different matter. Male chimpanzees patrolling group borders may kill every member of a weaker neighboring group they encounter.

With humans the patterns of male dominance vary widely from tribe to tribe and from culture to culture. Generalizations are hard to come by and there is no consensus among social psychologists about the operations of male dominance in any human society including our own. In some hunting and gathering societies males live apart from females and male dominance is evidenced in displays of bravery and achievement. Displays of valor and skill which have the appearance of boasting actually function to reinforce courage against the forces of darkness, ignorance and the malevolence of neighboring groups.

In times of drought and famine, courage and sacrifice can reach heroic heights, crucial to group survival. In some primitive societies a direct expression of male dominance occurs in the forceful removal from their mothers of pubescent males and the expunging of all traces of feminine influence on behavior by intensive and brutal, often sexually exploitative, rites of passage. The male role in enforcing genital mutilation of females has only recently occupied media attention.

Dominance expressed as tribal raids has, of course, been a male preserve from the beginning; captives were necessary for the practice of cannibalism. Females with sexual attractiveness were probably the first to be spared and females may have inspired the invention of slavery preferable as a creative alternative to cannibalism. Females may also have played a crucial role in the invention of trade and commerce—an alternative to the repeated male option of war and plunder. Females were an early if not the first objects of barter and such transactions probably entailed female input and cooperation as they still do in contemporary tribes.

Where female food gatherers are the main contributors to the food supply, male dominance seems to be muted. Still, the males maintain separate dwellings, have their own secret myths and activities. Anthropologists describe female attitudes toward such behavior as less than serious. Male behavior in general, particularly male courtship-sexual activity, is viewed with veiled amusement and secret giggles by females—one of the best kept feminine secrets.

True gender egalitarian cultures are rare but in a few small isolated South Pacific islands where intertribal warfare and headhunting were forbidden by missionaries a century ago, cultural traditions of female inferiority seem to be absent, men share child caring chores, the language is described as gender neutral and both male and female may strive for the highest title the culture can award which translates as "giver. There is no special male meeting house and all members of the community participate in decision making. Is equality possible?

Civilization brought great changes. The domestication of plants and animals led to food storage, food surpluses, lessened danger of famine, increased trade and commerce and sharply increased populations gathered in towns and cities. Another great change was a substantive alteration in the behaviors of male and female which had a profound and bewildering effect, not only on male-female relationships but on the very nature of human society.

As cities came into existence spatial relationships between male and female changed radically. The male moved from his roving, peripheral position of the social group to join the females and, along with infants and juveniles, established the family as the center of urbanized social life. He brought not only himself—along with food and other dividends—but his dominance as well. His dominance had always been evident but, peripheral and diluted by spacing, it could be ignored or avoided. No longer. The female has ever since been on the receiving end of male domination although myth, ballad, and poesy overflow with claimed exceptions and with accounts of the male's abject devotion, enslavement and sufferance.

An awesome demonstration of power is the adult male gorilla's dominance display of stomping, uprooting and hurling vegetation climaxed by thunderous chest thumping that can be heard throughout a circle half a mile wide. Male dominance behavior after five million years of evolution remains immediately identifiable—right up to the early great civilizations ruled by an emperor god. Shelley's Ozymandias—*look on my works, ye mighty, and despair*—and the chest thumping, silver-back male gorilla are brothers under the skin.

History as we know it really begins with civilization and the institutionalization of male dominance. History is written by writers. Those who could write were male. The choice of subjects was male, and the mode of expression was male. Philosophy, literature, jurisprudence, technology were all male productions. Those who ruled—with powers of life and death—were male. All others with their goods and services were male possessions. The wisdom, the subtleties of female thought and behavior are submerged and virtually unreported. Any role of the female other than for service to the male and his offspring is not important.

A challenging question relates to the roots of male dominance behavior and the ancient emotional brain which controlled that behavior. Violence and aggression, once crucial to protecting the primate group, lies ready to be triggered into action long after the dangers have vanished. The brain of reason and judgment, comparatively new, seems so often to fail. More often, the ancient emotional brain, asserts command. Even as violence is muted, selfishness, greed and anger prevail; individuals unceasing in their avarice grasp for power and security, typical of male dominated society at its competitive, adversarial worst.

For those who have reached higher levels of maturity with the brain of reason and logic firmly established in its executive role there are still vulnerabilities, not the least of which is a glorification of the cerebral cortex, not as a challenge to understand, something useful and interesting—which it is but as something magical. Humans, males especially, have identified with cortical function of "thought." Everything else—sensation, emotions, intuition, states of consciousness—is secondary. Reminiscent of Little Jack Horner we males have held up the human cortex and said not only cogito ergo sum—but how great I am. Preoccupation with possessing such a magical instrument dulls the appreciation of the emotional nuances that color thinking, enabling its owner to disdain most everything including his relationship to other humans, indeed, to living things in general. Things become something for the magic brain to work on, a kind of imperious intellectualism, imperious logic, imperious scientism. The indifference to others which results from this excess of emotional inhibition can only lead to increasing alienation, fear and absence of hope— in both self and other.

Religion, too, has within recent years been charged with patriarchal exclusivity, and, increasingly, has had to deal with the question of male dominance. Previously it was not so clearly labeled, and much was written about the origins and development of religion as a crucial component of humankind's cultural evolution. Sir James Frazer's, *The Golden Bough*. Sigmund Freud's, *The Future of an Illusion* and William James' *Varieties of Religious Experience*, familiar to many students do not question male domination. The awakening feminine consciousness, challenging the patriarchal nature of organized religion, has brought with it a renewed interest in matriarchal religions and ancient Goddesses and calls for a reexamination of the role of the female in religious history.

The evolution of the human species is marked by the lengthening period of dependence on the mother of both male and female offspring. In all primate groups, human or non-human, the male, nearing adolescence, leaves maternal protection to join other adolescent males and tag along after the mature males. In the human male, the memory of the early phase of this dependency buried deep within his psyche provides the hint for the myth of a mother goddess as well as the myth of a matriarchy, a period projected on to human history characterized by the dominance of the female.

Male awe and terror of female creative power and magic— to which, after all, males owe their existence—supported by a reservoir of imagery and long forgotten memories abetted matriarchal myth-making. Secondary reinforcement of such beliefs resulted from prolonged periods of plunder or hunting when males were separated from females who did, in fact, assume management of hearth, home and tribal relics, further extended in instances where the male population was largely destroyed. Male-made myths, more heroic than truthful, characterize human cultures generally and females, understandably, might have welcomed a myth such as matriarchy that carried hope of female empowerment. Such myths, however, had no more substance than myths of females assuming animal guises enabling them to indulge fantasies of freedom from bondage to males, to offspring or to both.

Female animistic beliefs and goddesses were countless, elaborate, and characteristic of ancient cultures generally. They depict female creativity, power and independence but do not provide evidence of female dominance over males. With civilization, culture evolved beyond the magical stage, as Frazer has described, and entered the religious phase. With new kinds of pair-bonding, myths and religious beliefs—as one would predict—underwent significant modification. Male belief in matriarchal myths was replaced by the pagan religions of the Hellenistic age patterned on new strivings and cultural institutions. Zeus and Hera, along with the dramatic carryings on of their extended clans on Olympus certainly reflect the realities of pair-bonding at the time, a time before the accumulations of civilization ushered in armed conquest as the reigning function of human society. The squabbles of dwellers on Olympus were no longer functional as a model of either government or religion. Female cults and goddesses came under male attack as, eventually, did paganism in general. Conquest demanded patriarchal religions, conquerors required the status or sanction of the Deity. Every government and every major religion practiced today, reflects formalized male dominance. As I write this the first female priests are being ordained in the Church of England.

The major religions, however, clearly reveal their female roots and female inspiration in their codes and canon. No male, observing mother and child over the many millennia of evolution could have ignored two idealized truths already stored in his heart, the supreme protective power of maternal nurturance on one hand and her infinite compassion and love on the other. Examples are numerous. The great religious leaders, in providing relief from suffering, routinely proffered directives for finding inward peace. Buddha, for example, after a few suggestions as to ethical and correct behavior, told his listeners to hold tenaciously during every waking moment—whether they were standing, walking, sitting or reclining—to a single thought, may all beings live happily and safe and may their hearts rejoice.

Lest his listeners think this unreachable, he chose a simple, everyday example as a model, the model based, not on theory, but on fact.

"Just as a mother," he explained, "at the risk of life, loves and protects her child, her only child, so one should cultivate this boundless love to all that live in the whole universe . . . ." Carrying out Buddha's suggestion, the unceasing cultivation of this single thought, led to its becoming an operating attitude, a characteristic mental state, culminating in Enlightment.

For Christianity, too, five centuries after Buddha, there need be no doubt about the origins of the model for religious behavior, the experience of and yearning for the loving mother.

"Suffer the little children to come unto me and forbid them not for such is the Kingdom of Heaven."

The failure of humanity to reach its religious or idealized goals should, of course, surprise no one. The political history of the Western world from some five thousand years ago, from the Egyptian civilization through Greek, Roman, monarchical and, eventually, representative or democratic government is largely the story of the gradual dissipation of dominance concentrated in the being of a single male and the dissemination of male power to the male populace at large. History details the many variations—all male—along the way, the migrations of power and its oscillations between the secular and the clergy, between emperors and popes, and, with the rise of capitalism, the shift of political power to the merchants and middle class, the century of confrontation by labor and the proletariat leading to revolution, dictatorships—Communist and Fascist—and war.

In an enormity of tragedy the Nazi crimes dispel forever any illusions about the operation of male dominance. In our own century—in the memory of many of us—male, female, infants and children were exterminated on an equal basis. When tomorrow's history is written, however—in full realization of the horrors of the Holocaust—it will be clear that no minority or defeated ethnic or religious group have suffered a fraction of the destructive behavior visited upon females in the millions of years of human history. While we have stopped burning females labeled as witches, such destructive behavior continues today. What safety the female has ever experienced was as property of a dominant male— as long as she remained in his favor. Only in the democracies has she had a vote and only recently has that taken on other than a "me, too" duplicate of her husband's political views. The problem of today's world-wide political, ethnic, economic, ecological crisis with its haves and have-nots, the third world, the rights of women and minorities, hinges on the degree of male dominance.

The single most important phenomenon of the great sweep of history as well as the truth of the here and now is the gradual modification of the operation of male dominance, dominance well illustrated in such historic struggles as those associated with the Magna Carta and The Rights of Man. Male dominance—expressed as nationalism—has slowed only with the threat of mutual destruction which included the planet itself.

With the development of methods to handle ethnic antagonisms and the eventual decline of nationalism, healthier governments will arise. They will reflect the heretofore disenfranchised, unrepresented females along with a new kind of male, males—minority or otherwise—who had been largely left out of power struggles. As new leaders emerge—male and female—not driven by dominance and power, their leadership based on inspiration and example, the cries of humans in need will be answered, conflicts and divisions will atrophy, the feeding frenzy of greed and consumerism will cease, and with the final cessation of male dominance, justice, equality and compassion will be reborn in forms greater than ever.

It will be a world of caring, of service and of peace. The female principle, the principle of mothering, millions of years old—that the "other" is more important than the "self"—will have come into its own. Her "fuzzy" thinking will be recognized for what it has always been, "thinking for two." Men will get back their rib and a little child shall lead them.

With the abandonment of domination as a governing behavior, anger—and its crystallization in hate and violence—as a prevailing human emotion will wither away. With the joy of inward peace, the wonder and mystery of being can be explored, the adventure of life can begin, free of fear, uncluttered with defenses, unconcerned with Self, responding effortlessly—and joyously—to the flow of experience in a world of no strangers and no enemies.

APPENDICES

The research and reasoning behind Dr. Rule's theory go back many years. For those interested in the foundations and background of his views, reprints of Dr. Rules's scientific papers are presented in the appendices complete with footnotes and bibliographical references. They are as readable now as when they were written.

In *UNCOVERING THE SOURCES OF LOVE AND HATE* Dr. Rule presents for the general reader the same basic theses set forth in his scientific papers. He shows that human behavior has roots in the animal kingdom that are traceable and understandable, he asserts that mothering behavior is the key to understanding the evolution of human social skills and, finally, he suggests new ways of understanding emotions which lead to destructive human behavior and new relationships to prevent such behavior.

Articles by Colter Rule, M.D.

The Speaker and the Speechless
A Theory of Human Behavior Based on Studies of Nonhuman Primates
The Graduate Journal, University of Texas
Vol. VIII, Number I, 1968   p. 228

A Theory of Human Behavior Based on Studies of Non-human Primates
Perspectives in Biology and Medicine, University of Chicago
Vol. 10, No.2, Winter, 1967   p. 266

A Biologically Based Theory of Human Behavior and Its Implications for Psychiatry. Speculations Derived from Recent Studies of Social Behavior of Non-Human Primates
The American Journal of Psychiatry
Vol.121, No. 4, October, 1964   p. 291

VOLUME VIII
NUMBER 1
1968

The

GRADUATE

JOURNAL

Colter Rule practices psychiatry in New York City. His professional life has been divided into three nearly equal portions: research in physiology, practice of internal medicine, and practice of psychiatry. The efforts reflected in this article were motivated by Dr. Rule's questioning of the validity of the vocabulary (or language) of psychiatry. He also makes a case for a very human sort of specifically focused social science designed first to come to adequate understanding of nonhuman primates and then to be extended to human beings without loss of respectful attention to the capacities of man's nonhuman ancestors.

First presented to psychiatrists (AMERICAN JOURNAL OF PSYCHIATRY, October 1964), the article was expanded for life scientists in PERSPECTIVES IN BIOLOGY AND MEDICINE, Winter 1967. At the invitation of THE GRADUATE JOURNAL Dr. Rule prepared this version for an even wider audience.

In a considerably different sense from that of Marshall McLuhan, the JOURNAL is concerned with communication. It sees something significant in Dr. Rule's observation that when verbal communication becomes prominent, behavior tends to become covert. This trend has hardly changed despite the number of new methods of communication. Though largely nonverbal, they are increasingly far from the fundamental behavior patterns of man's ancestors. Perhaps, after all, we do need to look more closely at the mothering behavior of the nonhuman primate or his posture when angered before we get too involved in abstract forms of communication.

⊸§   THE UNIVERSITY OF TEXAS   §⊷

A THEORY OF HUMAN BEHAVIOR BASED ON STUDIES OF NONHUMAN PRIMATES

TTEMPTS TO build a unified and solid theory of human behavior based on animal studies, while implicit in all thinking which compares man and other animals, have fallen far short of success or acceptability. Hopefully, a new multidisciplinary specialty, primatology, still loosely organized and without an established niche in the academic world, may contribute relevant data and a new perspective for consideration of the animal underpinnings of human behavior. Information on the social behaviors, communications, and organization of the natural dwelling primate troop, balanced by detailed studies under captive or laboratory conditions, has become increasingly interesting and increasingly reliable. (1, 2) Along with primatology other disciplines have, of course, been important contributors to the theory presented here. (See Note a)

Much prejudice (conscious or unconscious) must be overcome before an objective appraisal of a theory of human behavior based on other animals becomes feasible. Psychiatry and psychology alike are more or less outright in their rejection. A few theorists have extended ethological concepts to man (3, 4, 5) and a couple of best sellers about man have been based on ethology, but the majority of theorists seem to doubt the possibility of illuminating human behavior by studies of the behavior of other animals, a resistance not limited to professionals. Western man in general is closed-minded; even the child and the primitive are more open-minded in comparing human beings with other animals. The child never even considers that his pet dog or cat is not just as "human" as he is. I recently heard my twelve year old nephew speak drowsily but clearly to his dog, Sugar, who is given to snuggling in bed with him at night, "for heaven sakes, move over, Sugar." The child simply accords greater weight to behaviors such as care solicitation, nonaggression, play, etc., than he does to refined sophisticated but, nevertheless, fragments of behavior like verbalization or tool-making. He has yet to be trained in the ways of dualistic prejudice. The primitive or savage maintains a comparable degree of open-mindedness and even when he partially differentiates himself from the animal he does so with thoughtful consideration, and with compensatory awe or reverence which he accords the totem animal.. Only tongue-in-cheek vestiges of this, e.g., in Aesop, La Fontaine, and miscellaneous children's stories, remain in Western thought.

The origin of the wide conceptual gap between man and other animals goes back to the Greeks and to the roots of the Judeo-Christian thought; that is, to dualistic philosophies. The Eastern nondualistic systems seem not to have set up this unbridgeable chasm. Buddha is said to have dismissed dualism with a wave of his hand. Western thought, continuing the Platonic division between "thing" and "idea of thing," developed and extended dualism to its highest reaches. Western preoccupation with "things" (or, perhaps better, "things-in-motion") led through the centuries to the rise of industrialism, the scientific-technological revolution, and mass production. Increasing power enabled man to move mountains, to change the course of rivers. But with exploding populations this increased power also brought with it alterations in the vast but delicate web or balance of living things in their environment. Such unknowns carry an ominous portent. Dualism (typically) also carried the opposite, a promise of the first realizable human brotherhood because of freedom from toil. Philosophers urge that our enthusiasm for technological ingenuity not be confused with wisdom.

Whatever else is said about dualism it certainly led man to view the other animals as "things." Man (as exemplified, for instance, by the Athenian citizen in contrast to the slave) was accorded a "soul" by Judeo-Greco-Christian dualism; animals (and, presumably various classes of "nonhuman" human beings) were accorded a consolation prize, "instincts."

Whatever this distinction was meant to convey it seems certain that according a "soul" to man had much to do with (1) the privilege of life after death and (2) free-will, i.e., that man had some influence over the outcome of item 1. If free-will is defined as "knowledge of the proper choice" it cannot be made exclusively human but is simply a matter of degree. A more appropriate area for study is the phenomenon of "self-consciousness" or "self-awareness" best thought of simply as the natural outcome of a more highly developed cerebral cortex. Among the first products of that self-awareness were these very questions, immortality and free-will, representative of philosophy in its "toddling" or its "Little Jack Horner" stage.

The attempt to adapt the term "instinct" to science has led to Procrustean maneuvers. When, within recent times, Western man's rural existence ceased and was replaced by ever-growing megapolis, his day-to-day life with other animals was no more. Up to this point man's intelligence had rightfully accorded him trusteeship over his fellow creatures but certainly not claim to being more divine. With habituation to and preoccupation and obsession with gadgets and gadgeteering Western man took leave of the animal world without having clarified the distinction between his trusteeship and his divinity, a significant philosophic "hang-up." Little wonder that for Western man the possibility of an open-minded appraisal of his relationship to his fellow living creatures was lost.

In primitive societies religion and science are embodied in one institution, the medicine man. With the dawn of Western society these functions split and soon the dominant clergy decreed that man was modeled after the Gods (and, with the advent of monotheism, in the image of God), a view that would prevail through two millennia till Darwin. A comment about monotheism is necessary. Scholars may disagree but it is likely that the shift from polytheism to monotheism had something to do with the shift from early forms of "family" structure (gens, clan, matriarchy, etc.) to the familiar and modern patriarchal forms. One gets the feeling after wading through much confusing anthropological writing that the emphasis on "who lives with whom under what roof" shifted to "whose children are whose" and that "who owns what" added a confusing note to both. The proposition submitted here is that monotheism parallels and is related to the development of the patriarchal family, and that monotheistic religion represents the re-emergence of infantile, preverbal "imprintings," i.e., memories and images of "life with father." Conversely, the pantheist may well have had a "pan-parental" infancy. The relevance of this to the thesis of this paper will become obvious.

Darwin and the evolutionists dealt the church a severe blow by challenging the view that man was created in the image of God, and by asserting that man was descended (actually ascended) from ape-like ancestors. Darwin's assertions held up for structure (anatomy) but his attempt to extend them to function (behavior, excepting physiology) never came off. His book, THE EXPRESSION OF THE EMOTIONS IN MAN AND ANIMALS, is a cornerstone in the study of comparative behaviors but, in contrast to THE ORIGIN OF SPECIES and THE DESCENT OF MAN it was generally overlooked even by his scientific colleagues. The storm of controversy blew over, the conceptual antagonism, man as imperfect god versus man as intelligent animal, remained unresolved, the clergy feeling a little less divine (and tending to be comforted by the miracle of life per se, rather than the divinity of man) and the scientists (physicists leading off) humbly admitting the divine origin of the universe and, tangentially, of themselves. The stand-off had been achieved, in essence, by both parties retreating from an over-extended dualism. Western man remains suspended or swings between the alternatives and generally remains somewhat apathetic toward both religion and philosophy. Theist and atheist share the same platform today and the debate really comes down not to the previous definitions of God, or not God, but whether or not the universe has a purpose, i.e., makes "sense."

Hopefully, this historical-philosophical "snap-shot" is not too distorted and will provide a helpful background necessary for a discussion of the animal roots of human behavior.

The seed of the new specialty, comparative behaviors, remained dormant for perhaps half a century, its germination delayed, first by the rediscovery of Mendel's work and the development of genetics, then by the "reductionist" period of behavioral research with the countless studies of learning and conditioned reflex—a period rightfully labeled "the study of learning in white rats and college sophomores." (6) In the 1920's and 1930's a shift in the study of behavior began with the first studies of "sociality" and social organization as a crucial phenomenon in animals. Such studies as territoriality in English song-birds and the dominance hierarchy ("pecking order") in barnyard fowl (7, 8) set behavioral research on a new course and were important in opening up the new discipline, ethology, which emphasized the study of animals in their natural environment and meticulous investigations to distinguish between social and nonsocial modes of experience and learning. Animal behavior took on new meanings and opened new vistas; primatology marked this emergence.

The discipline of primatology is scarcely a decade old. In the mid-fifties only two centers for the study of primate behavior existed; now there are ten multimillion-dollar centers in this country alone and a number of others in major countries throughout the world. The number of field investigators has quadrupled and is rising rapidly. The volume of literature has already become unwieldy and two surveys in book form, one mainly of field studies, the other concerned with laboratory research, were published in 1965. (1, 2) A bibliography limited to the chimpanzee is approximately 400 pages long (9); one on the baboon is approximately 650 pages (10); both now have supplements. Conferences, congresses, and meetings are increasingly frequent. The interest of the scientific world has carried over to the general public where news and picture stories of chimps in space, of Jane Van Lawick-Goodall's work with wild chimpanzees and George B. Schaller's work with the mountain gorilla have been widely circulated. Anecdotal fictions of past eras and ages concerning our primate cousins are being replaced by corrected observations and somewhat startling discoveries. The social patterns governing primate groups may be much closer to early human social phenomena than was previously realized. A day spent observing the life of a primate troop (even as observed on film) is sufficient to rid one of the concepts obtained from zoo and circus, to mark the difference between captive animals and free animals so admirably fitted to cope and adapt to many natural environments.

Of some two hundred and fifty species of primates only twenty or so have been studied in sufficient depth to merit scientific conclusions; a thousand observation hours are presently considered minimal for a field study. When it is noted that the habitat of a given species may be restricted to a narrow layer high in a tropical rain forest, the difficulties and vastness of the work ahead can be appreciated. Further, complementary laboratory studies in many species may be impossible to obtain if the species neither thrives nor breeds in captivity. Most studies to date have been done on baboons, macaques, langurs, chimpanzees, gorillas, and gibbons; even these raise more questions than they answer. Indeed, we have barely scratched the surface, and while we have fairly reliable demographic data for a few species, the amount of data available for the many other crucial aspects of primate life is woefully sparse. We are, in short, still largely in the descriptive phase of the specialty. In studying individual animals an investigator characteristically uses a list of behavioral categories. The following list with nine headings is a generally accepted one: (*1*) ingestive, (*2*) shelter-seeking, (*3*) agonistic, which includes both aggressive fighting and escape behavior, (*4*) sexual, (*5*) care-giving, (*6*) care-soliciting, (*7*) mimicry (the technical term is allelomimetic and includes such activities as flocking in birds, schooling in fishes), (*8*) eliminative, (*9*) investigative. All of these can be social, including eliminative, when used to mark territory. Some must be social. (11) In studying primates, the social aspects and the accompanying communication increase the variables manifold, and many studies will be called for. Indeed, the paucity of data led a professional primatologist to remark that the amount of interest in primatology was out of all proportion to the amount of information available. (12) A possible explanation for this unusual degree of interest is an intuitive realization on the part of many that in primatology the predawn origins of human behavior may be revealed.

It is not possible in this short account to give other than an overview of the primate world. Of free-ranging monkeys, the greater number are arboreal, some never leaving the trees. Gorillas, chimpanzees, baboons, and various rhesus species are terrestrial, spending much time on the ground. All sleep in trees at night, except, on occasion, the gorilla. Primates other than man are primarily vegetarians, eating a wide variety of fruits, leaves, grasses, roots, nuts, and shoots. Birds eggs, nestlings, even small game are, however, occasionally eaten by baboons and chimpanzees. Evidence for hunting by any troop is unestablished.

Several phenomena often described under "population statistics" are fundamental to understanding animal behavior, although their precise application to man is not yet known.

Localization

Perhaps fundamental to his being a social animal, man is primarily an organism that is attached, and remains attached, to a particular geographical spot usually near which he was born and for which he formed a firm attachment early in life. (If his social nature stems from psychological phenomena classified under "figure," this might be classified under "ground.") Regardless of the excitement created by the conquest of space—regardless of wars, migrations, and modern transportation—the vast majority of the world's people are born and die within the radius of a few miles. Compared to nonhuman primates, of course, the range over which early man traveled was great, hundreds as compared to a few dozen square miles. But man is no nomad; that is, he is not an animal born to wander. Indeed, in the whole animal world nomads are a rarity; much of what was thought to represent nomadism turns out to be migration between primary and secondary localization, for example, summer and winter migration.

Man differs from other animals in having overcome most barriers to free movement; much of this, of course, is the result of the accumulated gadgetry of the past few decades. No limitation of bodily equipment now holds him back. Few physical obstacles, no insurmountable food shortages, and no hostile alien species contest his advance into new territory. Indeed, the main barriers to unrestricted movement may be those deep in his own nature, concepts as vague and yet as powerful as "home and mother," or "my people, my land, my country."

Population size

Man, though not a nomad, is surely a colonizer, and this has enabled him to multiply in vast numbers. The Malthus theory, with which Darwin concurred, stated that starvation, disease, and war were the sole factors operating to restrict the unlimited multiplication of individuals, including man. Such a formulation was grossly misleading and has required modification. Animals do not blindly reproduce themselves. Rather, animals organize themselves into orderly populations and societies which have various and characteristic ways of controlling population growth. Just what natural laws operate and whether man follows them is one of the most important questions confronting society today. (13) Current scientific studies are seeking to uncover the determinants, not only of total populations, but of the lesser units of population, such as societies, colonies, and groups. For such studies, nonhuman primate societies offer helpful material; for behavioral studies seeking to uncover other natural laws, nonhuman primate societies are excellent. They are composed of small numbers of individuals. Many occupy habitats where visibility is good so that recognition of individuals is possible. Wide choice of environments, often for the same species, offers an unusual opportunity to study the relationship of behavior and environment.

Group size of nonhuman primates under natural conditions is not great, usually not much above thirty individuals. Group size, the differences between birth and death rates, is a vector of various forces, for example, food supply, predator, and other pressures. The limited data-processing capacity of nonhuman primates seems to preclude the maintenance of well-integrated groups much above the figure of thirty mentioned above. The magnitude of the data-processing requirements for a member of a primate troop can be appreciated when one realizes that with a group of say thirty members each individual must be able to recognize every other individual quickly and accurately, regardless of partial or complete view, regardless of posture or position, and in various states of light and darkness. And data processing in communication is only the "social" component involved in successful adaptation. Aggregations up to several hundred animals have been described, but these may represent temporary associations of several groups coming together at night or congregating because of food supplies or other factors. The loose structure of certain chimpanzee groups, with individuals, mother-infant-juvenile, and adult male subgroups wandering at considerable distances from one another, has not yet been fully studied but may represent decreasing danger from predation and an increase in sociality rather than the opposite. The frequent intermingling of more than one group without agonistic behavior seems to bear this out. (14) Under captive or semicaptive conditions, as at Cayo Santiago or in certain of the Japanese primate centers where central provision stations have been installed, larger groups and different behaviors from those occurring under natural conditions are described.

Population density

Like localization and population size, the density of a population cannot properly be called a "behavior." Indeed, it may be viewed as the result of behavior. At the same time, like environmental factors, it determines behavior.

Although multiple variables related to birth and death rates enter into the determination of population density, the number of individuals in a given unit of space, that is, density, is an index of sociality. The psychological counterpart of density has been called "cohesiveness" and represents the final balance between positive and negative social responses. It is also a figure that is the final average of "spacing," the social behavior regulating one's distance from other individuals of the group; spacing will be defined later. The various primate species have distinctive densities and scatter patterns under natural conditions. Groups of howler monkeys are characteristically closely knit and cohesive. (15) Capuchins and baboons scatter widely during the daytime but gather closely together at night. The patas male (a swift-running, savannah-dwelling monkey) remains at a considerable distance from the main body of the group during the day and chooses a distant sleeping tree at night as well. (The patas male also thrashes around and makes much more noise than the rest of the group, suggesting that the behavior relates to his drawing predator pressure toward himself and away from the group. (16) The scatter pattern of the chimpanzee was touched on previously. Much needs to be learned about spacing, cohesiveness, density, and intergroup mixing. In addition to group size and density, adult male-female ratio, and the numbers of infants, juveniles, and transitional solitary males vary with the species. A figure for a howler group on Barro Colorado Island, for instance, included three males, eight females, three infants, four juveniles, and a few peripheral males. Such a figure could apply to other groups such as langurs, chimpanzees, and gorillas. Groups have a home range, the borders of which are soon learned by a field worker, and within this range there is a much used core area determined by food, water, and good sleeping trees.

The difficulty in obtaining data in field studies and the necessity of developing some system of classification can well be appreciated. C. R. Carpenter, a pioneer in these studies, evolved the formula, $N(N-1)/2$, where N equals the number of individuals in the group, to express the number of dyadic (interaction involving two individuals) relationships in a given group. Considering the variety of transactions between two individuals, the problem facing the field worker becomes clear. To simplify record-keeping, data are kept for interactions between types rather than individuals—for example, male-male, male-female, female-infant, and juvenile-juvenile. Other data categories include intergroup and interspecies phenomena, climatic and other ecological data. (15) These and other arbitrary procedures necessary for the early phase of a science are being modified and, indeed, a whole new methodology with new recording equipment is evolving. (17, 18)

Furthermore, certain postulates about social interactions have characterized early primate studies and should be noted. (15) First, all social relationships are reciprocal, the aroused motivation of one finds its satisfaction in an interacting organism. In the mother-infant situation, the infant satisfies its hunger, while the mother relieves the tension in her breast, derives satisfaction from holding, and the infant from being held. She derives some status or prestige gratification from exhibiting her infant. Second, each interaction involves a complex of both negative and positive drives. A typical example would be an interaction over a preferred feeding location where hunger drives an individual toward the preferred spot and fear of another individual keeps him away. Third, paired social relationships are subject to modification, specialization, differentiation, and generalization through learning and conditioning. Fourth, interactions accumulate in both negative and positive aspects, e.g., during the positive phase of the mother-infant relationship, each early interaction strengthens the positive affectional bond.

The total number of paired relationships determines to a large extent the overall pattern of group organization, or the group social structure. Conversely, the freedom of the so-called "free-ranging" monkey or ape is strictly limited by the social pattern, or structure, of the group.

The Fundamental Primate Social Behaviors (Including Man)

Primates are social animals. The social group is the unit, and the individual is a fragment of that unity. Separated from the group, the individual neither develops nor long survives; in the vast majority of primate species, the individual is born, lives, and dies never once out of sight or earshot of his social group. While this is not strictly true of the more evolved species, real exceptions are, even for man, rare and trivial. Separateness is an artificial condition; studies of the individual (or of two individuals or, indeed, of any fractions of the totality) are, hence, studies of artifacts, however defended—for example, in psycho-therapy—as practical and necessary. (b)

INFANT-MATERNAL BEHAVIOR

The individual at birth is totally dependent upon mothering behavior from one or more individuals for survival and growth. This dependence decreases gradually with growth into and through the peer-play period of behavior and tends to disappear with the attainment of physical maturity.

PEER-PLAY BEHAVIOR

The individual after infancy embarks on a prolonged period of peer-play behavior. This phase of physical and intellectual growth is devoted to practicing and mastering social behaviors appropriate to each sex and establishing social rank.

COURTSHIP-SEXUAL BEHAVIOR

The individual, using components developed during the peer-play phase, develops the capacity for integrated courtship-sexual behavior. This initiates the period of maturity along with dominance behavior, leadership-follower behavior, maternal behavior, all of which continue until the period of aging and decline.

SPACING BEHAVIOR

The individual under natural conditions of social life maintains an appropriate and specific distance between himself and every other member of his social group. This distance, corrected for known variables and averaged over time, indicates the strength and the nature of the social bond existing between any two individuals. (c)

TERRITORIAL BEHAVIOR

The individual with other members of the social group will defend by threat or fight the territory over which he ranges. He will defend, as well, certain products of that territory—for example, food, tools, trinkets—that he finds, makes, or accumulates.

DOMINANCE BEHAVIOR

The individual strives throughout life to attain and/or maintain a dominant position in the hierarchy of power and privilege that exists in every primate society.

Alliance behavior is classified under dominance behavior because as observed in nonhuman primate societies it has thus far been restricted to dominance interactions. Several forms of behavior involving more than two individuals have been observed. The following are examples:

1. Two individuals may suspend, more or less permanently, dominance interactions between themselves to join forces against a third individual.

2. An individual losing a dominance interaction to a second may forestall this loss by insinuating and ingratiating himself close to a larger or more dominant third individual, who "protects" him. (This must not be mistaken for philanthropy on the part of the dominant animal. It occurs in nonhuman primates apparently because the third and dominant animal automatically responds to the aggression directed toward himself, not noticing that the aggression is really directed at the ingratiating animal that has come close to him. Often, the ingratiating animal will "present" to the dominant individual in typical female fashion, a characteristic position of submission while he continues a threatening posture and facial expression directed toward the animal with whom he is still involved in a dominance interaction, i.e., he is aggressive from the front and submissive from the rear. Indeed the dominance interaction may "degenerate" into the question of which of the two animals can get closest to the third, i.e., the largest and most dominant.) (19)

3. Dominance rank is accorded the offspring of a high-ranking mother or family group. A female may be accorded dominance rank because she is the consort of a dominant male.

In this paper no detailed description of these behaviors or their ranges and variations will be undertaken. They were described briefly in an earlier paper, (20) and extensive material is available at several levels of detail in the literature. (1, 2, 21, 22, 23) Again, observing these behaviors, at least on film, is most helpful; seeing is still believing and, in this case, understanding. Good film footage on the various primate species illustrating their full behavioral repertoire is greatly needed. Further detailed analysis of these six basic categories into their constituents and the determination of the relationships between the categories is an important field for future study. We are concerned here only with an overview and with deriving principles that will help apply these categories to human behaviors. In spite of the range and complexity of each behavior category, the fact remains that these behaviors are identifiable, easily distinguishable one from the other, and are basic to all primate groups studied thus far. There is no reason to believe that the same behavioral categories will not extend to all the approximately 240 living subhuman primate species. It is inconceivable that such categories of behavior would not have characterized one additional species, namely, early man. The question becomes not whether man exhibited these behaviors but rather what happened to them, and the thesis of this paper is, of course, that they have not disappeared but continue to operate following their own rhythms and can be demonstrated, monitored, and often measured with little difficulty.

The Mystery of Speech

Why did these basic behaviors seem to disappear? Or perhaps a more blunt question: what blinded us? One thinks immediately of the vast, often glaring, accumulations of human culture and civilization which distract, preoccupy, fascinate, and often obsess us and which are traceable in almost linear fashion from television and automobiles back to the wheel, fire, and stone-flake weapons. (Not all human societies make fire, some borrow it from neighbors). (24)

But the real, perennial, stumbling block to understanding is always the mystery of human speech. It is this that blocks the awareness of man's continuity with the animal world mainly because it illustrates man's abstracting ability, his consciousness of self and, indirectly, his religiousness. It is this that is always submitted as final proof of the unbridgeable gap between man and beast. This barrier to understanding can disappear only with new concepts of the communication process. (25) When one compares communication among, say, apes with that among humans, one is tempted to propose that what the ape lacks in speech he makes up for by posture, gesture, facial expression, and nonverbal vocalizations. Indeed, it has been said that he communicates about as well as the average excitable human being trying to communicate with another human being who does not speak the same tongue. Further, as others have noted, human beings equipped with verbal skills oftentimes make a pretty messy business of communication, even at rather low levels of abstraction.

Human verbalization arose out of a communications matrix that once included posture, gesture, facial expressions, and nonverbal vocalization—all more or less undifferentiated. (d) The origin and development of speech made posture, gesture, facial expression, and some vocal characteristics obsolete for many communications functions, and these nonverbal components tended to drop out. The separation is a tenuous one; in certain emotional states the entire communications complex reappears, and the verbal component becomes relatively small. (e) The dropping out of the nonverbal components of communication means that behavior and the underlying motives tend automatically to become covert. Man, of course, discovered the social benefits of covertness and has refined it to an infinite degree. In implementing covertness he naturally used speech. We have for so long thought of speech as a communications vehicle that we have difficulty seeing that it also served the function of furthering covert behavior. Speech may or may not convey something, but it always hides something; it is noteworthy as much for what it conceals as for what it reveals. This is not accidental or incidental; this has been its function. In summary, speech, paradoxically, subserves the function of noncommunication. To understand what a person says, we must fully understand what he does not say or, more practically, what he does not wish to say. (f) This may help clarify why our clues to the basic primate behaviors were lost in man; they simply became covert. The evidence for the continued operation of these behaviors, therefore, is no longer visual but has to be, primarily, verbal-auditory. Proof of their continued operations requires, furthermore, not only sensitivity and awareness but an ongoing intimate and unthreatening, possibly even tender, social transaction which permits the communication of such awareness.

Additional difficulty in trying to understand the differences and the similarities between human and nonhuman primates stems from a real lack of understanding and a constant, unscientific exaggeration of the importance of speech, that is, a verbal in contrast to a nonverbal communications system. (The written word and all other communications advances that follow the discovery and development of speech are secondary matters.) If speech is seen simply as the natural outcome of increasing differentiation and refinement in the evolution of communication—a breakthrough phenomenon at a certain point in the process of cephalization and hierarchization in the evolution of the nervous system—it loses much of its awesome, miraculous uniqueness. (g) More and more evidence is accumulating that this is, in fact, true.

Speech, "Thought," and Their Relationships

The laws of speech seem to follow the same general laws of the development of the nervous system and of the intelligence. In severe aphasia, for instance, when an individual is unable to say "yes" or "no," he cannot convey this by shaking or nodding his head either. Nor can he do so with his hands, although muscles of both head and hands work well for other purposes. What is lost is the ability for conceptual thought, and both gesture and speech go with it. (26)

This paper is not the place to discuss abstract, symbolic, conceptual mental activity, or, in short, "thought," but certain relevant generalities should be mentioned.

First, the attainment of higher degrees of abstract thought as exemplified in man is the result of three interrelated factors operating over hundreds of thousands of years: (1) the marked increase in size of the cerebral cortex, (2) the prolonged immaturity and dependency on mothering behavior with its extended period of distraction-free learning, (h) and (3) an increasingly different physical, biological, and social environment.

Second, at a certain point, possibly early to mid-Pleistocene, a symbolic language, namely, speech, arose which, by bringing an unusual selective premium to the possessors, led to acceleration in each of the three factors mentioned above. Words, because of their great contribution to social collaboration and survival, rapidly supplanted visual images, neuromuscular sensation, and emotion as both the repository and the vehicle of concepts at various levels of generality. For example, one might cite the words Black Beauty, horse, animal, food; or Black Beauty, horse, beast-of-burden, vehicle, status symbol. In general, words and language not only document the distinctions and qualities of the environment—the basic elements of concepts—but permit a great increase in their number, subtlety, and efficiency of storage. It is clear that language multiplies what one sees and, hence, much of what one understands. The discovery of "the word" and the evolution of language gradually gave rise to an increasing complexity of concepts, including such things as the idea of time. Man became a "time-binder." He was taken out of his imbeddedness in immediacy. He acquired a past that he crystallized as history and a future attended with a degree of predictability. As he accumulated concepts he accumulated material goods (the precipitates of concepts) and even the kinds of material goods, such as dictionaries, libraries, and data-processing and computer machines, that permit the storage and processing of concepts. Words determine man's world, and the worlds in which different language groups live are distinct worlds, not merely the same worlds with different labels. (27) This statement, in essence, applies quite well to a comparison of the communication systems of human and nonhuman primates.

In short, psychologically, speech indicates the arrival at a certain level of conceptual thought. Anatomically, speech indicates the arrival at a certain level of complexity of the developing organism. (i)

Hopefully, it is clear at this juncture why comparisons of the intelligence of man and of the nonhuman primate as exemplified in laboratory studies are unfruitful. What distinguishes man from other primates, and one man from another, is not the laboratory kind of intelligence but the kind he accumulates and uses for social purposes. (28) It is this failure to measure and appreciate social intelligence as it operates under natural conditions that made the gap appear so vast, so unbridgeable, and that has interfered with valid studies. The potential for accumulation, for sharing, for collaboration, and for sociality, this—not intelligence per se—is the area where we have outdistanced the nonhuman primate. (j) One cannot help observe that we are still short of the sociality imperative for today's world.

Man's Modifications of Fundamental Behavioral Categories

The foregoing, it is hoped, has made clear that neither the fact of human speech nor the increased capacity of man to be guided by abstract concepts has removed man from the six vast categories of behavior that characterize all primate societies. Future studies will refine our knowledge of these categories, their relationship to one another, and the laws governing the rhythms of their operation, particularly in their relationship to environment. Indeed, much has been done and is now being done that we cannot go into here. The affectional maternal-infant system, its components, and its reciprocal relations with the peer-play affectional system has been much studied, particularly in the laboratory. (29) Psychiatrically, this simply means that if you are "short changed" as regards "mothering," the peer-play group may make up for it. The varieties of territorial behavior as well as variations in dominance behavior open wide vistas of endeavor. But in this paper we can state only generalities; namely, that these behaviors are as fundamental to human existence as such short-rhythm phenomena as respiration and the heart beat, intermediate (circadian) rhythms like sleeping, waking, eating, drinking, and longer rhythms like sexuality and seasonal changes.

The development of man is characterized by the ongoing process—now having operated for millennia—of refinement and elaboration, and it is this process that has so altered the six primate behavioral categories as to account for their being ignored. The study of how they have been elaborated and refined is now open to all and should provide for stimulating investigation and speculation. Toolmaking, for instance, can give us a clue to what happens as elaboration and refinement operate over great lengths of time. Regardless of ups and downs of history or circumstance, there is an unbroken line of tool development in which the tool becomes complex and specialized and the toolmaker becomes an ever-larger multimembered team, with each team member having a function and an area of endeavor. The chimpanzee toolmaker fashions a probe by stripping leaves from a small branch or a twig and uses it to explore a termite hill, hopefully to extract termites. (30) Man organizes a vast complex team of toolmakers to make a tool to explore space. The same holds true for each of the basic categories of behavior. (Take mothering.) Mothering behavior is defined as "care given with satisfaction if not joy and leading to growth and maturity in the one receiving the care. Care is understood to include every nuance of giving from nursing and physical support to protection, teaching, and encouragement." (20) Since these must lead to growth, each must be given in appropriate quantities ending in cessation (or a stronger term, rejection). This definition is broad but is well supported by observation of nonhuman primates; it is also definitive in that there is little blurring or overlapping with the other five categories. Man has refined and elaborated this category much as he has toolmaking. Mothering is no longer the province of one individual, the biologic mother, but is the province of a team, and the composition of this team varies widely with history and culture. In our society, the biologic father usually plays the second most important role on the team. (The question of the adult male's interest in and protection of the young varies widely among various species of nonhuman primates. It will require much more study.) (18, 31) For humans such team functions may be assumed by older siblings, other relatives, or paid employees. But, most importantly, the extended team includes teachers, ministers, doctors (and the personnel of institutionalized forms: church, YMCA, Girl Scouts, etc.) All occupy a place on this team whether they are fully aware of it or not. Sometimes there is nothing that could even be called a team, and the child exhibits the manifold, often pathetic, distortions of conflict and unguided growth. Fathering, it is clear, is best defined as "mothering behavior learned and performed by a male." (20) The father, theoretically capable of every mothering chore except breast feeding, is often associated for historical and other reasons with the late stages of peer-play behavior, namely, puberty rites in the male child or the introduction to formal courtship behavior in the female child. In view of the male domination of the female throughout history, the mental gymnastics called for in the acceptance of the concept of the "mothering male" can be appreciated. This is a challenge to every male, whether husband or lover or psychiatrist. Many males resist this simple formulation possibly because they feel it reflects on their maleness, whatever that is. Certainly, it need not be confused with sexual potency. It is difficult for the human male, who throughout history has so generally dominated the female, to appreciate fully how much he has learned by observing and mimicking her.

Relationship to Other Theories

We cannot dismiss the foregoing assertions by stating that the difficulty is semantic; that is precisely not the case. The term "mothering" or "mothering behavior" is not chosen arbitrarily, nor are the other category headings. They are chosen in spite of alleged vague or controversial aspects, instead of words like "dependency" and "counseling." The word "mothering" is a term used and understood by biologists, by psychologists, and by sociologists and is by no means a vague, bulky, or nebulous term. It is subject to analysis and measurement by each of these disciplines. This term, along with the other five, offers a way out of the private language problem, which reaches Tower of Babel proportions in present-day psychiatry. (k)

It may be helpful to take another look into the past. It was the scientist who pointed out the great similarity in structure and physiology of man and animal. The burden of proof should be on the psychiatric scientist to demonstrate the animal nature of human behavior, not to stubbornly assert how unlike are man and animal.

The doctrine of evolution established the fundamental tenet that, while evolution is irrevocable, never returning to an earlier state, neither does it eliminate all traces of earlier states. No psychiatric theory ever effectively embodied this as part of its structure; all were concerned, not with what and how animal behaviors operate in man, but if they operated at all.

From the evolutionist's point of view, the gap between nonhuman and human primates is limited mainly to minor changes in the skeletal structure and to increase in size and area of the cerebral cortex. These are small when compared to other evolutionary changes, for example, the change from sea to land, or from land to air, or a number of other evolutionary advances. The change from nonhuman primate to human, though small, was critical and, operating over years, accounts for the accumulations of culture and civilization. One can hear the call *vive la différence* and agree, but these differences must not blind us to the similarities between human and nonhuman primates which are crucial for psychiatry. Since structure determines function (behavior) minor structural changes indicate minor behavioral changes, a principle that should hold good in comparing man to the nonhuman primate. Indeed, theorists readily accept the data of the fossil record and the data of comparative anatomy, which confirm the close structural relationship of all primates. The same holds true for the data on physiological functions. But this open-mindedness is blocked when the question of comparative behaviors is raised. Actually, what lies at the root of the inability to resolve the question (in addition to the previously mentioned conceptual "blindness" which accompanies dualism) is the phenomenon of covertness discussed previously. Man's evolving cortex made it possible for him to inhibit, camouflage, and modify the basic primate behaviors far beyond the ability of any other primate, and the ability increased steadily. This gave rise over the years to the thesis that man does not have basic primate behaviors. The explanation given was that evolution is, periodically, "emergent" and that man was the sole recipient among millions of species of this wonderful gift. Such a view, of course, is closely related to the phenomenon of transcendence, the dualistic theological roots of which are more easily identified.

The error is easy to spot. We have conceptualized man as the top of a pyramid representing the animal world (viz., primate), and this conception with roots in the arrogance (and terror) of animism and primitive religion has contaminated scientific thought, in spite of denials to the contrary. A better conceptual scheme would be concentric circles, with man being represented by the outer layers, thus indicating that man does not obliterate animal behaviors but simply extends their dimensions, including the ability to inhibit. Such a scheme explains why man can be more "beastly" than the animal. Neither torture nor cannibalism, for instance, exists in nonhuman primates; either they are unable to conceive it or unable to carry it out. Further study is required. A baboon did not eat the carcass of an infant baboon killed by a predator, though baboons are known to kill and devour small animals they happen across. Whether they can hunt or do hunt is unsettled. (32)

Theorists—both philosophers and psychiatrists—faced with the task of constructing nonanimal behavioral models have been given to all kinds of imaginative pursuits. Usually, however, they have selected such models as gods, heroes, saints, philosophers, artists, scientists, or, latterly and modestly, the products of man's mind, such as chemical, mechanical, or electronic systems. Actually, none of these is a behavioral model; they have no blood and guts, so to speak. (1) Rather, they represent a succession of man's preoccupations in his evolution from protocultures through savagery and barbarism to the religious and scientific attitudes of later times. They may actually be things he is not, that is, they are rationalizations to cover terror or, possibly, tabooed behaviors, probably of a sexual or agonistic nature. (m)

The models of human behavior espoused by the various psychiatric and psychoanalytic schools cannot be discussed at length here. A few remarks, however, are called for since these theories have crystallized into schools (alliance behavior) which treat thousands of people, have a deep and vested economic interest, and seek to establish spheres of dominance within medical schools, hospitals, clinics, and welfare departments.

The first and most significant of these stemmed from Freud. From a philosophical point of view Freud represents the culmination of a long line of thinkers who challenged Descartes. If the Cartesian essence is characterized by *cogito ergo sum* or given more emphasis as "I think *logically*, therefore, I exist," it is clear that Freud's view was anti-Cartesian, i.e., "I do not (nor do you) think logically; your thought is largely unconscious, you simply rationalize." To this extent Freud's contribution to the history of thought is of great significance. But the storm of controversy arose, not from the above, but because of his attack on the church. The doctrine of the dynamic unconscious (challenging free-will) and the doctrine of the ubiquity of childhood sexuality were challenges to the "territory" of the church rather than any other segment of the community. All ethical and moral considerations involving sex and violence had, long since, been the province of the church. This is what Freud pre-empted, and the cry of outrage clearly came from the direction of the church, already restless and overzealous to protect its shrinking territory. Business, in essence, is amoral, but it does keep its eye on every other segment of the community. It took a neutral position in the interminable controversy that raged between science, as represented by Freud, and religion. Indeed, reasoning from primatology, the controversy, if anything, would tend to help business, since business could pursue its own interests free from any moral restraints by the otherwise preoccupied church. The same could be said, in general, of the law.

What has been responsible for the continued existence of the Freudian cult? The reason lies in several areas. First, it is a profession, and second, it is itself a business, so the powerful laws of dominance status and territoriality continue to operate. Further, it continues also to thrive on the original controversy set up with the church and has enlisted as disciples, adherents, and customers many of those whose quarrel was with the church. In retrospect, one sometimes wonders why the controversy over sex would ever have been taken so seriously. Primate studies show that under natural conditions sexual behavior follows the rhythms of the days and the seasons without turmoil. Under conditions of capture, restraint, and crowding, it becomes a frantic preoccupation and a cause for vicious fighting. (It is to be noted that the pell-mell, crowded, distracting, struggling, competitive nature of man's evolving social life distorts his natural bent in other areas than the sexual, it perverts motherhood and can turn it to murder. Peace turns to carnage, quietness to frenzy. These are laws of primate behavior, human, or nonhuman.) It was impossible for Freud, embedded in his time, to sense this simple reciprocal relationship. For Freud society was repressive, the sexual "instinct" was immutable; these were the essences. He rebuffed those who took issue with him with most unscientific intensity, accusing them of lacking courage to face facts.

Jung and Adler pointed out the Freudian bias but submitted biased views of their own. Freud had noted and documented modern (and anxiety-ridden) man's preoccupation with sex. Jung noted man's desire to relieve anxiety by meditation and fantasy, and Jung's "mystical" views found an excellent market among those whose lives had been dry and prosaic. Adler documented man's tendency to react to the anxiety of being "low man on the totem pole" by dominance interactions. It is probably no coincidence that Adler's views were popular among a socially impotent group; namely, the school teachers who have struggled to extricate themselves from the onus of being society's baby sitters. These statements are simple overviews but they carry a point. Once the factors concerned with dominance struggles (professional influence) and territoriality (business and marketing) are cleared away, it can be seen that there is truth in all three points of view but, like the three blind men of Gotham describing the elephant, each view is erroneous because of its narrowness. But at the same time these three pioneers were forthright and courageous: the Nina, the Pinta, and the Santa Maria of the voyage to "a far country." Each described important facets of many-faceted man.

The main splinter movements after this early period of psychoanalysis were the "social-cultural-interpersonal" theorists who pointed out that Freud, Adler, and Jung all emphasized the "individualistic" and all overlooked the social (interpersonal) nature of man. But in so doing, the new theorists discounted the animal roots of man—throwing the baby out with the bathwater—and cut themselves off from vast areas of scientific endeavor, including the medical profession, itself. H. S. Sullivan, an outstanding theorist of the cultural-interpersonal group, illustrates this. In his fundamental book, (33) under a section headed "One-Genus Postulate," he states that the human being, no matter how badly damaged or abnormal, is still much more like a human than he is like the nearest animal genus, and that the only worthwhile study for psychiatry is of things ubiquitously human. This is a conceptual error, unusual and curious in a man of Sullivan's brilliance. The "mental patient" has long been subject to humiliation, (34) and one of many forms of this has been classing him with the beast, e.g., being beastly, or his agreeing (desperately) to the friendly suggestion of the psychiatrist that he must feel "beastly." Sullivan's determination to remove him from this category is, of course, praiseworthy. The fact is, however, that the "normal" person in our society is much more "beastlike" than is the "abnormal" person. The beast though unevolved is integrated. Our "patient" though evolved is un- or dis-integrated. Integration, not evolvement, is the key. We are not seeing animal behavior in our "disintegrated patients"; we are seeing jagged, fragmented human behavior. (n)

What future for all these therapies? As for Freudian therapies, i.e., therapies that are dyadic and essentially nonresponsive ("projective"), their futility for severe behavioral disturbances, as Freud predicted, has been well established. In their "classical" form they are prohibitively impractical for extensive use in even the less serious disorders. In a purely research setting, however (freed, i.e., of status and commercial contaminants), they may serve as a continuing source of meaningful data obtained under conditions we now recognize as sensory deprivation. Freud, too, felt that psychoanalysis was a questionable therapy, and was, frankly, pessimistic, a view ignored or denied by those who make a living from it.

Much confusion has resulted from the ever-extending range of the responsive ("nonprojective, reactive, suggestive, counseling") therapies. The medical profession including psychiatry has been bewildered by the ever-growing influx of a wide variety of "nonprofessionals" in the field of therapy. It senses something is wrong, almost out of hand, yet it has had no unified theory to serve as a criteria to describe, criticize, and evaluate the psychologists, marriage counselors, hypnotists, social-service caseworkers, spiritual and religious counselors, and various other "lay therapists" who have entered the field. These trends become understandable in the light of the present theory. (o)

In conclusion: it is time we dropped the interminable controversies and feuds which characterized theories of human behavior. They are, at last, history. It is time we paid homage to the Freuds, the Adlers, the Jungs as we have to the Pasteurs, the Claude Bernards, the Pavlovs. The grim data of present-day living demands that the gaggle of psychiatric cults with their rituals and dialects, isolated from one another, be replaced with a broad and integrated view of man, scientific without denying man's spiritual aspirations, proud of man's achievements without an arrogance that removes him from the animal world. Human behavior and emotion are not technologies for a few, they are the proper concern of everyone, leaders and led, weak and strong, young and old. Only when they become the stuff of society itself, its very philosophy, can we expect man to accept the responsibility for the planet we call Home.

NOTES

(a) The "information explosion" created new disciplines, like primatology, and expanded old ones which have variously contributed to an increased understanding of human behavior. Archeology, reinforced by new finds and new fossil-dating techniques, is illuminating previously barren areas in the origins of early man, primarily, that he was truly bipedal and a tool user with a brain volume not much greater than that of present-day apes. (35, 36, 37, 38) Animal behaviorists using electronic equipment and operant conditioning have revolutionized the experimental approaches of the early learning theorists (and Pavlovians). Sparked perhaps by the ethologists, the field of animal behavior, if occasionally contentious, is lively and productive. (39, 40, 41, 42, 43) Many other disciplines relate to primatology as well as to a knowledge of man at a cellular, organismic (both physiological and psychological), and a sociological level. The following partial list gives an idea of the diversity of relevant disciplines: enzyme and protein chemistry, behavioral genetics, neurophysiology and neuroendocrinology, studies of dreaming, of sensory deprivation and excess (with its challenge of delineating concepts of sensory "harmony"), of circadian rhythms, psychopharmacology, the behavioral basis of perception, figure-ground phenomena, brain and computer circuitry, communications and information theory, games theory, comparative philology and microlinguistics. All are contributors, and most of them were nonexistent until recently. They make theory-building complex but they make it possible. (44, 45)

(b) The bias we acquire as members of a society that stresses "individualism" renders this rather simple concept difficult to grasp and retain. We tend to feel that our individualism, which was secondary to our break with the rigid political-economic-religious dominances of Europe, is a fundamental and independent fact of human nature. This "individualism" entertains such fictions as survival of the individual separated from the group when clearly, except for short intervals after maturity, separateness is impossible. Even the hermit has had years of human tutelage, and his world is probably inhabited with imaginary people anyway. Concepts like these remain implicit in much of our thinking. The terms "asocial" and "antisocial" are really misnomers since, like separateness, they are not compatible, except temporarily, with development or survival. Relative terms like "dyssocial" or "disharmonious social behavior" are more precise. As for "personality" as being a human prerogative, no error could be greater. The "personalities" of individual non-human primates are notorious and well known to primatologists.

(c) This behavior has been referred to as "spatial equilibration" and is most easily demonstrated for mature males during the breeding season but is observable for other group activities as well. (46, 47) A field investigator states that if she had a helicopter photo of a troop of langur monkeys raiding a farmer's fields she could (even though the individuals appeared only as black spots) identify every member of the troop, infants, mothers, juveniles, etc., simply by measuring the distances between the spots. If the field would "spatially" accommodate only, say, twenty-three of the thirty individuals constituting the troop, she could tell which seven remained outside the borders of the field. This indeed demonstrates how literal is spacing behavior in the non-human primate. The human "metaphorical" form of spacing, e.g., "we are very close" often—with emotional tension—becomes literal! (18)

(d) The least evolved human groups, e.g., the natives of the Kalahari Desert, simple food gatherers and hunters, have a vocabulary estimated at eighty words, and their communications system is so embedded in posture and gesture that they have difficulty communicating in the dark. Nonhuman primates have a range of sounds conveying distinguishable meanings, according to some observers, of, perhaps, fifteen to thirty, divisible into five or six groups of calls. There is a fair degree of specificity. A warning call occurring and recorded when a leopard threatens a primate group is not confused with a warning call recorded when the group has spotted a snake or hawk. When the calls are played back over loud speakers to the animals, they assume postures and behaviors appropriate to the nature of the threats. Similarly a tape recording of chimpanzees when it was raining sent them scurrying for cover when it was played back during fair weather. These examples are not submitted to illustrate any closeness between nonhuman primate and human communication. The Kalahari native has speech, i.e., it is phonetic, a sound substitutes for an idea, and the sounds are formalized statements of relationships between things. The nonhuman primate does not. But the two systems can still be discussed together. This is no commentary on any limitation of the Kalahari native's intelligence but reflects the utter and monotonous simplicity of his environment and daily activity.

[Since writing this passage I have been informed through the kindness of Dr. Doyle and Professors John Blacking and Desmond Cole, all of the University of Witwatersrand, Johannesburg that the statement is false, that the Bushman vocabulary, like that of any Bantu tribe, is deficient only in terms for (Western) gadgetry, and is approximately twice the size of the vocabulary employed by Shakespeare.

I leave this note as originally written, first, out of understandable desire for self-flagellation, and, second, in the pious hope that some master of comparative linguistics will be sympathetic to my plight and furnish some example to support my thesis. I am groping for some understanding between vocalization-verbalization and the external world. Certain Amerind languages have one word for bird and one other word for all other airborne objects. On the other hand, the Laplander has a dozen or so words for our one word, snow. In short, the thesis here espoused is that sounds—simply vocal or verbal—serve as potential or actual and meaningful communicable "slices" of the universe of things, actions, or relationships, tending toward the "involuntary-unaware" in nonhuman primate and toward the "voluntary-aware" in human beings. The phylogeny of human speech will forever be as "the snows of yesteryear," and so much is unsettled in its ontogeny that we cannot discuss it here. C. F. Hockett's work (25) must again be recommended.]

(e) The fate of these obsolete or vestigial nonverbal communication forms has been studied. (48, 49) In nonhuman primates they serve as components of display behavior, which probably serve to let off excess "energy-emotion." In human beings this applies also, but to the extent that they do not contaminate verbal communications they seem to have branched off into ritual and ceremony, at first with powerful implications of magic and supplication, but later as the taproot for many of our cultural pursuits. This is not, of course, to be construed as indicating a superiority of verbal over nonverbal communication. Indeed, the nonverbal is usually the language of beauty and tenderness. Colloquially, pretty is as pretty does.

(f) Psychiatrists, of all people, should understand this. Yet, here is an example from a current journal. The author is quoting Freud: ". . . the character of the ego is a precipitate of abandoned object-cathexes and . . . it contains the history of those object-choices." We can launch discussions of this statement in a number of directions, e.g., the use of the word "object" when referring to human beings, or which individuals or groups in our culture would understand the statement or which would not, etc. But the more interesting point is that the author holds it up as an example of an "elegantly simple statement." And further, this is from an article dealing with the phenomena of "cultural exclusion." (50) The simple fact is that we all exclude others, and we all hide our meaning, and we all use language to do so.

(g) We do not wish to discredit speech. It is given its full role in the subsequent accumulations of man—material, religious, artistic, and otherwise. Overevaluation of the spoken word is characteristic of the primitive-magic stage of development. We can still excuse that in the poet and others. But it has no place in psychiatry, where speech is merely a communications tool and a means to an end. A quote from H. S. Sullivan is relevant here: "There are people who seem completely staggered when one talks about nonverbal referential processes—that is, wordlesss thinking: these people simply seem to have no ability to grasp the idea that a great deal of covert living—living that is not objectively observable but only inferable—can go on without the use of words. The brute fact is, as I see it, that most of living goes on that way." (51)

(h) Man maintains fetal characteristics throughout life, a biological phenomenon called neoteny. But psychologically, too, he tends to remain immature, and, while we may resent the Peter Pan within us, we also retain for a long time the wonderment and imagination that leads to new things and new ways. The implications of this are considerable for the grave problems facing society in developing meaningful and wholesome attitudes toward the young. With automation, cheap power, a consuming as opposed to a productive social emphasis, the peer-play period of life is being stretched and lengthened to a remarkable degree. In this lengthened spectrum both family and school functions dwindle in significance and influence. The adults are confused, perplexed, even angered by this simple fact. The young know it, turn elsewhere for experience crucial for new forms of growth, breaking communications with parents and school and, naturally, increase the incidence of serious "goofs" whether with drugs, sex, violation of ethical moral precepts, obsessions with "my mother, the car" and other mechanical gadgets.

(i) The term "developing organism" is preferable to the term "developing nervous system" because conceptual or thinking behavior requires the participation of parts of the organism other than just the nervous system. Thinking, at least the form of thinking called for in problem-solving under experimental conditions, is regularly accompanied by an increase in muscle tension (not to mention many other physiological changes), which usually is not visible but is detectable by electrically measured action potentials taken of the muscles themselves. This is true even of the muscles of speech. On occasion, a word used in solving a problem may be identified by the configuration of the electrical potential readings; that is, the experimenter can tell what word the subject had in mind. (52) In deaf people who talk with the hands, the changes in electrical potential during thought occur in the muscles of their hands, not in the muscles of speech. Whether there exist forms of thought involving nervous tissue only will require further study and sharper definitions. Recent studies show that the forms of thought change with sensory deprivation, with variant states of the nervous system as obtained in changes of levels of arousal and dreaming and, of course, with drugs and with alterations in chemical or metabolic states. The relationship of speech and other aspects of the symbolic-conceptual processes to the metabolic and endocrine phenomena ongoing in the organism is a crucial and very large field for continuing study. At this time, we can assert only that all forms of conceptual thought require a relatively intact organism, certainly for most of the time involved in the process.

(j) Not that laboratory studies have been misleading; indeed, it is the reciprocity that exists between laboratory and field study that has made modern primatology the science it is. Laboratory studies established the fact that the chimpanzee is for a number of years more intelligent than the human infant of the same age, as measured by learning and by tests of problem solving. These years cover that period of development which is crucial for future socialization and psychological well-being.

An anecdote that leaked out of a government research laboratory in Texas has it that a well-conditioned (and obviously well-motivated) chimpanzee defeated a visiting general in a game of tic-tac-toe; since then, the number of challengers has dwindled. This, too, indicates a certain sharpness of intelligence, even in a laboratory setting. But true intelligence is best estimated under natural conditions whenever possible.

(k) My psychiatric training required the study of a number of distinct psychiatric languages, e.g., Meyerian, Freudian, Sullivanian, Jungian, Adlerian. Few terms or concepts are interchangeable even within psychiatry; they are virtually useless for other scientific disciplines. (See also 53)

(l) The untenability of disembodied "cognitive" behavior to a physician or anyone well grounded in physiology can be appreciated. (54)

(m) One could, perhaps, classify these models as examples of "ruminative" or "investigative" or "appetitive" behaviors, although these are not strictly behavioral entities. Appetitive behaviors are best conceived of as vague "rest-lessnesses" out of which more definitive behavior arises. Indeed, thought, medi-tation, and curiosity, particularly, can be imagined as forms of "appetitive" behavior carried to a peculiar length in man and, hence, most difficult to trace to the particular behavioral entities they give rise to. In other words, man focusing with exquisite refinement on a state of being we can call sentience came up with an image of himself as godlike, heroic, or whatever. The only difficulty is that he was wrong and that these images probably had much to do with defenses against his feeling the opposite.

While any behavior is ongoing, other behaviors, covert or inhibited, are building up, largely outside of awareness, preparatory to overt manifestation. We are faced with the problem of dealing with behaviors that are not yet mani-fest. Hopefully, the study of circadian rhythms and other biologic rhythms will give us clues to understanding these. For this, the human furnishes a good sub-ject because verbal clues may be the earliest available in spotting incipient behavior, at least until better chemical or electrical methods are developed. And we can understand a communication, as with any form of behavior, only when we understand what is not being communicated as well as what is. A communication is simply a wave in a vast sea, and we cannot understand that wave without understanding nonwaves, i.e., swells, tides, currents, winds, shore-lines, all of which determine that wave which is part of "the sea around us."

We know so little about the substrates of cognition and concept formation that theories remain idiosyncratic, even if artistic and delightful. This paper does not, therefore, recommend that as a theory it be accepted. It recommends that the data be processed again and again.

(n) Much interesting data for understanding animal behavior continues to come from the laboratories of the neuroendocrinologists and it invites specu-lation about human behavior as well. A generation ago the concepts of Sir Charles S. Sherrington, the reflex arc, and the concept of the pituitary as the "master gland" dominated the thinking in this field. Transection of the spinal cord and brain stem was the general experimental technique for studying CNS function. This has been replaced for brain study by techniques studying longitudinal structures and function. The work of H. W. Magoun and others in elucidating the ascending reticular substance has brought about important discoveries and a number of new views.

Recent theory views the brain as possessing three "analyzor-integrator" mechanisms: *(1)* the brain stem reticular formation, *(2)* the limbic-striatal system, and *(3)* the thalamo-neocortical system. The first system seems to be related to integrating the data connected with "posture," i.e., maintaining the orientation of the organism in space, and includes visceral adjustments as well as muscular. The second system subserves visceral and endocrine adjustments connected with alertness and focussing of attention, and, even with the neocortex removed, this system can control behaviors as complex as fighting, flight, food procurement, and sexual behavior. What components of mothering behavior it controls are naturally of relevance to the thesis outlined in this paper and may be delineated in future studies. The third system, the thalamo-neocortical, is the sole recipient of the major epicritic lemniscus afferents, but it also receives major input from systems 1 and 2. Thus, the thalamo-neocortical system is an analyzor-integrator mechanism which is connected with the organism's environment in two ways. First is the connection by direct, fast-acting sensory nerves, an evolutionary development which is characteristic of primates. The second is by indirect input from the "old" protopathic centers which have to do with "feelings," with behavioral attitudes or moods, such as anxious, angry, predatory, relaxed, sexual, and maternal. (55)

What comments can we make about the neocortex, man's most vaunted possession?

First, complex behavior such as fighting, food-procuring, and sexual behavior is possible without the neocortex.

Further, the unique ability of the neocortex lies, primarily, in sensory discrimination and analysis, and it is in this area that man so greatly surpasses his nearest primate relatives. Though our motor potential does not greatly exceed our primate relatives, and in some spheres we are not their equals, our ability to form sense percepts and to combine these into infinite concepts is what really underlies our superior ability to design complex and intricate behavioral patterns. While the neocortex can inhibit basic behaviors for indefinite periods of time, or can institute modifications of these basic behaviors to the point where they are virtually unrecognizable (particularly if the organism wishes to conceal them), the neocortex cannot change basic behavior. The forms of basic behavior are both determined and limited by structures below the neocortex.

Much work lies ahead in differentiating between "learned" as opposed to "instinctual" behavior. Probably no behavior exists which is purely instinctual; effects of learning have been demonstrated for earthworms and even ameba. An interesting relationship between so-called instinctual and learned behavior is illustrated in the development of male sexual behavior. Early castration of the human male prevents the development of male sexual behavior. If, however, castration follows the establishment of the male sexual behavior, the behavior pattern is not destroyed. The "learned" pattern makes the male hormone, necessary for learning, unnecessary for maintenance. Incidentally, subcortical EEG's of man and chimpanzee are virtually indistinguishable, an interesting and potentially crucial lead for understanding basic mood-behavior phenomena. (56) The word "instinct" will drop out of the vocabulary of behavioral scientists. DNA-RNA is as close to the concept of instinct as we can come. The hereditary organism can be said to exist previous to interchange (experience) with the environment only momentarily. From then on experience is physico-chemical, a division of which we can label social learning, or social communication.

(o) Application of this theory to Psychotherapy.

Having applied the present theory to psychotherapy over the past decade and having found it workable—sometimes remarkably so—I would make some remarks on its advantages which may be found interesting and, possibly, useful.

First, a definition of the therapist is important in clarifying the "therapeutic transaction." Freud defined the therapist as a scientist whose science is psychoanalysis which deals with the wanderings of a hypothetical biological energy, libido, and with its stasis in the hypothetical Oedipus complex. Sullivan defined the therapist as an expert in interpersonal relationships whose expertise is a saleable commodity, the sale of which is an honest way to make a living. (He further implied that it is, perforce, one of the most backbreaking, heartbreaking, agonizing ways of making a living one can choose. I know of no one truly involved in doing therapy who would disagree.) I think of Jung as one who helped "the other" explore the poetry of the soul, and of Adler as a teacher, but I do not have their precise definitions of the therapist. Fromm and some of the Existentialist groups postulate a kind of quasi-mystical relationship as the essence of the therapeutic transaction. Just how these various groups define the therapist is difficult to grasp, and there are probably hotly debated differences between the groups. Clues to their beliefs can be obtained from the study of Zen Buddhism, Soren Kierkegaard, Martin Buber, Martin Heidegger, Ludwig Binswanger, Jean-Paul Sartre, and others. Relationships of the "I-Thou" type characterize several of these schools, suggesting an origin of their basic views in peer behavior, (57) the logical extension of which would be the "brotherhood of man." If this is so there would seem to be little justification for the overtones of mysticism which so often surround them. This implies no disrespect for Existentialism or Zen Buddhism or other modes of nondualistic experience. As these have been presented in Western society, however, they seem little more than intellectual bubbles. Even in the Orient, Zen Buddhism is not submitted as the answer to "behavioral-emotional-social" breakdown. Zen (and a number of other philosophies invading psychiatry) can be thought of as the cutoff point, where psychiatry ends, i.e., when the "mothering team's" job has been finished and the choice of a mature philosophy is faced. Cases of "interminable" therapy are often those where the therapist neither sees nor understands his "mothering" role and is either unable or unwilling to fulfill it. The disdain of "social activists" toward psychiatrists who "cocoonize" the patient, eschew social protest, and cling to the cloistered security of the "nursery" becomes understandable.

In the present theory the therapist is simply defined as "society's specialist in corrective foster mothering," a most important, indeed, a key member and honorable member of the "mothering team."

While one can enact the roles of therapist as previously defined, I do not, truthfully, understand how one can *feel* any of them. On the other hand, once the idea had occurred to me—probably sparked by primatology where one sees no fathering, only siring—I found no difficulty in *feeling* that I am *a mother* or, since I am anatomically a male, that I feel capable of *mothering behavior.* Again, it is to be emphasized that I do not say, fathering, because it is redundant; fathering is simply mothering learned and performed by a male. I am capable of mothering behavior because I learned it from both my mother and father and a long list of parental surrogates and "assistants" who had, in turn, learned it from others. Once I felt no conflict with the idea of my "feeling" or showing mothering behavior, I began to feel comfortable with "the patient," not only in exploring the miscarriages of mothering behavior (i.e., from the entire mothering team) as the "patient" experienced it, but I began to feel quite capable of offering "corrective foster mothering" behavior in whatever form my imagination and judgment dictated as appropriate. This could include anything from doing nothing, but simply providing the passive presence and comfort of another human, to various degrees of activity such as help, advice, teaching, shared investigation, or simply verbal and nonverbal communication of appreciation and respect. Since patients' experience with and attitudes toward "mothering behavior" vary all the way from terror, often reported by those labeled "schizophrenic," to lesser degrees of negativism, I offer mothering behavior only as the patient senses the need of it, does not confuse it with any of the remaining five categories of primate social behavior, can ask for it, or can, at least, accept it without fear, guilt, or the feeling that his or her mother (real or fancied) will be jealous. It takes very little time for "patients" (at least those without brain damage or severe disorientation) to sense that I have no hidden desires to win a dominance struggle, expand my "territory" at their expense, enforce my spacing desires, literal or figurative, rather than theirs, or to answer my sexual needs actively or vicariously, and also to sense that I will not force friendship, indeed, though I am friendly. The question of their choosing me or my choosing them as friends will be decided in the future as their needs for mothering disappear or, stated another way, I can be "friendly and playful" but it is clear that we are not playing. (The nonhuman primate mother does not play with her offspring but rather teaches it to play. Play is with peers only.) It will be clear to anyone who has done therapy how often difficulties occur which can be easily recognized as falling into the above five categories. Once it is clear that we are involved in a "mothering transaction," the discrimination that is called for from the patient is simply that he not confuse my mothering behavior with that of anyone else, whether the other happens to be his biologic mother or any member of his mothering team. This, to me, is the essence of transference distortions; I am inclined to think it the only one.

The therapist must be on guard against offering mothering behavior for unwholesome motives, i.e., motives not totally and directly related to the welfare of the person one is dealing with. The danger is that the therapist offer (even force) mothering behavior on the patient to demonstrate (possibly to the therapist's mother) that the therapist needs no mothering, that, on the contrary, he is a supplier, and that his kind of mothering is far superior to anything he received. This unresolved competition with the mother (or some member of the mothering team) by the therapist is a common one, even in experienced therapists, and often evokes conflict and confusion in the therapeutic transaction which is variously mislabeled as Oedipal, homosexual, separation anxiety, none of which is basic but which simply obscures unresolved "intrapsychic" conflict between therapist and his mother.

"Mothering behavior" by the therapist is denied officially by both Freudian and Sullivanian therapists. Confidential talks with therapists from both schools lead me to believe, however, that it is constantly present; it is "bootlegged" in, so to speak, under one guise or another. The fact that a therapist becomes an expert in the language of the "unconscious" or the language of the "psychotic," or in the nuances of interpersonal transactions is no proof that his behavior is not derived from mothering. "Mothering behavior" includes all kinds of technical skills from removal of splinters to sharp observations on where one's thinking, feeling, and behavior is amiss.

My conception of the therapist in Freudian, Sullivanian, and Fromm-Existentialist therapies is not to be construed as a blanket indictment. The assertion is made, simply, that they are best examined as showing "mothering behavior" and that the awareness of this fact may lead, not only to the improvement of therapy, but also to the possibility of studying the therapeutic transaction as having a biologic base. The absence of signs of affection toward the patient in either Freudian or Sullivanian therapists is not proof of no "mothering behavior," indeed, for a particular patient at a particular time it may be the best possible "mothering behavior." The following from Darwin is worth noting: "No emotion is stronger than maternal love; but a mother may feel the deepest love for her infant and not show it by any outward sign. . . ." (58)

One wonders at times why the thesis outlined here was not developed long ago. Certainly a number of thinkers, Margaret Mead and Ian D. Suttie, to mention two, have made key statements on "fathering" and "mother love." One wonders why, with the emphasis on subjectivity that is called for in the training curricula to do psychoanalysis or "deep" or "intensive" psychotherapy, the awareness of the simple identity between therapy and "mothering behavior" is not completely reported and discussed. Perhaps male therapists are threatened by such awareness and females too timid to report it. In any event, many psychiatrists understandably being so opposed to "bad mothering" have overlooked the infinite patterns and uses of "good mothering."

If, indeed, "mothering behavior" has entered the therapies of all the schools, unlabeled and unrecognized, we have at last some basis of understanding why studies of all schools show essentially the same benefits. The common ingredient of all therapies may be the "mothering behavior."

The basic question in psychotherapy, whether implied or asked, is not, "What is your mother like?" Rather, it is, "From what persons did you receive mothering behavior?" "What were they like, what was good and bad about each, were they in conflict, how much appreciation did each demand?" The number of times that a patient suddenly realizes that the father, or a nurse-maid, or occasionally a neighbor, really deserved the label "mother," according to the patient, will surprise many therapists. And the ease with which the patient is able to accept foster-mothering as reflected in the life story and as demonstrated in the therapeutic relationship is a good measure of the patient's capacity for improvement.

Having given up "projective" therapy, the whole concept of waiting for a transference neurosis to develop is discarded. "Transference distortions," i.e., misunderstandings and miscommunications, are the very stuff of living and therapy, and the quicker one gets to work on them (gently, brother) the better. As for what the "patient" learns or wants to learn about me, my only task is to evaluate the reasons for his interest, mention possible morbid motives in passing, but to respond openly and candidly. "Tell me about when you were young, mommy (daddy)," is a natural and healthy manifestation of childhood growth. Not only do I respond to that simply and candidly, but I am quite ready to tell a story, even one with a moral. Further, six categories of social behavior are being monitored in our relationship. I have no hesitancy in sharing my view of how they work, since these are the very same categories of behavior the patient is encountering in day-to-day living. It should be unnecessary to say that these are not forced or imposed on the "patient"; further, evidence of satisfaction—if not joy—in the therapist need not be hidden either. Joy, like measles, is contagious.

Any controversy arising over these views of the therapist's role will most likely relate to conflicts in the definitions of "mothering," and, indeed, extended definitions (including, alas, the acceptance of the multiple factors and the Principle of Indeterminacy in human behavior) are necessary. The thesis here is, of course, that the essence of mothering is not "total acceptance," a term often heard in therapy conferences and emphasized in the writings of Fromm and others. The Pieta symbolizes mothering only under extremely heroic circumstances, a situation which occurs but rarely in therapy, although the patient often claims otherwise. Mothering is that artful combination of acceptance and rejection which stimulates growth, leads to skill in peer-play behavior, and eventually to full maturity.

REFERENCES

1. Irven DeVore, ed., PRIMATE BEHAVIOR: FIELD STUDIES OF MONKEYS AND APES, New York: Holt, Rinehart & Winston, 1965.

2. Allan M. Schrier, Harry F. Harlow, and Fred Stollnitz, eds., BEHAVIOR OF NONHUMAN PRIMATES: MODERN RESEARCH TRENDS, New York: Academic Press, 1965.

3. A. H. Esser, A. S. Chamberlain, E. D. Chapple, and N. S. Kline, *Territoriality of Patients on a Research Ward,* RECENT ADVANCES IN BIOLOGICAL PSYCHIATRY (VII), Joseph Wortis, ed., New York: Plenum Press, 1965.

4. N. G. Blurton Jones, *An Ethological Study of Some Aspects of Social Behavior of Children in Nursery School,* PRIMATE ETHOLOGY, Desmond M. Morris, ed., London: George Weidenfeld & Nicholson, 1967.

5. John Price, *The Dominance Hierarchy and the Evolution of Mental Illness,* LANCET, 2: 243, 1967.

6. Frank A. Beach, *The Snark Was a Boojum,* AMERICAN PSYCHOLOGIST, 5:115, 1950.

7. Henry Eliot Howard, TERRITORY IN BIRD LIFE, London: John Murray, 1920.

8. Thorleif Schjelderup-Ebbe, *Beitrage zur Sozialpsychologie des Haushuhns,* ZEITSCHRIFT FÜR PSYCHOLOGIE UND PHYSIOLOGIE DER SINNESORGANE, 1 Abteilung, 88: 226, 1922.

9. F. H. Rohles, Jr., THE CHIMPANZEE: A TOPICAL BIBLIOGRAPHY, 6571st Aeromedical Research Laboratory, Holloman Air Force Base, New Mexico, June 1962.

10. THE BABOON, an annotated bibliography compiled by the Biological Sciences Communication Project, The George Washington University, for The Southwest Foundation for Research and Education (Harold Vagtborg, director), San Antonio, Texas, 1964.

11. J. P. Scott, ANIMAL BEHAVIOR, Chicago: University of Chicago Press, 1958.

12. Stuart A. Altmann, *Primate Behavior in Review,* SCIENCE, 150:1440, 1965.

13. V. C. Wynne-Edwards, ANIMAL DISPERSION IN RELATION TO SOCIAL BEHAVIOR, Edinburgh: Oliver & Boyd, 1962.

14. Jane Van Lawick-Goodall, *New Discoveries Among Africa's Chimpanzees,* NATIONAL GEOGRAPHIC MAGAZINE, 128:802, 1965.

15. Clarence R. Carpenter, *A Field Study of the Behavior and Social Relations of Howling Monkeys,* COMPARATIVE PSYCHOLOGY MONOGRAPHS, 10:1, 1934.

16. K. R. L. Hall, *Social Interaction of Adult Males and Adult Females in Patas Monkey Groups,* Paper read for the American Association for the Advancement of Science, Montreal, December 1964.

17. Stuart A. Altmann, *Communication and Language,* Behavioral Sciences Seminar, The Rockefeller University, October-December, 1967.

18. Phyllis Jay, personal communication.

19. Hans Kummer, *Sociales Verhalten einer Mantelpavian-Gruppe*, BEIHEFTE ZUR SCHWEIZERISCHEN ZEITSCHRIFT FÜR PSYCHOLOGIE UND IHRE ANDWENDUNGEN, Supplement 33: 1, 1957.

20. Colter Rule, *A Biologically Based Theory of Human Behavior and Its Implications for Psychiatry*, AMERICAN JOURNAL OF PSYCHIATRY, 121:344, 1964.

21. Sherwood L. Washburn, ed., SOCIAL LIFE OF EARLY MAN, Viking Fund Publications in Anthropology No. 31, distributed through CURRENT ANTHROPOLOGY for the Wenner-Gren Foundation for Anthropological Research, New York, 1961.

22. Anne Roe and George Gaylord Simpson, eds., BEHAVIOR AND EVOLUTION, New Haven, Conn.: Yale University Press, 1958.

23. C. H. Southwick, ed., PRIMATE SOCIAL BEHAVIOR, Princeton, N.J.: Van Nostrand, 1963.

24. Kenneth P. Oakley, *On Man's Use of Fire, with Comments on Tool-Making and Hunting*, SOCIAL LIFE OF EARLY MAN, *op. cit.*

25. C. F. Hockett, *Logical Considerations in the Study of Animal Communication*, ANIMAL SOUNDS AND COMMUNICATION, W. E. Lanyon and W. N. Tavolga, eds., (Washington, D.C.: American Institute of Biological Sciences, Publication 7, 1960), pp. 392–430.

26. Wilder Penfield and Lamar Roberts, SPEECH AND BRAIN MECHANISMS, Princeton, N.J.: Princeton University Press, 1959.

27. Edward Sapir, *The Status of Linguistics as a Science*, LANGUAGE, 5:207, 1929.

28. Jarvis R. Bastian, *Primate Signaling Systems and Human Languages*, PRIMATE BEHAVIOR: FIELD STUDIES OF MONKEYS AND APES, *op. cit.*, p. 585.

29. Harry F. Harlow, *Primary Affectional Patterns in Primates*, AMERICAN JOURNAL OF ORTHOPSYCHIATRY, 30:676, 1960.

30. Jane Van Lawick-Goodall, *Chimpanzees of the Gombe Stream Reserve*, PRIMATE BEHAVIOR: FIELD STUDIES OF MONKEYS AND APES, *op. cit.*, p. 425.

31. Phyllis Jay, *The Common Langur of North India*, PRIMATE BEHAVIOR: FIELD STUDIES OF MONKEYS AND APES, *op. cit.*, p. 197.

32. Stuart A. Altmann, *Social Behavior of Amboseli Baboons*, Film and remarks for American Association for the Advancement of Science, Montreal, December 1964.

33. Helen Swick Perry and Mary Ladd Gawel, eds., HARRY STACK SULLIVAN: THE INTERPERSONAL THEORY OF PSYCHIATRY, New York: Norton, 1953.

34. Michel Foucault, MADNESS AND CIVILIZATION: A HISTORY OF INSANITY IN THE AGE OF REASON, New York: Pantheon, 1965.

35. Kenneth P. Oakley, *A Definition of Man*, SCIENCE NEWS, 20: 69, Harmondsworth, Middlesex, England: Penguin Books, 1951.

36. Sherwood L. Washburn and Virginia Avis, *Evolution of Human Behavior*, BEHAVIOR AND EVOLUTION, Anne Roe and George Gaylord Simpson, eds., (New Haven, Conn.: Yale University Press, 1958), pp. 421–436.

37. Adolph H. Schultz, *Einige Beobachtungen und Masse am Skelett von Oreopithecus im Vergleich mit anderen catarrhinen Primaten*, ZEITSCHRIFT FÜR MORPHOLOGIE UND ANTHROPOLOGIE, 50: 136, 1960.

38. Kenneth P. Oakley, *Notes on L. S. B. Leakey's* "THE FIRST MEN:" RECENT DISCOVERIES IN EAST AFRICA, ANTIQUITY, 31:286, 1957.

39. Theodore C. Schneirla, *Aspects of Stimulation and Organization in Approach/Withdrawal Processes Underlying Vertebrate Behavioral Development*, ADVANCES IN THE STUDY OF BEHAVIOR, I, D. S. Lehrman, R. A. Hinde, and Evelyn Shaw, eds., (New York: Academic Press, 1965), p. 2.

40. Konrad Lorenz, INSTINCTIVE BEHAVIOR: THE DEVELOPMENT OF A MODERN CONCEPT, Claire H. Schiller, ed., (New York: International Universities Press, 1957), Chapters I, II, III, V, and VII.

41. J. P. Scott, *Critical Periods in Behavioral Development*, SCIENCE, 138: 949, 1962.

42. Theodore C. Schneirla and J. S. Rosenblatt, *Critical Periods in the Development of Behavior*, READINGS IN ANIMAL BEHAVIOR, T. E. McGill, ed., (New York: Holt, Rinehart & Winston, 1965), p. 287.

43. J. P. Scott, *Reply to Schneirla and Rosenblatt*, READINGS IN ANIMAL BEHAVIOR, *op. cit.*, p. 290.

44. George W. Brooks and Ernst Mueller, *Serum Urate Concentrations Among University Professors: Relation to Drive, Achievement and Leadership*, JOURNAL OF AMERICAN MEDICAL ASSOCIATION, 195: 415, 1966.

45. E. Orowan, *The Origin of Man*, NATURE, 175: 683, 1955.

46. Clarence R. Carpenter, *Societies of Monkeys and Apes*, BIOLOGICAL SYMPOSIA, Robert Redfield, ed., 8: 177, 1942.

47. Jacob von Uexküll, *A Stroll Through the Worlds of Animals and Men*, INSTINCTIVE BEHAVIOR: THE DEVELOPMENT OF A MODERN CONCEPT, *op. cit.*, pp. 5–82.

48. Jurgen Ruesch, THERAPEUTIC COMMUNICATION, New York: Norton, 1961.

49. ————— and Gregory Bateson, COMMUNICATION, New York: Norton, 1951.

50. Eugene B. Brody, *Cultural Exclusion, Character and Illness*, AMERICAN JOURNAL OF PSYCHIATRY, 122: 852, 1966.

51. H. S. Sullivan, Quoted in: J. Ruesch and Weldon Kees, NONVERBAL

COMMUNICATION, Berkeley: University of California Press, 1956.

52. Edmund Jacobson, *Electrophysiology of Mental Activities,* AMERICAN JOURNAL OF PSYCHOLOGY, 44: 677, 1932.

53. Roy R. Grinker, Sr., *The Sciences of Psychiatry: Fields, Fences and Riders,* AMERICAN JOURNAL OF PSYCHIATRY, 122: 367, 1965.

54. Silvano Arieti, *Conceptual and Cognitive Psychiatry,* AMERICAN JOURNAL OF PSYCHIATRY, 122: 361, 1965.

55. A. V. Nalbandov, ed., ADVANCES IN NEUROENDOCRINOLOGY, Urbana: University of Illinois Press, 1963.

56. J. M. Rhodes, M. L. Reite, D. Brown, and W. R. Adley, *Cortical-Subcortical Relationships in the Chimpanzee During Different Phases of Sleep,* ELECTROENCEPHALOGRAPHY AND CLINICAL NEUROPHYSIOLOGY, 17: 449, 1964.

57. Marian Hoppin, personal communication.

58. Charles Darwin, THE EXPRESSION OF THE EMOTIONS IN MAN AND ANIMALS, New York: D. Appleton & Co., 1873.

(Printed jointly with PERSPECTIVES IN BIOLOGY AND MEDICINE)

Reprinted from PERSPECTIVES IN BIOLOGY AND MEDICINE
Vol. 10, No. 2, Winter 1967
c 1967 by The University of Chicago. All rights reserved.
Printed in U.S.A.

A THEORY OF HUMAN BEHAVIOR BASED ON
STUDIES OF NON-HUMAN PRIMATES

COLTER RULE, M.D.

Throughout the Middle Ages, man, under the guidance of theological leaders, was preoccupied with his immortal soul, with life hereafter, and with the types of ethical behaviors that would win a favored position in the next world. The Age of Reason, the industrial and scientific revolutions, and materialist philosophies offset all this and replaced it with the conviction that, since man could triumph over nature and toil, he could, in effect, have his heaven here on earth. This belief, too, is running its course, and enthusiasm over technological advances has begun to fade. Man the toolmaker excites us less and less. (A telecast of a recent Gemini mission in space shared the screen with a college football game!)

Philosophers decry sterile mechanistic advances by stating that they have failed mankind. This disenchantment stimulates us to reappraise man's relatedness to nature and the animal world. Such an endeavor is made feasible by an ever increasing flood of data arriving anywhere from *A* to *Z*, anthropology to zoology, and much of this data bears directly on behavior. Less than two decades ago, a leading psychologist discussing research in behavior could define psychology as "the study of learning in white rats and college sophomores" [1]. Today, the "information explosion" has destroyed the boundaries of the academic disciplines; the multi-disciplinary study is the rule rather than the exception. Many fields and many studies contribute to knowledge of behavior whether at a cellular, physiological, psychological, or social level. Archeological discoveries have illuminated crucial areas in the origins of early man.[1] The controversy between the ethologists on the one hand and the classical learning theorists

---

[1] Primarily, that he was truly bipedal and a tool user with a brain volume not greatly exceeding that of present day apes [2–5].

(and Pavlovians) on the other has given rise to the somewhat contentious but productive science of animal behavior that exists today [6–10]. But there are many other contributors. Behavioral genetics, neurophysiology, neuroendocrinology, enzyme chemistry, brain and computer circuitry, communications and information theory, all have been deeply involved [11, 12]. Additional crucial and fruitful areas are the studies on circadian rhythms, sensory deprivation, physiology of dreaming, psychopharmacology, the behavioral basis of perception, figure-ground phenomena, etc.

One of the newest additions to the family of multidisciplinary specialties is primatology, barely a decade old. Ten years ago there existed only two centers for the study of primate behavior. Now there are many in both universities and government institutions; the number of field investigators has quadrupled and continues to increase, and the volume of literature is already unwieldy. Two surveys in book form, one mainly of field studies, the other reporting on laboratory research, were published in 1965 [13, 14]. One section of the annual convention of the American Association for the Advancement of Science two years ago was devoted entirely to primate behavior. In spite of accelerated effort, most primate studies raise more questions than they answer. Of the approximately 240 living species of non-human primates, reliable field studies are available for less than two dozen. Much work lies ahead. The absence of a solid foundation of reliable data has led a professional primatologist to remark that the amount of interest in primatology shown by scientists in general is out of all proportion to the amount of information available [15]. A possible explanation for this unusual degree of interest may be a rising ground swell of suspicion that in primatology the beginnings of human behaviors may be revealed. While the behaviors observed in non-human primates may be little more than seedlings when contrasted with the fully evolved behaviors as revealed in man, they seem, nevertheless, to be identifiable and to demonstrate crucial bridges between biological, psychological, and social man. For clinical psychiatrists, enough data has accumulated about primate social behaviors, about the ways their small societies (usually between fourteen and thirty individuals) are organized, and about dyadic behaviors (behaviors between any two individuals) to speculate about human behavior. Admittedly, the medical profession has never let the paucity of data interfere with its determination to build theories, however fanciful. Perhaps this privilege is justified by the ancient and awful responsibility medicine accepted from society, but another good reason for attempting to theorize about human behavior is the muddled, if not desperate, state of present-day psychiatric theory. Psychiatry was recently described by one of its leading thinkers as a kind of gaggle of cults exhibiting rituals and dialects, isolated from one another, none possessing a broad, integrated, and scientific view of man [16].

Several phenomena often described under "population statistics" are fundamental to understanding animal behavior, although their precise application to man is not yet known.

Localization.—Perhaps as fundamental to his being a social animal, man is primarily an organism that is attached, and remains attached, to a particular geographical spot near which he was most likely born and for which he formed a firm attachment early in life.[2] Regardless of the excitement created by the conquest of space—regardless of wars, migrations, and modern transportation—the vast majority of the world's people are born and die within the radius of a few miles. Compared to non-human primates, of course, the range over which early man traveled was great, hundreds as compared to a few dozen square miles. But man is no nomad, that is, he is not an animal born to wander. Indeed, in the whole animal world nomads are a rarity; much of what was thought to represent nomadism turns out to be migration between primary and secondary localization, for example, summer and winter migration.

Man differs from other animals in having overcome most barriers to free movement, much of this, of course, the result of the accumulated gadgetry of the past few decades. No limitation of bodily equipment now holds him back. Few physical obstacles, no insurmountable food shortages, and no hostile alien species contest his advance into new territory. Indeed, the main barriers to unrestricted movement may be those deep in his own nature, concepts as vague and yet as powerful as "home and mother," or "my people, my land, my country."[3]

Population size.—Man, though not a nomad, is surely a colonizer, and this has enabled him to multiply in vast numbers. The Malthus theory, with which Darwin concurred, stated that starvation, disease, and war were the sole factors operating to restrict the unlimited multiplication of

[2] If his social nature stems from psychological phenomena classified under "figure," this might be classified under "ground."

[3] Implications of such concepts may have importance for space exploration.

individuals, including man. Such a formulation was grossly misleading and has required modification. Animals do not blindly reproduce themselves. Rather, animals organize themselves into orderly populations and societies which have various and characteristic ways of controlling population growth. Just what natural laws operate and whether man follows them is one of the most important questions confronting society today [17]. Current scientific studies are seeking to uncover the determinants, not only of total populations, but of the lesser units of population, such as societies, colonies, groups. For such studies, non-human primate societies offer helpful material; for behavioral studies seeking to uncover other natural laws, primate societies are excellent. They are composed of small numbers of individuals. Many occupy habitats where visibility is good so that recognition of individuals is possible. Wide choice of environments, often for the same species, offers an unusual opportunity to study the relationship of behavior and environment.

Group size of non-human primates under natural conditions is not great, usually not much above thirty individuals. Group size, the differences between birth and death rates, is a vector of various forces, for example, food supply, predator, and other pressures. The limited data-processing capacity of non-human primates seems to preclude the maintenance of well-integrated groups much above the figure of thirty mentioned above. Aggregations up to several hundred animals have been described, but these may represent temporary associations of several groups coming together at night or congregating because of food supplies or other factors. The loose structure of certain chimpanzee groups, with individuals, mother-infant-juvenile, and adult male subgroups wandering at considerable distances from one another, has not yet been fully studied but may represent decreasing danger from predation and an increase in sociality rather than the opposite. The frequent intermingling of more than one group without agonistic behavior seems to bear this out [18]. Under captive or semicaptive conditions, as at Cayo Santiago or in certain of the Japanese primate centers where central provision stations have been installed, larger groups and different behaviors from those occurring under natural conditions are described.

Population density.—Like localization and population size, the density of a population cannot properly be called a "behavior." Indeed, it may be viewed as the result of behavior. At the same time, like environmental factors, it determines behavior.

Although multiple variables related to birth and death rates enter into the determination of population density, the number of individuals in a given unit of space, that is, density, is an index of sociality. The psychological counterpart of density has been called "cohesiveness" and represents the final balance between positive and negative social responses. It is also a figure that is the final average of "spacing," the social behavior regulating one's distance from other individuals of the group; spacing will be defined later. The various primate species have distinctive densities and scatter patterns under natural conditions. Howler monkeys are characteristically closely knit and cohesive [19]. Capuchins and baboons scatter widely during the daytime but gather closely together at night. The patas male (a swift-running, savannah-dwelling monkey) remains at a considerable distance from the main body of the group during the day and chooses a distant sleeping tree at night as well.[4] The scatter pattern of the chimpanzee was touched on previously. With hundreds of species still unstudied, indeed barely known, much needs to be learned about spacing, cohesiveness, density, intergroup mixing, etc.

The Fundamental Primate Social Behaviors (Including Man)

Primates are social animals. The social group is the unit, and the individual is a fragment of that unity. Separated from the group, the individual neither develops nor long survives; in the vast majority of primate species, the individual is born, lives, and dies never once out of sight or earshot of his social group. While this is not strictly true of the more evolved species, real exceptions are, even for man, rare and trivial. Separateness is an artificial condition; studies of the individual (or of two individuals or, indeed, of any fractions of the totality) are, hence, studies of artifacts, however defended—for example, in psychotherapy—as practical and necessary.[5]

---

[4] The patas male also thrashes around and makes much more noise than the rest of the group, indicating that the behavior relates to his drawing predator pressure toward himself and away from the group [20].

[5] The bias we acquire as members of a society that stresses "individualism" renders this rather simple concept difficult to grasp and retain. We tend to feel that our individualism, which was secondary to our break with the rigid political-economic-religious dominances of Europe, is a fundamental and independent fact of human nature. This individualism entertains such fictions as survival

A. INFANT-MATERNAL BEHAVIOR

The individual at birth is totally dependent upon mothering behavior from one or more individuals for survival and growth. This dependence decreases gradually with growth into and through the peer-play period of behavior and tends to disappear with the attainment of physical maturity.

B. PEER-PLAY BEHAVIOR

The individual after infancy embarks on a prolonged period of peer-play behavior. This phase of physical and intellectual growth is devoted to practicing and mastering social behaviors appropriate to each sex and establishing social rank.

C. COURTSHIP-SEXUAL BEHAVIOR

The individual, using components developed during the peer-play phase, develops the capacity for integrated courtship-sexual behavior. This initiates the period of maturity along with dominance behavior, leadership-follower behavior, maternal behavior, all of which continue until the period of aging and decline.

D. SPACING BEHAVIOR

The individual under natural conditions of social life maintains a specific distance between himself and every other member of his social group. This distance, corrected for known variables and averaged over time, indicates the strength and the nature of the social bond existing between any two individuals.[6]

---

of the individual separated from the group when clearly, except for short intervals after maturity, separateness is impossible. Even the hermit has had years of human tutelage, and his world is probably peopled with imaginary people anyway. Such concepts remain implicit in much of our thinking. The terms "antisocial" and "asocial" are really misnomers since, like separateness, they are not compatible, except temporarily, with development or survival. Relative terms like "dyssocial" or "disharmonious social behavior" are more precise.

[6] This behavior has been referred to as "spatial equilibration" and is most easily demonstrated for mature males, especially during the breeding season. The breakdown of spacing behavior into its many components, e.g., operational, tactile, visual, auditory, and olfactory space, as well as abstract concepts involving time, are a few of the areas for stimulating multidisciplined research. We are concerned here only with the basic "behavioral envelope," which can be clearly differentiated from the other basic "behavioral envelopes" [21, 22].

E. TERRITORIAL BEHAVIOR

The individual with other members of the social group will defend by threat or fight the territory over which he ranges. He will defend, as well, certain products of that territory—for example, food, tools, trinkets—that he finds, makes, or accumulates.

F. DOMINANCE BEHAVIOR

The individual strives throughout life to attain and/or maintain a dominant position in the hierarchy of power and privilege that exists in every primate society.

Alliance behavior.—(This is classified under dominance behavior because as observed in non-human primate societies it has thus far been restricted to dominance interactions.) Several forms of behavior involving more than two individuals have been observed. The following are examples:

1. Two individuals may suspend, more or less permanently, dominance interactions between themselves to join forces against a third individual.

2. An individual losing a dominance interaction to a second may forestall this loss by insinuating and ingratiating himself close to a larger or more dominant third individual, who "protects" him. [7]

3. Dominance rank is accorded the offspring of a high-ranking mother or family group. A female may be accorded dominance rank because she is the consort of a dominant male.

In this paper no detailed description of these behaviors or their ranges and variations will be undertaken. They were described briefly in an earlier paper [24], and extensive material is available at several levels of detail in the literature [13, 14, 25–27]. Observing these behaviors, at least on film, is most helpful; seeing is still believing and, in this case, understanding. Further detailed analysis of these six basic categories into their constituents and the determination of the relationships between the categories is an important field for future study. We are concerned here only with an overview and with deriving principles that will help apply these categories to human behaviors. In spite of the range and complexity of each behavior category, the fact remains that these behaviors are identifiable, easily distinguishable one from the other, and are basic to all

---

[7] This must not be mistaken for philanthropy on the part of the dominant animal. It occurs in non-human primates apparently because the third and dominant animal automatically responds to the aggression directed toward himself, not noticing that the aggression is really directed at the ingratiating animal that has come close to him [23].

primate groups studied thus far. There is no reason to believe that the same behavioral categories will not extend to all the approximately 240 living species. It is inconceivable that such categories of behavior would not have characterized one additional species, namely, early man. The question becomes, not whether man exhibited these behaviors, but rather what happened to them, and the thesis of this paper is, of course, that they have not disappeared but continue to operate following their own rhythms and can be demonstrated, monitored, and often measured with little difficulty.

The Mystery of Speech

Why did these behaviors seem to disappear? Or perhaps a more blunt question, what blinded us? One thinks immediately of the vast, often glaring, accumulations of human culture and civilization, which distract, preoccupy, fascinate, and often obsess us and which are traceable in almost linear fashion from television and automobiles back to the wheel, fire, and stone-flake weapons.[8]

But the real, the perennial, stumbling block to understanding is always the mystery of human speech. It is this that blocks the awareness of man's continuity with the animal world (mainly because it illustrates man's abstracting ability, his consciousness of self and, indirectly, his religiousness). It is this that is always submitted as final proof of the unbridgeable gap between man and beast. This barrier to understanding can disappear only with new concepts of the communications process [29]. When one compares communications in, say, apes with humans, one is tempted to propose that what the ape lacks in speech he makes up for by posture, gesture, facial expression, and vocalizations. Indeed, it has been said that he communicates about as well as the average excitable human trying to communicate with another human who does not speak the same language. Further, as others have noted, humans equipped with verbal skills ofttimes make a pretty messy business of communication, even at rather low levels of abstraction.

Human verbalization arose out of a communications matrix that once included posture, gesture, facial expression, and vocalization—all more or less undifferentiated.[9] The origin and development of speech made

---

[8] Some human societies do not make fire, they borrow it from neighbors [28].

[9] The vocabulary of the least evolved human groups, e.g., the natives of the Kalahari Desert, simple food gatherers and hunters, have a vocabulary estimated at eighty words, and their communications

posture, gesture, facial expression, and some vocal characteristics obsolete for many communications functions, and these non-verbal components tended to drop out. The separation is a tenuous one; in certain emotional states the entire communications complex reappears, and the verbal component becomes relatively small.[10] The dropping out of the non-verbal components of communication means that behavior and the underlying motives tend automatically to become covert. Man, of course, discovered the social premium on covertness and has refined it to an infinite degree. In implementing covertness, he naturally used speech. We have for so long thought of speech as serving as a communications vehicle that we have difficulty seeing that it also served the function of furthering covert behavior. Speech may or may not convey something, but it always hides something; it is noteworthy as much for what it conceals as for what it reveals. This is not accidental or incidental; this has been its function. In summary, speech, paradoxically, subserves the function of non-communication. To understand what a person says, we must fully understand what he does not say or, more practically, what he does not wish to say.[11] This

system is so embedded in posture and gesture that they have difficulty communicating in the dark. Non-human primates have a range of sounds conveying distinguishable meaning, according to some observers, of, perhaps, fifteen to thirty, divisible into five or six groups of calls. There is a fair degree of specificity. A warning call occurring and recorded when a leopard threatens a primate group is not confused with a warning call recorded when the group has spotted a snake. Played back to the primate group, they assume postures and behaviors appropriate to the appearance of these threats. A tape recording taken while it was raining sent chimpanzees scurrying for shelter when it was played back during fair weather. These examples are not submitted to illustrate how close non-human primate communications are to human. The Kalahari native has speech, i.e., it is phonetic, a sound substitutes for an idea, and the sounds are formalized statements of relationships between things. The non-human primate does not. But the two systems can still be discussed together. This is no commentary on any limitation of the Kalahari's intelligence but reflects the utter and monotonous simplicity of his environment and daily activity.

[10] The fate of these obsolete or vestigial non-verbal communications forms has been studied [30, 31]. In non-human primates they serve as components of display behavior, which probably serve to let off excess "energy emotion." In humans this may apply also, but to the extent that they do not contaminate verbal communications they seem to have funneled off into ritual and ceremony forming the taproot for many of man's cultural pursuits. This is not, of course, to be construed as indicating a superiority of verbal over non-verbal communication. Indeed, the non-verbal is usually the language of beauty and tenderness. Colloquially, pretty is as pretty does.

[11] Psychiatrists, of all people, should understand this. Yet, here is an example from a current journal. The author is quoting Freud: ". . . the character of the ego is a precipitate of abandoned object-cathexes and . . . it contains the history of those object-choices." We can launch discussions of this statement in many directions, e.g., the use of the word "object" when referring to human beings, or which individuals or groups in our culture would understand the statement or which would not, etc. But the more interesting point is that the author holds it up as an example of an "elegantly simple

may help clarify why our clues to the basic primate behaviors were lost in man; they simply became covert. The evidence for the continued operation of these behaviors, therefore, is no longer visual but has to be, primarily, verbal-auditory. Proof for their continued operation requires, furthermore, not only sensitivity and awareness but an ongoing intimate and unthreatening, possibly even tender, social transaction which permits the communication of such awareness.

Additional difficulty in trying to understand the differences and the similarities between human and non-human primates stems from a real lack of understanding and a constant, unscientific exaggeration of the importance of speech, that is, a verbal in contrast to a non-verbal communications system.[11] If speech is seen simply as the natural outcome of increasing differentiation and refinement in the evolution of communication—a breakthrough phenomenon at a certain point in the process of cephalization and hierarchization in the evolution of the nervous system —it loses much of its awesome, miraculous uniqueness.[12] More and more evidence is accumulating that this is, in fact, true.

Speech, "Thought," and Their Relationships

The laws of speech seem to follow the same general laws of the development of the nervous system and of the intelligence. In severe aphasia, for instance, when an individual is unable to say, "yes" or "no," he cannot convey this by shaking or nodding his head either. Nor can he do so with his hands, although muscles of both head and hands work well for other purposes. What was lost is the ability for conceptual thought, and both gesture and speech go with it [34].

---

statement"! And further, this is from an article dealing with the phenomena of "cultural exclusion" [32]. The simple fact is that we all exclude others, and we all hide our meaning, and we all use language to do so.

[11] The written word and all other communications advances that follow the discovery and development of speech are secondary matters.

[12] We do not wish to discredit speech. It is given its full role in the subsequent accumulations of man—material, religious, artistic, and otherwise. Overevaluation of the spoken word is characteristic of the primitive-magic stage of development; we can still excuse that in the poet and others. But it has no place in psychiatry, where speech is merely a communications tool and a means to an end. A quote from Sullivan is relevant here: "There are people who seem completely staggered when one talks about nonverbal referential processes—that is, wordless thinking: these people simply seem to have no ability to grasp the idea that a great deal of covert living—living that is not objectively observable but only inferable—can go on without the use of words. The brute fact is, as I see it, that most of living goes on that way" [33].

This paper is not the place to discuss abstract, symbolic, conceptual mental activity or, in short, "thought," but certain relevant generalities should be mentioned.

First, the attainment of higher degrees of abstract thought as exemplified in man is the result of three interrelated factors operating over hundreds of thousands of years: (1) the marked increase in size of the cerebral cortex, (2) the prolonged immaturity and dependency on mothering behavior with its extended period of distraction-free learning,[14] and (3) an increasingly different environment, physical, biological, social.

Second, at a certain point, possibly early to mid-Pleistocene, a symbolic language, namely, speech, arose and by bringing an unusual selective premium to the possessor led to acceleration in each of the three factors mentioned above. Words, because of their great contribution to survival, rapidly supplanted imagery, neuromuscular sensation, and emotion as both the repository and the vehicle of concepts at various levels of generality, for example, Black Beauty, horse, animal, food; or Black Beauty, horse, beast-of-burden, vehicle, status symbol, etc. In general, words and language not only document the distinctions and qualities of the environment—the basic elements of concepts—but permit a great increase in their number, subtlety, and efficiency of storage. It is clear that language multiplies what one sees and, hence, much of what one understands. The discovery of "the word" and the evolution of language gradually gave rise to an increasing complexity of concepts, including such things as the idea of time. Man became a "time-binder." He was taken out of his imbeddedness in immediacy. He acquired a past that he crystallized as history and a future attended with a degree of predictability. As he accumulated concepts, he accumulated material goods (the precipitates of concepts) and even the kinds of material goods, such as dictionaries, libraries, and data-processing and computer machines, that permit the storage and processing of concepts. Words determine man's world, and the worlds in which different language groups live are distinct worlds, not merely the same worlds with different labels [35]. This statement, in essence, applies quite well to a comparison of the communication systems of human and non-human primates.

[14] Man maintains fetal characteristics throughout life, a biological phenomenon called neoteny. But psychologically, too, he tends to remain immature, and, while we may resent the Peter Pan within us, we also retain for a long time the wonderment and imagination that leads to new things and new ways.

In short, psychologically, speech indicates the arrival at a certain level of conceptual thought. Anatomically, speech indicates the arrival at a certain level of complexity of the developing organism. The term "developing organism" is preferable to the term "developing nervous system" because conceptual or thinking behavior requires the participation of parts of the organism other than just the nervous system. Thinking, at least the form of thinking called for in problem-solving under experimental conditions, is regularly accompanied by an increase in muscle tension (not to mention many other physiological changes), which usually is not visible but is detectable by electrically measured action potentials taken of the muscles themselves. This is true even of the muscles of speech. On occasion, a word used in solving a problem may be identified by the configuration of the electrical potential readings, that is, the experimenter can tell what word the subject had in mind [36]. In deaf people who talk with their hands, the changes in electrical potential during thought occur in the muscles of their hands, not in the muscles of speech. Whether there exist forms of thought involving nervous tissue only will require further study and sharper definitions. Recent studies show that the forms of thought change with sensory deprivation, with variant states of the nervous system as obtained in changes of levels of arousal and dreaming, and, of course, with drugs and with alterations in chemical or metabolic states. The relationship of speech and other aspects of the symbolic-conceptual processes to the metabolic and endocrine phenomena ongoing in the organism is a crucial and very large field for continuing study. At this time, we can assert only that all forms of conceptual thought require a relatively intact organism, certainly for most of the time involved in the process.

Hopefully, it is clear at this juncture why comparisons of the intelligence of man and of the non-human primate as exemplified in laboratory studies are unfruitful. What distinguishes man from other primates, and one man from another, is not the laboratory kind of intelligence but the kind he accumulates and uses for social purposes [37]. It is this failure to measure and appreciate social intelligence as it operates under natural conditions that made the gap appear so vast, so unbridgeable, and that has interfered with valid studies. The potential for accumulation, for sharing, for collaboration, and for sociality, this—not intelligence per se

—is the area where we have outdistanced the non-human primate.[15] One cannot help but observe that we are still short of the sociality imperative for today's world.

Man's Modifications of Fundamental Behavioral Categories

The foregoing, it is hoped, has made clear that neither the fact of human speech nor the increased capacity of man to be guided by abstract concepts has removed man from the six vast categories of behavior that characterize all primate societies. Future studies will refine our knowledge of these categories, their relationship to one another, and the laws governing the rhythms of their operation, particularly in their relationship to environment. Indeed, much has been done and is now being done that we cannot go into here. The affectional maternal-infant system, its components, and its reciprocal relations with the peer-play affectional system has been much studied, particularly in the laboratory [38]. The varieties of territorial behavior as well as variations in dominance behavior open wide vistas of endeavor. But in this paper we can state only generalities, namely, that these behaviors are as fundamental to human existence as such short-rhythm phenomena as respiration and the heart beat; intermediate (circadian) rhythms like sleeping, waking, eating, drinking; and longer rhythms like sexuality and seasonal changes.

The development of man is characterized by the ongoing process—now having operated for millennia—of refinement and elaboration, and it is this process that has so altered the six primate behavioral categories as to account for their being ignored. The study of how they have been elaborated and refined is now open to all and should provide for stimulating investigation and speculation. Toolmaking, for instance, can give us a clue to what happens as elaboration and refinement operate over great lengths of time. Regardless of ups and downs of history or circumstance, there is an unbroken line of tool development in which the tool

---

[15] Not that laboratory studies have been misleading; indeed, it is the reciprocity that exists between laboratory and field study that has made modern primatology the science it is. Laboratory studies established the fact that the chimpanzee is for a number of years more intelligent than the human infant of the same age, as measured by learning and by tests of problem solving. These years cover that period of development which is crucial for future socialization and psychological well-being.

An anecdote that leaked out of a government research laboratory has it that a well-conditioned (and obviously well-motivated) chimpanzee defeated a visiting general in a game of tic-tac-toe; since then, the number of challengers has dwindled. This, too, indicates a certain sharpness of intelligence, even in a laboratory setting. But true intelligence is best estimated under natural conditions whenever possible.

becomes complex and specialized and the toolmaker becomes an ever larger multimembered team, with each team member having a function and an area of endeavor. The chimpanzee toolmaker fashions a probe by stripping leaves from a small branch or a twig and uses it to explore a termite hill, hopefully to extract termites [39]. Man organizes a vast complex team of toolmakers to make a tool to explore space. The same holds true for each of the basic categories of behavior. Take mothering. Mothering behavior is defined as "Care given with satisfaction if not joy and leading to growth and maturity in the one receiving the care. Care is understood to include every nuance of giving from nursing and physical support to protection, teaching, encouragement, etc." [24]. Since these must lead to growth, each must be given in appropriate quantities ending in cessation (or a stronger term, rejection). This definition is broad but is well supported by observation of non-human primates; it is also definitive in that there is little blurring or overlapping with the other five categories. Man has refined and elaborated this category much as he has toolmaking. Mothering is no longer the province of one individual, the biologic mother, but is the province of a team, and the composition of this team varies widely with history and culture. In our society, the biologic father usually plays the second most important role on the team, although such team functions may be assumed by older siblings, other relatives, or paid employees.[16] But, most important, the extended team includes teachers, ministers, doctors (and the personnel of institutionalized forms: church, YMCA, Girl Scouts, etc.), ad infinitum. All occupy a place on this team whether they are fully aware of it or not. Sometimes the biologic mother plays no role to speak of, and sometimes, tragically, there is nothing that could even be called a team, and the child exhibits the manifold, often pathetic, distortions of conflict and unguided growth. Fathering, it is clear, is best defined as "mothering behavior learned and performed by a male" [24]. The father, theoretically capable of every mothering chore except breast feeding, is often associated for historical and other reasons with the late stages of peer-play behavior, namely, puberty rites in the male child or the introduction to formal courtship behavior in the female child. In view of male domination of the female throughout history, the mental gymnastics the acceptance of the concept

---

[16] The question of the adult male's interest in and protection of the young varies widely among various species of non-human primates. It will require much more study [40].

of the "mothering male" will call for can be appreciated. This is a challenge to every male, whether husband or lover or psychiatrist. Many males resist this simple formulation possibly because they feel it reflects on their maleness, whatever that is. Certainly, it need not be confused with sexual potency. It is difficult for the human male, who throughout history has so generally dominated the female, to appreciate fully how much he has learned by observing and mimicking her.

The Relationship of Psychiatry to the Six Behavioral Categories

It is clear that no matter what the theory or technique espoused by the psychiatrist, and by now even the most rigid of us admit that many theories and therapies are helpful, we are, from the standpoint of primatology, society's "specialists in corrective foster mothering." Whether we are shocked or honored by this label, we cannot remove it without losing our real identity. It should be clear that the behavior of the psychiatrist cannot possibly be stretched to fit into any of the other categories. To establish this beyond doubt, we would have to explore in detail what the endless processes of elaboration and refinement have done to the categories we cannot cover in this paper. The processes of elaboration and refinement work largely outside of awareness, which makes the tracing of each category into the past difficult. But we all have a pretty good idea of what dominance behavior is, and unraveling its history and operation is by no means impossible. The same is true of territorial behavior, which appears to be the taproot of property rights. Spacing behavior in the human is of particular interest because it swings back and forth between the literal and the abstract (figurative) so constantly. Our language forms, of course, reflect many of these abstractions, for example, I feel close to him, etc. Fortunately, since there are only six categories, the task of getting to the essence of a disjunctive social transaction is generally easy. To take a simple example, for instance, prostitution becomes essentially a social transaction in which one party is involved in territorial behavior (money and property) and the other, not without exception, is involved in courtship-sexual behavior.

The above should add to the clarification of the psychiatrist's role. How commonly it is significantly contaminated unknowingly by the intrusion of the other behaviors, overtly or covertly! A stimulating controversy arises when it is argued that classical psychoanalysis is by no stretch of the imagination an example of "corrective foster mothering." It is, nevertheless. That it exhibits only one of the many facets of mothering behavior is not significant; mothering permits of wide variations. Mothering of a newborn monkey, for example, is accomplished by a wire frame covered with terry cloth [38], and good results often seem to be accomplished by "terry-cloth-covered" psychoanalysts. The miracle, however, lies in the monkey or the patient, not in the wire frame. It is clear, on the other hand, that classical analysis can level many charges at other therapies, usually in the category of poorly conceived activity on the part of the therapist. The mother, for instance, strictly speaking does not play with her child but, rather, teaches it to play. Play is with peers. And so it is with psychiatry. The psychiatrist may or may not be friendly, but he is not a friend of the patient. (Personally, I feel he should be friendly to the extent that it is unthreatening to himself or his patient.) The psychiatric transaction ends with the development in the patient of the capacity for true friendship. Whether the psychiatrist ever becomes a friend is incidental or coincidental.

Certain of the disjunctive sequences that take place in the psychiatric transaction are due to distorted definitions of mothering. The essence of mothering is not total acceptance, contrary to much psychiatric opinion. Even the "Pietà" cannot be conceived of as symbolic of this essence, as moving as it may be. The "Pietà" symbolizes mothering only under extremely heroic circumstances. This, fortunately, occurs but rarely in the therapeutic transaction, although the patient often claims otherwise. Mothering is that artful combination of acceptance and rejection which stimulates growth leading to maturity by way of full peer-play behavior.[17]

Other disjunctive possibilities in therapy derive from the basic categories. Sexual-courtship behavior is probably a common contaminant to the ongoing foster mothering with persons of the opposite sex, as well as dominance behavior (in the form of professionalism) and territorial behavior (in the form of money matters). With surprisingly little effort, these behaviors can be monitored by the psychiatrist once he "gets the hang of it." Further, since these are the precise behaviors the patient is involved with in his outside life, there is no particular harm in the psychiatrist sharing his knowledge of their operation if he does not force it

[17] Erich Fromm, for instance, has written much on the acceptance quality of "love," not spelling out the skilled and imaginative forms of rejection, which are growth-provoking.

upon the patient or interfere with the full development of the patient's capacity for self-assertion and self-discovery. Nice distinctions are called for and sometimes difficult ones. However, this is characteristic of most worthwhile endeavors. But a new freedom and a new spontaneity enter the transaction. For the first time, the psychiatrist can dip freely into the reservoir of experience and intuition that he possesses and can shift his responses as quickly and over as wide a range as any sensitive mother. Passivity and activity are variables routinely available to any mother in changing her tactics from one type of child to the next or for the same child at different times. To deny this principle is to restrict sharply the applications and dimensions of therapy. Another way of stating this is to say that the psychiatrist's role as foster mother, that is, an important member of the mothering team, is far more fundamental to the patient's growth than the psychiatrist's role as scientist (Freud) or professional selling a service (Sullivan); as the "I" in the "I-thou" concepts of the Existentialists; or, presumably, as Zen master in the Zen Buddhist views of recent years.[18]

History, Philosophy, Science: Relationship to This Theory

It would be tempting to dismiss this presentation by stating that the difficulty is semantic, but that is precisely not the case. The term "mothering," or "mothering behavior," is not chosen arbitrarily, nor are the other category headings. They are chosen in spite of alleged vague or controversial aspects, instead of words like "dependency" and "counseling." The word "mothering" is a term used and understood by biologists, by psychologists, and by sociologists and is by no means a vague, bulky, or nebulous term. It is subject to analysis and measurement by each of these disciplines. This term, along with the other five, offers a way out of the private language problem, which reaches Tower of Babel proportions in present-day psychiatry.[19]

[18] This implies no disrespect for Existential or Zen Buddhistic or other modes of non-dualistic experience. As these have been presented in Western psychiatry, however, they seem little more than intellectual baubles. Even in the Orient, Zen Buddhism is not submitted as the answer to "behavioral-emotional-social" breakdown. Zen (and a number of philosophies invading psychiatry) may represent the cutoff point where psychiatry ends, i.e., when the "mothering job" has been finished and the choice of a mature philosophy is faced.

[19] My psychiatric training required the study of a number of distinct psychiatric languages, e.g., Meyerian, Freudian, Sullivanian, Jungian, Adlerian. Few terms or concepts are interchangeable even within psychiatry; they are virtually useless for other scientific disciplines.

In view of the possibilities claimed for the present theory, it may be helpful to take another look into the past. It was the scientist who pointed out the great similarity in structure and physiology of man and animal. The burden of proof should be on the psychiatric scientist to demonstrate the animal nature of human behavior. But psychiatric theories stubbornly assert how unlike are man and animal.

The doctrine of evolution established the fundamental tenet that, while evolution is irrevocable, never returning to an earlier state, neither does it eliminate all traces of earlier states. No psychiatric theory ever effectively embodied this as part of its structure; all were concerned, not with what and how animal behaviors operate in man, but if they operated at all.[20]

From the evolutionist's point of view, the gap between non-human and human primates is small and is limited mainly to minor changes in the skeletal structure and to increase in size and area of the cerebral cortex. These are small when compared to other evolutionary changes, for example, the change from sea to land, or from land to air, or a number of other evolutionary advances. The change from non-human primate to human, though small, was critical and, operating over years, accounts for the accumulations of culture and civilization.[21] Since structure determines function, that is, behavior, minor structural changes indicate minor behavioral changes, a principle that should hold good in comparing man to the non-human primate. Indeed, theorists readily accept the data of the fossil record and the data of comparative anatomy, which confirm the close structural relationship of all primates. The same holds true for all the data on physiological functions. But this openmindedness is blocked when the question of comparative behaviors is raised. Actually, what lies at the root of the inability to resolve the question is the phenomenon of covertness discussed previously. Man's evolving cortex made it possible for him to inhibit, camouflage, and modify the basic primate behaviors far beyond the ability of any other primate, and the ability increased steadily. This gave rise over the years to the thesis that man does not have basic primate behaviors. The explanation given was that evolution

---

[20] Freud insisted upon a biological orientation supported more by stubborn intuition than by data. It is a shame that he coined a language unusable by biologists.

[21] One can hear the call "vive la différence" and agree, but these differences must not blind us to the similarities between human and non-human primates, which are crucial for psychiatry.

is, periodically, "emergent" and that man was the sole recipient among millions of species of this wonderful gift. Such a view, of course, is closely related to the phenomenon of transcendence, the theological roots of which are more easily identified.

The error is easy to spot. We have conceptualized man as the top of a pyramid representing the animal world (viz., primate), and this conception with roots in animism and primitive religion has contaminated scientific thought, denials to the contrary. A better conceptual schema would be concentric circles, with man being represented by the outer layers, thus indicating that man does not obliterate animal behaviors but simply extends their dimensions, including the ability to inhibit. Such a schema explains why man can be more "beastly" than the animal. Neither torture nor cannibalism, for instance, exists in non-human primates; either they are unable to conceive it or unable to carry it out.[22]

Theorists—both philosophers and psychiatrists—faced with the task of constructing non-animal behavioral models have been given to all kinds of imaginative pursuits. Usually, however, they have selected such models as gods; heroes; saints; philosophers; artists; scientists; or, latterly and modestly, the product of men's minds, such as mechanical or electronic gadgets. Actually, none of these is a behavioral model; they have no blood and guts, so to speak.[23] Rather, they represent a succession of man's preoccupations in his evolution from protocultures through savagery and barbarism to the religious and scientific attitudes of later times. They may actually be things he is not, that is, they are rationalizations to cover tabooed behaviors, probably of a sexual or agonistic nature.[24]

[22] Further study is required. A baboon did not eat the carcass of an infant baboon killed by a predator, though baboons are known to kill and devour small animals they happen across. They do not hunt [41].

[23] The untenability of disembodied "cognitive" behavior to a physician or anyone well grounded in physiology can be appreciated [42].

[24] One could, perhaps, classify these models as examples of "ruminative" or "investigative" or "appetitive" behaviors, although these are not strictly behavioral entities. Appetitive behaviors are best conceived of as vague "restlessnesses" out of which more definitive behavior arises. Indeed, thought, meditation, and curiosity, particularly, can be imagined as forms of "appetitive" behavior carried to a peculiar length in man and, hence, most difficult to trace to the particular behavioral entities they give rise to. In other words, man focusing with exquisite refinement on a state of being we can call sentience came up with an image of himself as godlike, heroic, or whatever. The only difficulty is that he was wrong and that these images probably had much to do with defenses against his feeling the opposite.

While any behavior is ongoing, other behaviors, covert or inhibited, are building up, largely

Final Remarks

Having ventured so far in speculation, it would seem abrupt to end this paper without at least a few remarks concerning the specific theories that determined the course of psychiatry. Earlier theories have now become institutions, but when launched they were often directed against institutions if only for the reason that the beliefs they challenged were held by institutions. Institutions in primate terminology represent alliance behavior, the beginnings of which we identified in non-human primate societies and which have been carried forth with the expected elaboration and refinement by man.

Freud's views, regardless of any stated intent, were clearly directed against the institution, the church. Since neither the scientific nor the business institutions have any direct interest in determining moral or ethical practices, if and when they attack Freudian doctrines, they do so simply as allies of the church.[25] Both the doctrine of a dynamic unconscious and the doctrine of the ubiquity of childhood sexuality were challenges to the territory of the church rather than any other segment of the community. Why Freud selected theses that were primarily antagonistic to the church, long since deposed from the seats of power, poses an interesting question. All ethical and moral considerations involving sex and violence had, long since, been the province of the church. This is what Freud pre-empted, and the cry of outrage clearly came from the direction of the church, already restless and overzealous to protect its shrinking territory. Business, in essence, is amoral, but it does keep its eye on every other segment of the community. It took a neutral position in the interminable controversy that raged between science (as represented

---

outside of awareness, preparatory to overt manifestation. We are faced with the problem of dealing with behaviors that are not yet manifest. Hopefully, the study of circadian rhythms and other biologic rhythms will give us clues to understanding these. For this, the human furnishes a good subject because verbal clues may be the earliest available in spotting incipient behavior, at least until better chemical or electrical methods are developed. And we can understand a communication, as with any form of behavior, only when we understand what is not being communicated as well as what is. A communication is simply a wave in a vast sea, and we cannot understand that wave without understanding non-waves, i.e., swells, tides, currents, winds, shorelines, all of which determine that wave which is part of "the sea around us."

We know so little about the substrates of cognition and concept formation that theories remain idiosyncratic, even if artistic and delightful. This paper does not, therefore, recommend that as a theory it be accepted. It recommends that the data be processed again and again.

[25] We emphasize "doctrine" rather than secondary professional or status considerations.

by Freud) and religion. Indeed, if our reasoning based on observation of non-human primates is correct, the controversy, if anything, was helpful to business, since it allowed the business community to pursue its own course of growth free from any moral restraints from the otherwise pre-occupied church.

What has been responsible for the continued existence of the Freudian cult? The reason lies in several areas. First, it is a profession, and second, it is a business, and the laws of survival of these entities continue to oper-ate. It continues also to thrive on the original controversy set up with the church and has enlisted as adherents and customers many of those whose quarrel was with the church.

In retrospect, one sometimes wonders why the controversy over sex would ever have been taken so seriously. Primate studies show that under natural conditions sexual behavior follows the rhythms of the days and the seasons. Under conditions of capture, restraint, and crowding, it becomes a frantic preoccupation and a cause for vicious fighting. Em-bedded in his time, it was impossible for Freud to sense this simple truth. The few who challenged him were accused of lacking the courage to face facts.

Thinkers who took issue with Freud were rebuffed with most unscien-tific intensity. Both Jung and Adler pointed out the Freudian bias but submitted biased views of their own. Jung's mysticism found an excellent market among those whose lives had been dry and prosaic. Adler's doc-trines of power found a comparable market among the socially impotent, namely, the teachers, who have struggled constantly to extricate them-selves from the onus of being society's baby-sitters.

Once the factors involved in dominance or status struggles (professional considerations) and territorial behavior (business and market aspects) are cleared away, it can be seen that there is much truth in all three points of view. They were the Niña, the Pinta, and the Santa Maria of the voyage to "a far country." Each described important facets of many-faceted man.[26]

The pell-mell, crowded, distracting, struggling, competitive nature of man's evolving social life does do a number of things to man, and it does distort his natural bent. We can actually measure the rather dreadful things that crowding and restriction do to our primate cousins. It de-

---

[26] This paper has tried to keep theory as its sole target, not psychiatrists or psychiatry.

stroys and perverts natural sex, motherhood, and peaceful living together. Sex becomes a nervous preoccupation, ofttimes an obsession, sometimes a perversion, and tragically gets hooked up with violence. Motherhood can turn to murder. Peace can turn to carnage. And so it is with man.

Freud noted and documented man's preoccupation with sex, Jung noted man's desire to experience relief by meditation and fantasy, and Adler noted man's tendency to react to being "low man on the totem pole" by dominance struggles.[27]

They all raised questions that sent us scurrying to the clinic, to the laboratory, and to the library. And in these places we have found answers to some of the questions. This paper has suggested one more place to go, the field and forest.

It is time we paid homage to all of the early theorists as we have to the Pasteurs, the Claude Bernards, the Pavlovs. It is time we dropped

[27] Space forbids dealing with (1) the splinter movements of latter-day psychiatry and (2) with methodology of therapy.

1. The main splinter group after Freud, Jung, and Adler were the "social-cultural-interpersonal theorists" who pointed out that all of the earlier "individualistic" theories overlooked the social (interpersonal) nature of man. But in so doing, they made the error of discounting man's biologic roots and cut themselves off from vast areas of scientific endeavor, including the medical profession itself. H. S. Sullivan, an outstanding theorist of the social-interpersonal group, illustrates this. In a passage from his fundamental book [43], under a section headed "One-Genus Postulate," he states that the human, no matter how badly damaged or abnormal, is still much more like a human than he is like the nearest animal genus and that the only worthwhile study for psychiatry is of things ubiquitously human.

This is a conceptual error, unusual and curious in a man of Sullivan's brilliance. The "mental patient" has long been subject to humiliation [44], and one of many forms of this has been classing him with the beast, e.g., being beastly, or his agreeing (desperately) to the friendly suggestion of the psychiatrist that he must feel "beastly." Sullivan's desire to remove him from this category is, of course, praiseworthy. The fact is, however, that the "normal" person in our society is much more "beastlike" than is the "abnormal" person. The beast though unevolved is integrated. Our "patient" though evolved is un- or dis-integrated. Integration, not evolvement, is the key. We are not seeing animal behavior in our "disintegrated patients." We are seeing jagged, fragmented human behavior.

2. As for methodology, the future of Freudian therapies, i.e., therapies that are dyadic and essentially non-responsive ("projective"), is still pretty much up in the air. Their futility for severe behavioral disturbances, as Freud predicted, has been well established. They are prohibitively impractical for extensive use in even the less serious disorders. In a purely research setting, however (freed, i.e., of status and commercial contaminants), they may serve as a continuing source of meaningful data (incidentally, this also is a prediction by Freud).

Most confusing of all, of course, has been the ever extending range of the responsive ("non-projective, reactive, suggestive, counseling") therapies. The medical profession, including psychiatry, understandably has been bewildered. It senses something is wrong, almost out of hand, yet it has had no theory to serve as a criteria to describe, much less to criticize, the rapid influx of a wide variety of non-professionals into the field of therapy. Under this heading are listed psychologists, marriage counselors, social-service caseworkers, hypnotists, and spiritual counselors in ever increasing numbers. Such phenomena become understandable in the light of present theory.

controversies that now have only historical validity. The best refutation of the theory presented in this paper is not to point out flaws in the data or the reasoning but to stand quietly and look at a beautiful cathedral, or listen to Brahms' Second Symphony, to immerse one's self, that is, in the creativity that is man. To know the dimensions of man's heroism and sacrifice and to lose one's self in the moving greatness of man at his best—then the data of this theory and the theory itself recede into insignificance.

But if we are concerned with man broken—if we are concerned with collective man in his agonies and antagonisms, with his disintegrating roles as father and mother, brother and sister, lover, leader and follower —then we must use this theory, we must sharpen and tighten it, or forge another of comparable dimensions to take its place.

REFERENCES

1. F. A. BEACH. Amer. Psychol., 5:115, 1950.
2. K. P. OAKLEY. A definition of man. Sc. News, No. 20. Baltimore: Penguin, 1951.
3. S. L. WASHBURN and V. AVIS. In: A. ROE and G. G. SIMPSON (eds.). Behavior and evolution. New Haven, Conn.: Yale Univ. Press, 1958.
4. A. H. SCHULTZ. Z. Morphol. Anthropol., 50:136, 1960.
5. K. P. OAKLEY. Antiquity, 31:199, 1957.
6. T. C. SCHNEIRLA. In: D. S. LEHRMAN, R. HINDE, and E. SHAW (eds.). Advances in the study of behavior, vol. 1. New York: Academic, 1965.
7. K. LORENZ. In: C. H. SCHILLER (ed.). Instinctive behavior, the development of a modern concept, part 11, chaps. i, ii, iii, v, and vii. New York: International Univ., 1957.
8. J. P. SCOTT. Science, 138:949, 1962.
9. T. C. SCHNEIRLA and J. S. ROSENBLATT. In: T. E. McGILL (ed.). Readings in animal behavior, p. 287. New York: Holt, Rinehart & Winston, 1965.
10. J. P. SCOTT. In: T. E. McGILL (ed.). Readings in animal behavior, p. 290. New York: Holt, Rinehart & Winston, 1965.
11. G. W. BROOKS and E. MUELLER. J. Amer. Med. Ass., 195:415, 1966.
12. E. OROWAN. Nature, 175:683, 1955.
13. I. DEVORE (ed.). Primate behavior, field studies of monkeys and apes. New York: Holt, Rinehart & Winston, 1965.
14. A. M. SCHRIER, H. F. HARLOW, and F. STOLLNITZ. Behavior of non-human primates: modern research trends. New York: Academic, 1965.
15. S. A. ALTMANN. Science, 150:40, 1965.
16. R. G. GRINKER, SR. Amer. J. Psychiat., 122:367, 1965.
17. V. C. WYNNE-EDWARDS. Animal dispersion in relation to social behavior. Edinburgh: Oliver & Boyd, 1963.

18. Jane Van Lawick Goodall. Nat. Geogr., 128:802, 1965.
19. C. R. Carpenter. Compar. Psychol. Monog., 10:1, 1934.
20. K. R. L. Hall. Paper read at the American Association for the Advancement of Science Convention, Montreal, December, 1964.
21. C. R. Carpenter. Biol. Symp., 8:177, 1942.
22. J. von Uexkull. *In:* C. H. Schiller (ed.). Instinctive behavior. New York: International Univ., 1957.
23. H. Kummer. Beih. Schweiz. Z. Psychol., Suppl. 33:1, 1957.
24. C. Rule. Amer. J. Psychiat. 121:344, 1964.
25. S. L. Washburn (ed.). Social life of early man. Chicago: Aldine, 1961.
26. A. Roe and G. G. Simpson (eds.). Behavior and evolution. New Haven, Conn.: Yale Univ. Press, 1958.
27. C. R. Southwick (ed.). Primate social behavior. Princeton, N.J.: Van Nostrand, 1963.
28. K. P. Oakley. *In:* S. L. Washburn (ed.). Social life of early man. Chicago: Aldine, 1961.
29. C. F. Hockett. *In:* W. E. Lanyon and W. N. Tavolga (eds.). Animal sounds and communication, p. 392. Washington, D.C.: American Institute of Biological Sciences, 1960.
30. J. Reusch. Therapeutic communication. New York: Norton, 1961.
31. J. Reusch and G. Bateson. Communication. New York: Norton, 1951.
32. R. B. Brody. Amer. J. Psychiat., 122:852, 1966.
33. H. S. Sullivan. Quoted *in:* J. Reusch and W. Kees. Nonverbal communication. Berkeley: Univ. California Press, 1956.
34. W. Penfield and L. Roberts. Speech and brain mechanisms. Princeton, N.J.: Princeton Univ. Press, 1959.
35. E. Sapir. Language, 5:21, 1929.
36. E. Jacobson. Amer. J. Psychol., 44:677, 1932.
37. J. Bastian. *In:* I. DeVore (ed.). Primate behavior, field studies of monkeys and apes, chap. xvii. New York: Holt, Rinehart & Winston, 1965.
38. H. F. Harlow. Amer. J. Orthopsychiat., 30:676, 1960.
39. Jane Goodall. *In:* I. DeVore (ed.). Primate behavior, field studies of monkeys and apes, chap. xii. New York: Holt, Rinehart & Winston, 1965.
40. P. Jay. *In:* I. DeVore (ed.). Primate behavior, field studies of monkeys and apes, chap. vii. New York: Holt, Rinehart & Winston, 1965.
41. S. A. Altmann. Film and remarks at American Association for the Advancement of Science Convention, Montreal, December, 1964.
42. S. Arieti. Amer. J. Psychiat., 122:361, 1965.
43. H. S. Sullivan. The interpersonal theory of psychiatry. New York: Norton, 1953.
44. M. Foucault. Madness and civilization, a history of insanity in the age of reason. New York: Pantheon, 1965.

A BIOLOGICALLY BASED THEORY OF HUMAN BEHAVIOR AND ITS IMPLICATIONS FOR PSYCHIATRY:

Speculations Derived from Recent Studies of Social Behavior of Non-Human Primates

COLTER RULE, M.D.

The quest for a biologically based theory of human behavior has been and continues to be a preoccupation of science. Workers in varied fields have contributed to this quest in greater or lesser measure; few have equalled medical men. The quest for this theory, however, is more than a formal scientific project. It is implicit in all thinking which compares man and animal. Such thinking stretches back to Fontaine, Aesop and King Solomon to the roots of primitive civilization.

This paper continues that quest. Its bid for more serious consideration than is accorded the fables of a former day rests on two factors. One is the high quality of present day animal studies wherein fact replaces anecdote and anthropomorphism (14). The other is the increasing facilities for field and laboratory studies of non-human primates that will provide opportunities to check assertions and challenge speculation.

The paper is divided into two parts. Part I reviews studies of the social behavior of non-human primates (apes and monkeys). Part II considers the implications of these studies for a biologically rooted theory of human behavior and its applications to psychiatry.

PART I

Background. The scientific study of anatomy preceded the scientific study of behavior and the Darwinian theory of evolution rested primarily on the data of comparative anatomy. But Darwin, like all of us, was, in addition to his interest in man's origin, preoccupied with the riddle of man's behavior. His book *The Expression of the Emotions in Man and Animals*(15) marks the founding of a science of comparative behavior. Outstanding

scientists of the day followed his lead but the movement was short-lived. With the rediscovery of Mendel, science veered off into genetics and into studies of conditioned reflex and learning. Nearly three decades would pass before, in the late 1920's, studies of animal behavior would be renewed. Reliable field studies of the non-human primates are, with few exceptions, not yet ten years old. Recent studies include Washburn and Devore (baboons)(5); Southwick (howler and macaque)(6); Phyllis Jay (langur)(10); Jane Goodall (chimpanzee)(9); Schaller (gorilla)(7).

When these field observations are cross-checked against laboratory studies such as Wm. Mason (Yerkes Laboratory Primate Biology)(11) and H. and M. Harlow (Wisconsin Regional Primate Center)(12, 13), we can say that the sum total is exciting not only for the pathways of future research that are opened up, but for the speculations we are at last justified in making about human behavior and its biologic roots. There are 240 species of living non-human primates in the world; reliable field studies are available for less than 20, so there is a great deal more work ahead.

A field study of non-human primates is arduous and demanding. Schaller spent a gruelling year in Africa following a gorilla family group in terrain best left to one's imagination. Previous characterization of the gorilla depicted him as a bloodthirsty and ferocious beast with an amazing array of human and superhuman traits, all basically treacherous. A previous scientist, crediting these accounts, spent many days inside a cage in the forests of Africa waiting for the gorillas to come to him. His success, comments Schaller, was as restricted as he was(7). The roar and chest thumping of a 500-pound male gorilla is awesome, but so approachable did gorillas turn out to be that Schaller was able to share a tree with them and even the same branch. They are amiable and decent. A big male will put up with four infants clambering all over him or hitching rides on his back. A group will tolerate a strange gorilla, a visiting male gorilla was observed to join the troop for a few days without their showing overt signs of antagonism. Gorillas do not fight for a territory; when two troops meet, they may pass by or they may join up for an hour or two. They may even make their nests together and bed down for the night.

Jane Goodall's study of the chimpanzee is also formidable considering that an adult male chimpanzee is several times as strong as a strong man. She, too followed her "family" group over trails thought impassable for anything but chimpanzees. Fortunately, she says, she became increasingly arboreal as the study progressed. As in the gorilla study, her data requires a revision of earlier views of non-human primate behavior. Earlier studies were based on baboons in zoos and rhesus macaques under conditions of crowding or stress. A dominant male chimpanzee, for instance, contrary to what previous studies might have led one to suspect, does not battle to acquire a "harem" but may queue up and await his turn to copulate with a receptive female. The necessity to redefine and reevaluate the concepts of dominance and territoriality will be taken up later.

General Remarks about Non-human Primates. Understanding non-human primate behavior is facilitated by reviewing a basic classification of general animal behavior. The following list with 9 headings is a generally accepted one: 1) ingestive, 2) shelter seeking, 3) agonistic, which includes both aggressive fighting and escape behavior, 4) sexual, 5) care-giving, 6) care-soliciting, 7) mimicry (the technical term is allelomimetic and includes such activities as flocking in birds, schooling in fishes), 8) eliminative, 9) investigative. All of these can be social, including eliminative when used to mark territory. Some must be social(14).

Of free-ranging monkeys, the greater number are arboreal, some never leaving the trees. Apes, baboons, and various rhesus species are terrestrial, spending much time on the ground. All except the gorilla sleep in trees at night. (Snakes, predators and falling seem to be deep rooted sources of fear.) These primates are basically vegetarians, eating a wide variety of fruits, leaves, roots, nuts, shoots. Birds' eggs, nestlings, or even small game are only occasionally eaten by baboons and chimpanzees. This is interesting since these food sources would seem to be readily available(5, 9).

Group Size and Composition(3). Group size ranges all the way from a male and a female gibbon without young to 40 and upward for baboons and macaques. Average group size, adult male-female ratio, and the numbers of infants, juveniles, and transitional solitary males vary with the species. A figure for a howler group on Barro Colorado Island, for instance, included 3 males, 8 females, 3 infants, 4 juveniles, and a few peripheral males. Such a figure could apply to other groups such as langurs, chimpanzees, and gorillas. Groups have a home range, the borders of which are soon learned by a field worker, and within this range there is a much used core area determined by food, water, and good sleeping trees.

The difficulty in obtaining data in field studies, and the necessity of developing some system of classification can well be appreciated. Carpenter, a pioneer in these studies, evolved the formula, $\frac{N(N-1)}{2}$, to express the number of dyadic (interaction involving two individuals) relationships in a given group. Considering the variety of transactions between two individuals, the problem facing the field worker becomes clear. To simplify record keeping, data are kept for interactions between types rather than individuals—for example, male-male, male-female, female-infant and juvenile-juvenile. Other data categories include intergroup and interspecies phenomena, climatic and other ecological data. These and other arbitrary procedures necessary for the early phase of a science are being modified and, indeed, a whole new methodology is evolving(17).

Furthermore, certain postulates about social interactions have characterized early primate studies and should be noted(4). *First,* all social relationships are reciprocal, the aroused motivation of one finds its satisfaction in an interacting organism. In the nursing situation, the infant satisfies its hunger, while the mother relieves the tension in her breast and enjoys the sensation of holding. She derives some status or prestige gratification from exhibiting the infant. *Second,* each interaction involves a complex of both negative and positive drives. A typical example would be an interaction over a preferred feeding location where hunger drives the individual toward the preferred spot and fear of another individual keeps him away. *Third,* paired social relationships are subject to modification, specialization, differentiation, and generalization through learning and conditioning. *Fourth,* interactions accumulate in both negative and positive aspects, *e.g.,* during the positive phase of the mother-infant relationship, each early interaction strengthens the positive affectional bonds.

The total number of paired relationships determines to a large extent the over-all pattern of group organization, or the group social structure. Conversely, the freedom of the so-called "free-ranging" monkey or ape is strictly limited by the social pattern, or structure, of the group.

Spacing. Clues to an understanding of social relationships in primate groups can be revealed by observing spatial relations between individuals and subgroups, *e.g.,* females and juveniles. These clues are not usually evident if the group is relaxed but can be observed where food is limited or other stress situations exist. Under stress conditions the strength of the attachment between two individuals may be judged, or actually measured, by observing for a period of time the average distance that separates the two animals(3). "Group scatter" or spatial distribution varies with the species. Howlers are typically closely grouped, while capuchins range widely, and spider monkeys even more widely(16).

Territoriality. Territoriality is defined as behavior in defense of an area against another individual (or individuals) of the same or different species. First described for English song birds and a variety of animals, it was originally considered to be characteristic of non-human primate societies also(3, 4, 17). Conjecture indicated that it might be a special aspect of spacing, or that it was related to learning details of the home range, to the phenomenon of homing and to group defense. Territoriality as originally described, however, is not borne out by recent studies of free-ranging primates. It may appear only under conditions of stress brought about by artificial crowding. Further studies will be required.

Dominance(3-6). An individual is said to be dominant over another when it has priority in feeding, sexual and locomotor behavior and when it is superior in aggressiveness and in group control to another or other individuals. It is related to status or prestige. Emphasis on the competitive aspect of dominance behavior characterized early papers on monkey and ape groups. The harmonious aspects of dominance observed in free-ranging primates has only recently been fully appreciated(7, 9). From one point of view dominance behavior can be represented by the statement, "I'll get what I can," but from another point of view it becomes, "I'll find my niche."

A full discussion of complex dominance interactions is not possible here. The following points may be helpful:

1. Dominance is not an absolute, it can be measured only relative to another individual.

2. Dominance behavior involves both sexes and all ages, except newborns, and the behavior by which these hierarchies are established and maintained, or lost, are essential aspects of group integration.

3. Dominance gradients vary from species to species; dominance in arboreal species tends to be less aggressive.

4. Dominance interactions vary with the activity and with the situation, that is, individuals dominant in one circumstance may not be in another.

5. Under conditions of captivity or stress, dominance interactions may be in-

tense, leading to fighting and a high mortality which includes females and young.

6. In free-ranging species there is little or no fighting; often a mild threat by posture or facial expression suffices.

7. The female consort of a dominant male may receive dominance status because of her association with him. Similarly, the infant of a dominant female receives some prestige because of his mother's dominance.

8. In certain terrestrial species, dominance of a combined male (or female) combination occurs; the second and third ranking males together may outrank the dominant male. In other words, alliances are possible.

9. An interesting gesture of submission in a dominance interaction, observed in certain macaques, is a presentation in the female position of the less dominant male, e.g., number two ranking male may present to number one male, who may respond with abortive mounting. Number three male may on another occasion present to number two male and be mounted. Indeed, two equally ranked males greeting one another after a separation may present and be mounted in turn. This apparently is non-sexual and may be a sign of non-aggression.

Maternal-Infant Behavior(11, 12). Final and definitive statements about maternal-infant relationships in non-human primates are not yet possible. Until recently, detailed observations have come only from captive animals and caution in applying the findings to free-ranging primates, not to mention human behavior, is, of course, necessary. Available observations, nevertheless, justify speculation.

In captivity, monkey mothers vary greatly in their behavior toward their infants, from devoted and protective to neglectful and abusive. Under stress conditions, such as have obtained on occasion during excessive crowding in shipment, mothering may deteriorate rapidly, and mothers may kill infants. In free-ranging groups, however, it is rare to observe a monkey mother who is not at least moderately effective. Probably natural selection operates so

strongly against the ineffective mother that there are few around.

In free-ranging langurs the newborn is likely to be a center of attention of the females. It is passed from female to female being retrieved by its mother only if there is a cry of distress. The relative clumsiness of the several females in handling and reacting to the newborn is obvious to field workers(10). Mothers tend to become increasingly adept with successive offspring(17, 18). In a number of species the infant begins to supplement its diet of mother's milk after a few weeks by picking up droppings from the mother's mouth as she feeds on leaves and shoots. Soon he may reach up to take a small piece of food from his mother's lips. This may play a role in the infant's learning the dietary choices of the group.

The question of the mother actually "teaching" the infant is, of course, crucial. A quote from Barbara Harrison is interesting. "It is quite wrong to assume that the young Orang reacts to a large extent by instinct . . . the contrary is the case, most things are learned through direct teaching, even climbing (the mother Orang clasps the infant's hand around the branches) and fundamentals are quickly forgotten if they are removed from the mothers. This teaching continues for at least four or five years although from eighteen months on learning is accelerated by incentive from and imitation of playmates"(8). The description of the gorilla mother, backing away from her infant as it learns to walk(18), is also evidence for active teaching on the part of the mother.

The following description of maternal-infant relations is based on observations of captive monkeys. In general, the mother-infant interaction goes through three stages: mutual attachment, maternal ambivalence, and separation. The attachment stage in rhesus begins at delivery or shortly after and continues for about 90 days. Immediately after delivery, mothers show attachment and affection for all baby monkeys and will steal other babies than their own if given a chance. After a few days they will limit protective responses to their own offspring. The infant rapidly develops a strong grasping reflex but until it does the mother will carry the infant. She will also help the infant find the nipple by nudging it nippleward.

Mothers become aggressive toward other infants and other mothers about the time that their infants begin rough-and-tumble play. From 90 days onward, protective and comforting responses of the mother decrease and rejective responses increase. This period of ambivalence may be associated with size and color changes of the infant in certain species. The mother resists the infant's care-soliciting behavior in a decisive manner, though the infant will remain close to her and, at night, still remains in physical contact. In the third phase there is a steady rejection of the infant's care-solicitation.

If the infant is removed from its mother so that it is deprived of all mothering behavior except for artificial feeding, it passes a point where it is no longer able to establish satisfactory relationships with a foster mother or peers, with mates, and, later, with offspring. Normal healthy infants, born to behaviorally normal monkey parents, can be rendered "neurotic and/or psychotic" by controlling their early mothering and other social experiences. Depending upon the degree of deprivation of mothering, these monkeys show various behavioral aberrations. They sit passively in their cages staring vacantly into space, showing no interest in the surroundings including monkeys in adjoining cages. Stereotyped behavior includes clasping their own body or head in their arms and rocking back and forth for long periods of time. Others will seize one of their own arms in their teeth and tear at the flesh until the blood flows. With lesser degrees of maternal deprivation this "psychotic" behavior is not exhibited but the infants are unable to establish characteristic play responses to peers. What is worth noting is that they exhibit mainly fighting behavior.

Peer-Play Behavior (11, 12). Laboratory studies of the development of play indicate five stages: first, presocial, when first put together infants play with objects, not with each other. Second, infants tumble, wrestle and roll with each other al-

though no one gets hurt. Third, play involves approach and withdrawal with chasing back and forth. Fourth, integrated play involves a blending of all the above three behaviors; they show periods of "frantic-frenzy" including chase, withdrawal, tussling, and manipulations of objects. This may be where the phrase "more fun than a barrel of monkeys" originated. Following this, the fifth stage is one of aggressive, integrated play during which the dominance hierarchy is well established. None of this play behavior is observed in infants deprived of mothering behavior.

Heterosexual Behavior (11, 12). The third system is the heterosexual system. It begins in infancy and like the other systems can be divided into stages. Three can be easily identified: infantile sex, sex play, and mature sexuality. In the infantile, the sex behavior is fragmentary. From the first month the females tend to show behavior that is less aggressive and the males show behavior that is more aggressive. In subsequent months males show increasing tendencies to mount and thrust and decreasing tendencies to crouch and present. The opposite occurs in females. By six months of age, male and female traits are clearly defined. There is very little overlap. This remains unchanged without a latency period. When the females are three years of age and males four, mature sexuality begins. In general, no sexual behavior is observed in infants deprived of mothering. In the few observed cases of births to females deprived of mothering during their own infancy, maternal behavior is almost totally lacking; the infant's care-soliciting behavior fails to evoke even minimal nursing and care responses.

The preceding account is a brief survey of recent field and laboratory research in the social behavior of non-human primates. Space prevents inclusion of much interesting data. Such phenomenon as vocalization as a cultural tool, cultural innovations and how they are transmitted, deviate behavior, variations in temperament and behavior in individuals and in species are among the items that have been passed over as of lesser importance for the speculations that follow.

PART II

Discussion and Speculations. What inferences can we draw from these recent studies of non-human primates which are valid for understanding human behavior ?

Foremost, it would seem that there are three fundamental patterns, or forms, of social behavior leading to the maturation of the individual. These three great patterns of behavior are :

1. Mothering behavior. Defined as care given with satisfaction—if not joy—and leading to growth and maturity in the one receiving the care. Care is understood as every nuance of giving from nursing to support, protection, and teaching, a broad definition but well supported by observations of the behavior of non-human primates.

2. Peer or play behavior. For humans this could be called friendship behavior since in its evolved forms dominance interactions are minimal, the transactions are joyful or productive, and it is primarily non-sexual.

3. Reproductive behavior. Courtship and romance often leading to marriage and family formation are the best terms for this behavior in human society.

Several aspects are worthy of note. First, there is very little difficulty recognizing these three varieties of behavior, both objectively when one observes these behaviors in non-human primates and subjectively when one is engaging, or even endeavoring to engage, in these behaviors with other humans. Second, while there are many other forms of social behavior, *e.g.*, grooming, defensive fighting, dominance interactions and vocalization, these behaviors are clearly of lesser importance for understanding individual maturation than the three fundamental behaviors mentioned. Third, although mothering in all its major outlines is clearly observed in primates that lack fire, tools or symbolic language, fathering, as a social behavior, is not observed. Whether even rudimentary social fathering exists in non-human primates is debatable ; certainly biologic fathering is unrelated to social fathering. Fathering is a comparatively new behavior ; mothering

behavior goes back more than a million years. Indeed, fathering is best defined as "mothering behavior" learned and shown by a male.[2]

These assertions raise questions of interest for medicine and psychiatry. Does the discovery of fire, the development of tool and weapon making, the development of language and symbolic thinking remove man from his rootedness in these behaviors ? Do some of man's behaviors have no biological roots ? Or has the development of the neocortex so modified biologically based behaviors that, for all intents and purposes, man's behavior is non-biological ? For example, is the behavior of the physician (or the psychiatrist, the clergyman, the teacher, the scientist, and the artist as well) removed from the biologic forces which are so easily traced in the behavior of the non-human primates ?

Existing Theories. Much contemporary psychiatric theory contends that the answer is, yes, that man has taken leave of these biologic roots. Freud is the one major theorist who insisted that man's behavior is biologically rooted. Unfortunately, his insistence that Oedipal behavior was obligatory because of its instinctual, biologic roots caused so much controversy that a biologically rooted theory of human behavior was discarded by those who discarded the Oedipus complex. The baby was thrown out with the bathwater. The "cultural" schools deny these biological roots, or reject them as of no value for theory or therapy. Sullivan's view that we are all more simply human than otherwise expresses this. Indeed, he defines the therapist as an expert in interpersonal relations whose expertise is a saleable commodity, the sale of which is an honest way to make a living. Freud defined the therapist as a scientist whose

---

[2] In our society the human infant can be described as receiving mothering behavior from two main sources, the biological mother and a foster mother called father. The difficulty in organizing and integrating the experience of being "mothered," considering the varieties of "good" and "bad" mothering the infant receives, and from whom, can be appreciated. And, in the presence of even minor brain damage, anxiety or other chronic distraction such as pain, for instance, the task for the infant becomes well-nigh impossible.

science is pyschoanalysis, dealing with the wanderings of a hypothetical biological energy called the libido and its stasis in the hypothetical Oedipus complex. Fromm and some of the Existentialist groups postulate a kind of quasi-mystic relatedness as being the essence of the therapeutic relationship. Just how these various groups define the therapist is difficult to grasp. Indeed, there are hotly debated differences between the groups. Clues to their beliefs can be obtained from the study of Zen Buddhism, Kierkegaard, Buber, Heidegger, Binswanger, Sartre and others. Relationships of the "I-Thou" type characterize several of these "schools" which either deny a biological base in therapy or, at most, pay it lip service. It has been suggested that relationships of the "I-Thou" type have their biologic origins in peer behavior(19). If so, there would seem to be little justification for the overtones of mysticism which so often surround them.

In studies of human maturation the biologically based behaviors are clearly seen, in emotional disorders the miscarriage of these behaviors is painfully evident. For the psychiatrist to lose track of these behaviors in either his patient or himself forces him to construct a theory which ignores not only the language of biology but also the vast reservoir of biologic knowledge. It is no wonder that he has isolated himself from the other medical specialties.[3]

---

[3] Much interesting data for understanding animal behavior continue to come from the laboratories of the neuroendocrinologists and it invites speculation about human behavior as well. A generation ago the concepts of Sherrington, the reflex arc, and the concept of the pituitary as the "Master gland" dominated the thinking in this field. Transection of the spinal chord and brain stem was the general experimental technique for studying CNS function. This has been replaced for brain study by techniques studying longitudinal structures and function. The work of Magoun and others in elucidating the ascending retricular substance has brought about important discoveries and a number of new views.

Recent theory views the brain as possessing three "analyzor-integrator" mechanism: 1) the brain stem reticular formation, 2) the limbic-striatal system and 3) the thalamoneocortical system. The first system seems to be related to integrating the data connected with "posture," *i.e.*, maintaining the orientation of the organism in

Implications for Psychotherapy. The thinking which led me to the studies and conclusions described led me to new feelings about the nature of psychotherapy.

---

space, and includes visceral adjustments as well as muscular. The second system subserves visceral and endocrine adjustments connected with alertness and focussing of attention, and, even with the neocortex removed, this system can control behaviors as complex as fighting, flight, food procurement and sexual behavior. What components of mothering behavior it controls are naturally of relevance to the thesis outlined in this paper, and may be delineated in future studies. The third system, the thalamoneocortical, is the sole recipient of the major epicritic lemniscus afferents, but it also receives major input from system 1 and 2. Thus, the thalamoneocortical system is an analyzor-integrator mechanism which is connected with the organism's environment in two ways. First, by direct, fast acting sensory nerves, an evolutionary development which is characteristic of primates ; and by indirect input from the "old" protopathic centers which have to do with "feelings," with behavioral attitudes or moods, such as anxious, angry, predatory, relaxed, sexual, maternal, *etc.*(20).

What comments can we make about the neocortex, man's most vaunted possession ?

First, complex behavior such as fighting, food procuring and sexual behavior is possible without the neocortex.

Further, the unique ability of the neocortex lies, primarily, in sensory discrimination and analysis, and it is in this area that man so greatly surpasses his nearest primate relatives. Though our motor potential does not greatly exceed our primate relatives, and in some spheres we are not their equals, our ability to form sense percepts and to combine these into infinite concepts is what really underlies our superior ability to design complex and intricate behavioral patterns. While the neocortex can inhibit basic behaviors for indefinite periods of time, or can institute modifications of these basic behaviors to the point where they are virtually unrecognizable (particularly if the organism wishes to conceal them), the neocortex can not change basic behavior. The forms of basic behavior are both determined and limited by structures below the neocortex.

Much work lies ahead in differentiating between "learned" as opposed to "instinctual" behavior. Probably no behavior exists which is purely instinctual; effects of learning have been demonstrated for earthworms and even ameba. An interested relationship between so-called instinctual and learned behavior is illustrated in the development of sexual behavior in the human male. Early castration of the human male prevents the development of male sexual behavior. If, however, castration follows the establishment of the male sexual behavior, the behavior pattern is not destroyed. The "learned" pattern makes the male hormone, necessary for learning, unnecessary for maintenance.

While I can with some effort enact various therapists' roles, I am unable to feel any of them. On the other hand, I find no difficulty in feeling that I am *a mother* or, since I am anatomically a male, that I *feel capable* of mothering behavior. Again, it is to be emphasized that I do not say fathering because it is redundant; fathering is simply mothering learned and shown by a male. I am capable of mothering behavior because I learned it from my mother and my father and a long list of parental surrogates and "assistants" who had in turn, learned it from others.[4]

Since I feel no conflict with the idea of my showing mothering behavior, I feel comfortable with the patient, not only in exploring the miscarriages of "mothering behavior" as the patient experienced it, but I feel quite capable of offering corrective "foster mothering behavior" in whatever form my judgement dictates, whether this be help, teaching, shared investigation, encouragement, or simply appreciation and respect. Since the patient's experience and attitudes toward "mothering behavior" vary all the way from terror, often reported by the schizophrenic, to lesser degrees of negativism, I offer mothering behavior only as the patient senses the need of it, does not confuse it with either friendship or sexual behavior, can ask for it or can, at least, accept it without fear, guilt or the feeling that his or her mother (real or fancied) will be jealous.[5] In short, he must not confuse

my mothering behavior with anyone's else. This, to me, is the essence of transference, other distortions are unimportant.

Only if one has experienced good moth-

is no proof that his behavior is not derived from mothering. "Mothering behavior" includes all kinds of technical skills from removal of splinters to sharp observations on where one's thinking, feeling, and behavior is amiss.

My conception of the therapist in Freudian, Sullivanian, and Fromm-Existentialist therapies is not to be construed as a blanket indictment. The assertion is made, simply, that they are best examined as showing "mothering behavior," and that the awareness of this fact may lead, not only to the improvement of therapy, but also to the possibility of studying the therapeutic transaction as having a biologic base. The absence of signs of affection toward the patient in either Freudian or Sullivanian therapists is not proof of no "mothering behavior," indeed, for a particular patient at a particular time it may be the best possible "mothering behavior." The following from Darwin is worth noting: "No emotion is stronger than maternal love; but a mother may feel the deepest love for her infant and not show it by any outward sign . . ."(15).

One wonders at times why the thesis outlined here was not developed long ago. Certainly a number of thinkers, Margaret Meade, Suttie, to mention two, have made key statements on "fathering" and "mother love." One wonders why, with the emphasis on subjectivity that is called for in the training curricula to do psychoanalysis or "deep" or "intensive" psychotherapy, the awareness of the simple identity between therapy and "mothering behavior" is not completely reported and discussed. Perhaps male therapists are threatened by such awareness and females too timid to report it. In any event, many psychiatrists understandably being so opposed to "bad mothering" have overlooked the infinite patterns and uses of "good mothering!"

If, indeed, "mothering behavior" had entered the therapies of all the schools, unlabeled and unrecognized, we have at last some basis of understanding why studies of all schools show essentially the same benefits. The common ingredient of all therapies may be the "mothering behavior."

The basic question in psychotherapy, whether implied or asked, is not, "What is your mother like? Rather, it is "From what persons did you receive mothering behavior?" "What were they like, what was good and bad about each, were they in conflict, how much appreciation did each demand, *etc.?*" The number of times that a patient suddenly realizes that the father, or a nursemaid, or occasionally a neighbor, really deserved the label "mother" acording to the patient, will surprise many therapists. And the ease with which the patient is able to accept foster-mothering as reflected in the life story and as demonstrated in the therapeutic relationship is a good measure of the patient's capacity for improvement.

---

[4] Not only do individuals learn mothering as they develop, but they often offer mothering behavior to others, not entirely with wholesome motives and goals but 1) to demonstrate to their mothers that they need no mothering behavior, that, on the contrary, they are suppliers, and 2) that their kind of mothering behavior is a far superior kind anyway. This covert competition with the mother is often confused with Oedipal phenomena, homosexual behavior, separation anxiety, *etc.*, none of which are basic but simply obscure the competition.

[5] "Mothering behavior" by the therapist is denied officially by both Freudian and Sullivanian therapists. Confidential talks with therapists from both schools lead me to believe, however, that it is constantly present; it is "bootlegged" in, so to speak, under one guise or another. The fact that a therapist becomes an expert in the language of the "unconscious" or the language of the psychotic, or in the nuances of interpersonal transactions